Confessions
of a
Hero-Worshiper

ALSO BY STEPHEN J. DUBNER

Turbulent Souls:
A Catholic Son's Return to His Jewish Family

CONFESSIONS
of a
HERO-WORSHIPER

—❦—

Stephen J. Dubner

wm
WILLIAM MORROW
An Imprint of HarperCollins*Publishers*

Grateful acknowledgment is made to reprint the following:

Lyrics from "I Just Want to Make Love to You," by Willie Dixon, copyright © 1959 (renewed 1987) Hoochie Coochie Music (BMI)/Administered by BUG. All rights reserved. Used by permission of Blues Heaven Foundation (founded by Willie Dixon in 1981): www.bluesheaven.com.

Excerpt from Pindar's "Olympian 7: For Diagoras of Rhodes, Winner, Boxing, 464 B.C." Reprinted by permission of the publishers and the Trustees of the Loeb Classical Library from *Pindar: Volume I, Olympian Odes, Pythian Odes,* Loeb Classical Library Volume L56, translated by William H. Race, p. 133, Cambridge, Mass.: Harvard University Press, copyright © 1997 by the President and Fellows of Harvard College. The Loeb Classical Library® is a registered trademark of the President and Fellows of Harvard College. All rights reserved.

Excerpt from W. C. Heinz's "Brownsville Bum," *True,* 1951.

HarperCollins books may be purchased for educational, business, or sales promotional use. For information please write: Special Markets Department, HarperCollins Publishers Inc., 10 East 53rd Street, New York, NY 10022.

FIRST EDITION

Designed by Cassandra J. Pappas

Printed on acid-free paper

Library of Congress Cataloging-in-Publication Data

Dubner, Stephen J.
   Confessions of a hero-worshiper / Stephen J. Dubner.—1st ed.
      p. cm.
   Includes bibliographical references.
   ISBN 0-688-17365-9
     1. Harris, Franco, 1950—Appreciation. 2. Hero worship. 3. Dubner, Stephen J. 4. Football fans—United States. I. Title.
   GV939.H33 D83 2003
   796.332'092—dc21

[B]   2002032625

03 04 05 06 07 WB/RRD 10 9 8 7 6 5 4 3 2 1

For Solomon and Anya

CONTENTS

Book Three
A HERO AND HIS BOY

Book One

A BOY AND HIS HERO

1

THE HOUSE OF DREAMS

———··•◄∞►•··———

Y ES, I SHOULD HAVE KNOWN better than to go home
again. This couldn't end well, wouldn't end well, and I knew it
full well. But I was powerless to resist.

From New York City, my safe and distant metropolis—this was a few
years ago, before madmen had crashed airplanes into skyscrapers—I
drove in the back way, through the Catskills and up into the rolling low-
lands. I passed a junk shop, a self-serve farm stand, a rotted-out covered
bridge. Spring had just surrendered to summer. Far in the distance I
could see the sweet, straight line where the cornfields, a mile wide,
dead-ended at the base of steep woody hills. That line still excited me,
just as other lines now excite me—the curve of my new bride's bare
arm, the sight of my own byline.

Along Route 30, memories pounced at me. In Middleburgh: the high-
school ballfield where I broke up a no-hitter in the last inning. (We must
have lost the game but my own sliver of glory is all that comes to mind.)
In Schoharie: the ragged, shallow creek where my mother taught me to
fish. (We never caught a thing and lost all our lures.) I saw a flat-faced
man soaping up a flat-faced school bus and the thought of riding it—the
thought of childhood—made my insides sag.

Gallupville Road, my road, dipped and snaked through hayfields and hillocks, pea-green in the muted June light. I had biked these hills a million times, a million years ago. I cursed their steepness and the dogs that sprang silently, teeth bared, from behind the forsythia. Now I only had to nudge the gas pedal and the hills fell away.

For twenty minutes I didn't pass another car. It was taking forever. I checked the speedometer: 23 mph, it said. This was a homecoming retarded by memories; Odysseus had made better time.

Up the steepest hill yet and finally, there below, lay my Eden.

Right away I saw that it was all wrong. The house still stood but the yard did not. The yard was gone. It was now a gravel lot, filled with a couple dozen cars.

The yard was the reason I had come home. The yard was a long, sloping spit of crabgrass where we staked our cow and played ball and recited the Rosary in summertime, the eight of us kneeling in a tight circle around our parents. And a momentous event had taken place in that yard. I had come home to stand in the tall grass at its edge and maybe close my eyes and commune with that momentous event.

The momentous event was in fact a dream—a visitation, really—that came to me every single night for a few years. The Dream featured a man I never met but who meant more to me than any man, dog, or deity. Jesus included. In my parents' home, Jesus was the only thing that truly mattered and although there was some mystery as to how the family had gotten that way, his dominion was never challenged. Our world revolved around the goings-on at Our Lady of Fátima, where my parents were pillars and where I, the baby of the family, became an altar boy when I was five.

The church, I had been instructed, was named for the Virgin Mary's appearances to three shepherd children in the Portuguese mountain village of Fátima. I had further been instructed that it would be an honor to receive such a visitation myself, and that I should keep my eyes open.

So when my own visitation arrived, I took it seriously. My hero came to me with a force, a grace, a reality that neither Jesus nor Mary could muster. He left me quivering in my sleep, astir with joy and longing. In my waking hours I thought of him always, and tried to walk in his light.

But my hero was a football player. This was plainly a heresy, and I

therefore never as much as mentioned the Dream to anyone. Still, I depended on it. Every night I looked forward to bedtime—which may say
less about the Dream than about the unmoored, keening state of my
childhood. It wasn't a miserable childhood, only one with a chunk blown
out of its center, that chunk being my father. I had returned to the site of
this visitation because I had come to believe that it was my hero who
had kept me from crumbling into that hollow center.

JUST AS I PULLED onto the muddy roadside, another car turned in.
It was a pale green Honda. The man who got out wore khaki shorts, a
long-sleeve Oxford shirt, wire-rimmed glasses, loafers with no socks.
He walked with an uneasy, mincing gait, smoothing his hair, with no humility in his stride. He was obviously unaware that he was trampling
my sacred ground. From the looks of him, he could have been a school-
teacher. It was late June: maybe, I thought, the man who bought the
house from my mother was the principal and he threw a year-end party
for his employees?

I rolled down my window. "Hello," I called out, friendly. "Something's
happening here today, yeah?"

"Um, yes." He froze as he spoke, then started quickly toward the
house.

"What . . . what is it?" I asked.

He seemed to blanch. He froze again—"I don't know"—then unfroze,
hurried up the front steps, gave two quick knocks and slipped inside.

What a jerk. *Do you know who I am?*

Or maybe I misheard him. Or he misheard me? Or—I hadn't shaved
in a few days—he thought I was a hoodlum. Or perhaps there was a funeral going on? But he wasn't dressed for a funeral. . . .

For a few minutes I just sat and fumed. Then I drove toward town
and stopped at Wolfe's Market, where I had stocked shelves as a kid.
Mrs. Wolfe was working the counter. We did some catching up, talking
like two adults, which we were, but a part of me kept waiting for her to
ask why in the hell I shelved the mouse poison next to the cat food. (It
made sense to me.)

I told Mrs. Wolfe I'd been up to my old house. I didn't say that the site of my holy Dream had been ruined, only that I saw a lot of cars parked in my yard. "Any idea what's going on there?" I asked.

"You don't know?"

"Know what?"

"Oh boy," she said.

"*What?*"

She exhaled a long, thin stream. "Your house," she said, "is a sex club. A swingers' house. They call it the House of Dreams."

She wasn't kidding. Mr. Wolfe came in just then and together they told me all about it, soberly, the way you'd tell your child that, Well, no, Buster wasn't *really* sent to a farm for old dogs. They said that the man who bought our house fixed it up, installed a Jacuzzi, then bought ads in the kind of newspapers that swingers read. The House of Dreams had a PO box right there in Wolfe's Market. "My box is just below theirs," Mrs. Wolfe told me, "and I've gotten a couple of their letters. It's some pretty wild stuff."

Our house a sex club? *Our* house? That couldn't be. My parents were extremely chastity-minded. They were, I would be willing to bet, the only people to have had sex in that house during our long tenure. They rigorously monitored my sisters' boyfriends; they spoke of the Virgin Birth less as a miracle than a model. Once, when our dog began coupling off with a stray, my mother hurriedly explained that they must have gotten stuck together by a clump of burrs. (And I believed her.)

I drove back up to the house. All the shades were drawn, not a scrap of motion. The house, I had to admit, looked wonderful, far spiffier than in our day. It had been more than ten years since my mother sold the place and moved to Florida. She had called each of us kids, half-hoping, I think, that someone would step in to buy it. But none of us were in the market for a run-down, hundred-year-old farmhouse on thirty acres in the back of beyond. We were all gone and planned on staying gone. For so long the house thrived on our rambunctiousness but toward the end it atrophied, my mother and me rattling around all alone inside, and then just my mother. She could barely afford the heating bills, much less repairs. It fell apart piece by piece, like an old man who stops getting his teeth fixed—and once your teeth fall out, why bother keeping up the rest of your appearances?

Now, though, the chimneys stood straight, new windows sat flush in their frames, the roof gleamed. The old asphalt shingles, full of spidery cracks from years of errant baseballs, had been replaced by clean gray siding. The kitchen had been rebuilt, floor-to-ceiling windows lined with shiny silver reflective panels—the Jacuzzi room, I presumed.

Our old tire swing still hung from the maple tree. The nerve. I thought about knocking on the door, innocently, asking to look around my childhood home, as I'd intended. I then thought about posing as a swinger but I didn't think I could pull it off—and I knew I couldn't handle a Jacuzzi full of naked strangers splashing around the kitchen where my mother led us in Grace before every meal. I may have thirsted for heresy, even tasted a bit myself, but this was not what I had in mind. A priest I once knew told me about some kids who broke into his church and defecated on the altar. Now I understood how he felt. My entire childhood had been shat on.

I sat at the roadside, daring someone to come out and chase me away. Nothing moved. The cars in the lot stood smug and silent, nice cars and new, not like ours had been. I couldn't think of anything else to do—I had forgotten entirely about communing with my childhood hero—so, before driving off, I snapped pictures of all the license plates.

I had the film developed as soon as I got back to New York. The plates were from New York, Massachusetts, Connecticut. I had taken the pictures with blackmail in mind. My wife, Ellen, laughed when I told her. "That instinct," she said, "comes from your mother." She was right. My mother, although often mistaken for an emotionalist, was in fact a truth-seeker with a wide streak of pragmatism. And a moral sense that was high and hard, like a brushback pitch. When I was in junior high school, with just the two of us left in the house, there was a rash of car break-ins in Schenectady. My mother was outraged. Just thwarting the thieves, however, wouldn't suffice; she had to teach them a lesson. The next time she went shopping in Schenectady, she dumped a few pounds of compost—cucumber peels and apple cores and fish heads—in a cardboard box, wrapped it up like a fancy gift, and left it on the back-

seat with the doors unlocked. Nobody stole her present and it stank up
the car for weeks, but she felt better for having staked out the moral
high ground.

I never did resort to blackmail but I too felt better, knowing I could. I
did look up the House of Dreams website, which boasted "a hidden private club, a beauteous farmhouse sitting on 30 wooded acres." I had to
laugh. My father was a newspaperman, a word man through and
through, and *beauteous* was one of his all-time favorites. My father was
often withdrawn, sometimes for weeks on end, but when he was on an
upswing he'd sing and joke and chatter to make up for lost time. He used
his favorite words promiscuously, as if they were punch lines all on their
own, endowing them with melodies and an extra syllable: *bee-OOT-e-us!*
My mother's dress, a fresh glass of cow's milk, a good report card—any
of them might be *bee-OOT-e-us!* But I never heard my father, optimist
though he was, use that word to describe our slope-floored, shingle-
cracked, roof-sagging house, which was many things to many Dubners
for many years but to none of us beauteous.

The House of Dreams website told a different story. The decor was
"gracious," in a "neo-farmhouse style," while the three upstairs bed-
rooms were configured to suit every need: "an open swinging room,
semi-private and totally private." That would be my parents' room, the
Girls' Room, and mine.

For the next few weeks I hatched plans to shut down the House of
Dreams—anonymous threats, arson, a buyback. I called the state troop-
ers in Duanesburg. (They knew about the operation but couldn't do
anything. "Consenting adults and all that," I was told.) I called some
old neighbors. ("Yup, it's terrible," said Mr. Meader, the plumber. "We
used to call it the Dubner Farm but now everybody calls it the Sex
Farm.")

I called a few of my sisters and brothers. They gasped, asked if our
mother knew yet, then warned me not to tell her. Despite her output as a
mother, sex remained a topic one didn't raise with her. She had also been
having heart trouble. This news, they feared, might be the end of her.

I told her anyway. As the baby of the family, I had waited too long to have my say; as the baby of the family, I knew well the strength of her heart.

She took the news surprisingly well. "They're all swinging, huh?" she said. "Geez, it's a shame nothing can be done about it. But it's all in the free will of the individuals, you know. People can choose good or they can choose evil."

I was disappointed. Her moral dudgeon seemed to be fading with age. But after a time, I realized she was right. I had gotten all worked up about a desecration that wasn't. A house has no allegiance, no conscience; a pile of lumber and nails couldn't owe me anything, no matter how I longed to relive my childhood visitation. Besides, the Dream still glimmered on where it really mattered, where it really took place: in my mind.

As for my childhood hero? He, I'd recently learned, hadn't gone anywhere. He still lived in Pittsburgh.

FOR NEARLY TWENTY YEARS my hero had lain dormant in me. Then, one morning not long ago, walking to work through Times Square, I saw him, hanging from the rusty metal clip of a news kiosk, on the cover of a magazine called *Black Enterprise.*

He was a businessman now and wore a dull suit, but my heart began leaping about at the sight of him. Never mind that he was long past his playing days and that I wasn't the kid I used to be. (Or was I?) My reaction was purely chemical. I wasn't just reminded of him; I was reminded of how I once felt about him. A team of American and British scientists, I have read, claim to have isolated the areas of the human brain where love resides. They did this by using X-ray imagery to measure the chemical activity in the brain of an Infatuated Person while he views photographs of his Infatuee. I am confident that if those scientists had hooked me up in Times Square that morning, I would have blown their wiring. My infatuation may not have been lust, but if it wasn't love, nothing was.

I hadn't thought of him since I was a teenager. But in the days and weeks after seeing that magazine, I thought of little else. I knew my feelings for him hadn't *really* resumed, that I was only hearing a powerful echo. (Wasn't I?) I knew I wasn't one of those people who glom onto a guru, some famous stranger, and try to wring from him the mysteries of life. (Was I?)

Still, it set me to wondering. About him, about me, about the spell he'd cast. What had become of him? What kind of man was he? What kind of man was he back when I thought I knew everything there was to know about him? What kind of child was I to have latched onto him so devoutly? And most of all this: what kind of man does that child become?

I cannot say that my life was now unhappy, but it certainly did keep me guessing. After a brief, early marriage, I had just begun a second one, hoping this time for both harmony and children. To my mother's deepest chagrin, I had emigrated out of her fervent Catholicism. In my work, I had reached what seemed a peak, the *New York Times*, but the view didn't always live up to my expectations. Life had thrown any number of interesting pieces at me but I couldn't fit them together. I was a collage, not a complete picture, far less somehow than the sum of my parts.

When the sight of my childhood hero knocked me so squarely into the past, I had just begun to wonder if I could *ever* see myself whole without sifting through the pieces from long ago.

I wasn't trained for that. It is customary in my family to tamp down the past: it happened, it can't be changed, it's best left undisturbed. But the more I tried ignoring the past, the more brazenly my parents and my little-boy self and my childhood hero insisted on cluttering up my present.

That was when I made a seemingly clever and prudent plan—a trip back to the Dream site to wrestle with whatever ghosts my memory might rouse.

That, as we have seen, didn't work out as planned.

I probably should have let it go there. But I couldn't. I have more than a little of my mother in me—both the truth-seeker and the pragmatist—which is how, the following spring, I would come to find myself

clutching an airsick bag on a terrifically bumpy flight bound for Pittsburgh. There, perhaps, I'd find some answers. There, perhaps, I could finally understand why a little boy would reach out to some faraway
figure to usher him through a childhood that no one near to him could
penetrate.

2

Limbs and Loins

———◦∞◦———

I CAME OF AGE deeply ignorant of my parents' past, which was just how they wanted it. There were no long, laughing nights of reminiscence. No crinkled photographs or family heirlooms, no wool-coated visitors from the Old Country, which I knew to be a distant, exotic land called Brooklyn.

As it happened, my parents had sacrificed their hard history, torched it entirely, in order to build a future path to Heaven. As a child, what little I knew about them lay within the confines of our church and house. What I didn't know could fill a book (and it already has). I wouldn't learn their stories for many years, until my late twenties, at which point I unspooled and eventually wrapped myself up in the history they abandoned.

As it happened, my very Catholic parents had each started out Jewish. My mother, born Florence Greenglass, came from a fast-assimilating immigrant family of shopkeepers in Crown Heights. My father, Solomon Dubner, grew up in Brownsville, known then as Little Jerusalem, the son of a pious, rigid man named Shepsel. Even after twenty years, Shepsel Dubner lived his every day in Brooklyn as if he were still in Poland—the same clothes and food, the same curt Yiddish, the same neighbors praying the same prayers in a synagogue built to look like the one back home.

My mother was a comely, kind, and deeply willful ballerina. My father was an amiable, hopeful, but depressive dreamer. They met during the heart of World War II when my father, a soldier stationed in the South Pacific, came back to New York on furlough. By then they had each, implausibly, trudged through valleys of desperation and desire to fall completely in love with Jesus. Now they fell in love with each other. Fueled by their zeal, as converts tend to be, they reinvented themselves. Florence and Solly became Veronica and Paul; Catholicism encircled their every passion.

My mother's mother, though not religious, seethed with shame. My father's father, who was nothing but religious, entered a state of raging despair. Shepsel Dubner pronounced his son dead and sat shiva for him; he declared that he would never again speak to his son nor utter his name, and commanded the rest of the family to do the same. For the most part, Shepsel's harsh command was obeyed.

Paul and Veronica, meanwhile, hardly seemed to notice. They got fruitful and multiplied and, since their families weren't family anymore, they transplanted their expanding brood to the dilapidated farmhouse in Duanesburg, New York—just 150 miles but a world away from New York City—now known as the House of Dreams.

From Brooklyn they had carried forth only a few shards: an accent, a taste for strange, salty foods (my father stole a regular after-Mass nosh of gefilte fish on matzo), and a foggy reverence for the Brooklyn Dodgers.

My mother grew up a few blocks away from Ebbets Field. Her father kept the radio in his candy store tuned to the Dodgers game, enticing customers to linger all day. (The radio was set up near his most expensive cigars.) As a girl, my mother followed the team's on-field accomplishments only casually. It was their civilian activities that she and her girlfriends monitored, swapping sightings of this Dodger in a hat shop or that one riding the trolley.

My father, growing up a few neighborhoods over, rooted with his whole being for the Dodgers (as well as, owing to a Hebraic loyalty popular in Brooklyn, Hank Greenberg of the Detroit Tigers). Solly Dubner and his friends, who wanted nothing more than to get up and out of their fathers' Old World houses, saw no inconsistency in a bunch of asphalt kids devoting themselves to a green-grass game that was all about going home, home, home.

He badly wanted to play shortstop for the Dodgers and when that didn't pan out he wanted to cover them for the *Daily News*. But his talent was not commensurate with his dreams. In the end he settled for a correspondence course with the Newspaper Institute of America. This was after the war, after his conversion, after he'd been cast out from his family. He wrote his NIA assignments in the chinks of time between church, work (a series of clerking and lifting and selling jobs), and the ever-deepening duties of fatherhood. A boy, then three girls, a pair of boys, one last girl, and me.

He was in his forties by the time he won a real newspaper job, as a copy editor with the *Schenectady Gazette*. Stung by the Dodgers' defection to Los Angeles, he had become a Mets fan. He had also invoked a family rule that no two of us could root for the same baseball team. Upon birth, I was assigned the Baltimore Orioles. (The Mets, Yankees, Dodgers, Giants, Cardinals, and Red Sox had all been taken.)

I became genuinely devoted to the Orioles. I loved the goofy smiling bird on their caps; I loved the city of Baltimore—smelling, I imagined, all crabby and smoky. I depended on Boog Powell's big baggy presence at first base, and in the yard I tirelessly imitated the diving backhand stops of third baseman Brooks Robinson, the Human Vacuum Cleaner. I didn't much care for Earl Weaver, the Orioles' snarly little manager, but I did like that he grew tomatoes in the bullpen. We grew tomatoes too.

As soon as I learned to ride a bike, I took to the hills selling packets of flower seeds door to door. With my first earnings, I bought a subscription to *Sports Illustrated*, the better to follow my team. It didn't hurt that I inherited the Orioles just in time for a years-long winning streak. I never had occasion, therefore, to challenge my father's odd rooting rule or even wonder about it. But now I do. Was he only trying to be playful? To exercise control? To re-create the endless baseball debates of his youth?

Maybe all that is a little true. But I now suspect that he gave us each our own baseball team because it was the only big and grand and valuable thing he could afford to give us, with his $150-a-week salary and his eight children and the quiet poverty those two numbers conspired to levy. We were a family accustomed to sharing and doing without—but when it was finally your turn with the *Gazette* sports section, settling in under the breakfast clatter to study the box score, you were an *owner.* Once a day, you knew what it felt like to have more than enough.

Even my sisters rooted hard and sent off for autographed pictures. Baseball was a sort of satellite religion in our home. Like us, baseball was pious and reverent and rule-bound, neither boastful nor violent; it had its own saints, rituals, relics. Best of all, it had a history. We were free to rake through the players' lives, to learn who they were and how they got that way.

In our living room was a crooked bookcase jammed with Catholic biographies and prayer books and children's stories. There stood among them just one secular book, *A Tree Grows in Brooklyn*. This exception gave it great weight. My discovery of it was startling, as if I'd stumbled upon the Dead Sea Scrolls: hard evidence of a lost, vital era. My parents' era.

True, the Nolan family wasn't Jewish—I suspect the book wouldn't have been in our home if they were—but they did live in the same Brooklyn that produced my parents, a paved-over farmland packed with Italians and Irish and Jews, drunkards and preachers, trolley cars and ice trucks.

Knowing nothing about my parents as children, I read the book for clues, plugging them into every story. I pictured my little-boy father, grubby Spaldeen in grubby hand, kicking over his mother's wash bucket as he sprinted down the tenement stairwell. (So that's where his jumpiness came from.) I saw my little-girl mother staring down the butcher to make sure he kept his thumb off the scale. (So that's where her hardness came from.)

Sure, these were pilfered memories, and they weren't much, but they were all I had. My mother and father offered only glancing, innocuous tidbits about the past, and it was understood that we weren't to ask for more.

All that missing history troubled me, just as it troubled me that the New Testament couldn't account for Jesus between his dramatic birth and his dramatic ministry. What *happened* all those years? In Sunday School we read countless "Little Boy Jesus" books, but they were plainly fabrications. My father even knew a lady who wrote such books; they were no more authentic to Jesus than *A Tree Grows in Brooklyn* was to my parents. And not once, in all my reading, did I run across a teenage Jesus.

Even so, I knew far more about Jesus than I knew about my parents. Even Zeus and Superman had their origin myths. My parents, I was expected to believe, had been brought forth whole, Catholic, unmarked by their very births. There was only one ancestor they freely claimed, one affiliation they hadn't renounced, and that was the Brooklyn Dodgers.

The kinship seemed all the more real since the Dodgers had also fled Brooklyn. It hardly mattered that I was prohibited from rooting for them, either the Diaspora Dodgers or the Mets who popped up one borough over. The fact that the Dodgers of Brooklyn had existed, and were acknowledged to have existed by my parents, who acknowledged nothing else about their time in Brooklyn, gave the whole of baseball an imprimatur that, in my mind at least, rivaled the crucifix itself.

My mother tolerated baseball, even followed it, as long as it didn't interfere with the pursuit of Heaven. She kept her eyes on the prize. Like any good Catholic mother, she dearly wanted to send one of her sons into the priesthood. By now all three of my brothers were out of contention. Joe, learning to fly fighter jets in the Air Force, was already married. Peter was about to be (wearing a dashiki, no less). Dave had made it clear that his teenage disdain for the Church was permanent. I was my mother's last, best hope.

"Let Jesus come to you," she said, over and again, as if it were all up to me, and I did try. He had obviously come to my parents. I was slavishly obedient, praying and fasting and studying as prescribed. I genuinely revered Father DiPace, and I executed my altar-boy duties with feeling. From the outside I must have been the very picture of a young priest-in-training. In my heart, however, I believed in but one true religion, and that was baseball.

The Duanesburg Little League had only four teams. I was a very good player in a very small talent pool, and this led me to believe I was better than I was, bound for the Orioles if I worked hard enough. I threw myself fly balls until my arm throbbed. I spent so many hours at the Pitchback, a rebounding contraption designed for overzealous Little Leaguers, that I popped its springs. In the interest of maximizing my potential, I decided one day to become a switch-hitter. I set about teaching myself to bat left-handed. On my first swing I connected so well— with the back of my skull—that my mother heard the thump from the kitchen and came out to find me crumpled in the grass.

Mostly I tried to get someone else to play with me. Beth, my closest sibling, was, unfortunately, a girl. I begged Dave to hit me grounders but he had moved on to motorcycles and low-grade mayhem. My mother had a good arm but too many chores. My father was off at the newspaper or, just as often, "lying down" upstairs. This, I had gleaned, was code language for some condition far beyond exhaustion.

It was my father I wanted more than anyone. He felt about baseball as I did. Novices complained about the slow pace of the game, but he and I understood that each rare spasm of action was in fact the result of a thousand tiny, constant maneuvers. My father appreciated the importance of footwork in the field. He taught me about choking up on the bat with two strikes. He knew all about drag bunting and charging a ground ball and hitting the cutoff man, details that eluded my Little League teammates and even the coaches.

I did once get him to hit me some grounders in the yard. The sun had already set. I was so eager to show off that I bobbled the first three or four balls, easy ones.

"Shrug it off!" he hollered out. He knew I was nervous, and because I knew he knew, I settled down.

He handled the bat slickly, with a manly familiarity, the way the old soldiers from the VFW twirled their rifles in the Memorial Day parade. He was in his early fifties, short of breath but, as he would have said, full of pep. It was October and already we'd had some heavy frosts. The yard was pocked with cow hoofprints, half-frozen and deep. My father kept warning me to stay on smooth ground but I made him hit the ball farther and farther from my spot—I wanted to make those backhand dives like Brooks Robinson. We created a rhythm: the *kronk* of his bat, the ball sizzling through the tall fall grass, me diving, pivoting, throwing, the *smat* into his bare palm. Again and again and again. By now it was deep dusk. One dim bulb hung from the barn and the ball was so old and brown that it was shadow I followed more than ball. My father tried a few times to wave me in but I wouldn't let him go. I was having the time of my life. He hit again, a hard chopper to my right that, as I charged it, must have nicked one of those hoofprints, for it hopped up and hit me hard in the throat. I went down. When I came to, my father was so worried, his eyes quaking behind his glasses, that I guess he thought he killed me. He never hit me any more grounders after that.

A BABY LEARNS to play long before he talks, and if ontogeny truly recapitulates phylogeny, mankind probably did the same. We'll never know the exact games our prehistoric brethren played, but anthropologists believe they involved the hitting of a rock with a stick—in which case, our sports have evolved far less than other human endeavors.

That, psychologists tell us, is because sports fulfill our most primal urges: our sexual urges. In baseball, for instance, if the man with the phallic bat strikes the eggish ball just so, he produces a run. (Of course, he is just as likely to strike out.)

When I was in the first grade, I invited my teacher to our house one Saturday for what my mother called a brunch but which I knew to be a date. Her name was Miss Finch and I was in love with her. She wore nylons and skirts and eyeliner and swished past my desk in a sweet, ticklish cloud. I had asked my mother to make blueberry pancakes. My mother's cooking, which necessarily placed quantity above quality, was generally terrible, but her blueberry pancakes were all right. Miss Finch arrived exactly on time. I ran onto the porch to greet her but was struck dumb and blushing. I retreated, fetching an object I prided above all else and which, I now see, did my talking for me: my baseball bat. It was a full-size bat, originally thirty-two inches long, whose end my father had sawed off, leaving it not gracefully rounded but surgically flat and caked with the mud of a thousand playground hours.

The actual game of baseball, however, is more slyly sexual, laced as it is with long pauses and an almost gentlemanly decorum. Football is another matter. Football is, from start to end, carnal—one team ramming its way through the other, squiring its precious ball through a pit of limbs and loins, the men brutish and hidden and helmeted.

Our school was too small and poor to have a football team, and the two-hand touch we played on Saturdays hardly resembled the real thing. But I saw it on television. Football was another world; it was everything my family was not about. I began watching one Sunday and, surprised that no one made me stop, I kept at it. My love of baseball was a pure love, but because it was sanctioned by my parents, it was also chaste. Football tasted like forbidden fruit. And once I'd had a taste all I wanted was more. That it happened only on Sundays was an added excitement. To come home from church, feeling all somber and saintly, and go straight to a football game on television was almost too much to bear. A violent, enthralling, foreign Sabbath. Football was my first illicit thrill—as bold a rebellion as I, a shy and obedient boy, could manage.

And it went beyond rebellion. In a houseful of brothers and sisters and parents, all of them older and smarter and more capable than me, football was the most precious of commodities: football was mine and mine alone.

3

THE IMMACULATE RECEPTION

———◆◆◆◆◆———

IN 1972, the first year of my football obsession, I was nine and Christmas Eve fell on a Sunday. That meant no football for me. We'd go to early Mass, then hustle home to spend the day preparing for what my mother called Jesus' birthday party.

The television and couch would be shoved into a corner to make way for the tree. The tattered sheet music, jumbled stamp collections, and grinning school pictures were cleared from the top of the piano. That's where we set up the plaster Nativity scene—minus, for now, the Baby Jesus, who wasn't allowed until after midnight, and the Three Wise Men, who would arrive on January 6, the Feast of the Epiphany. The day got louder as the out-of-house siblings drove in from points north and west. In early afternoon, a bunch of us would tromp into the woods, my father with an ax over his shoulder, to hunt for a presentable tree to be chopped down, dragged through the snow, let to thaw in the bathtub, and decorated with paper chains, tinsel, and an angel on top. At eight o'clock my mother would make me get in bed so I'd be fresh for Midnight Mass, which was the performance of the year for an altar boy and which capped a long day full of anticipation and revelry but, alas, no football.

But it was the playoff season. This meant there would also be a game on Saturday, the day before Christmas Eve, the Oakland Raiders against the Pittsburgh Steelers.

I had begun studying football in the *Schenectady Gazette* and *Sports Illustrated*, but I didn't yet have a favorite team. This wasn't a problem. Whenever a boy sits down to watch a ballgame, his mind engages in a swift and subtle calculus to determine where his heart will spend the next three hours (and, in some cases, far beyond).

On this day the math was easier than usual. The Raiders, dressed in menacing silver, black, and white, were perennial winners but vain and nasty. The team's owner, a martinet named Al Davis, allowed no clocks on Raiders property because he didn't want his minions distracted by non-football matters. Davis routinely signed up players who'd been in trouble with the law; he'd had Raiders employees pose as sportswriters to scout an opponent's injuries.

The Steelers, meanwhile, outfitted in knightly black and gold, had won a division title for the first time in their forty years of existence. The Steelers played hard but not dirty; they were confident but not cocky. They were still owned by Arthur J. Rooney, who founded the team, a genial and generous man known as the Chief. A reformed horseplayer, boxing promoter, and ward healer, the Chief was still rough around the edges but for decades now had gone to Mass every morning and was said to have paid for more funerals than the City of Pittsburgh itself. Every Sunday he watched his Steelers in silence with a cigar in his mouth and a priest at his side; he was known to sprinkle Holy Water in the locker room before a big game. To all but a few aging cranks who remembered that the Chief had made his bones amid strong-arm men, women for hire, and votes for sale, he was considered a saint, a cheery but weary Moses given a glimpse, at long last, of football's Promised Land.

On that wintry Saturday, it required little further thought or effort to turn my heart over to the Steelers.

PRO FOOTBALL GOT its start in the Pittsburgh area and so did, it seemed, half the National Football League, from the loose-limbed quarterbacks (Johnny Unitas out of St. Justin's and Joe Namath from up in Beaver Falls) to the onomatopoeic head-bangers (Mike Ditka from Aliquippa and Cookie Gilchrist, who went from Har-Brack High straight to the pros). In the towns up and down the three rivers that converge in Pittsburgh, steelmaking and football were Jesus and Mary. On Friday nights, high-school games drew ten thousand spectators. Lots of those boys went on to college ball, the best of them to Penn State or Pitt. The others took jobs in the steel mills and played for the mill football team. And then there were the Steelers.

For much of the Steelers' history, some of those mill teams might have beaten them. The Steelers lost dully and they lost spectacularly, but almost always they lost. They had some good players over the years but managed to cut the greatest, Johnny Unitas—a move as cursed in Pittsburgh as, in Boston, the sale of Babe Ruth to the Yankees. The team's coaches, hired mainly from the Chief's circle of cronies, were generally ineffectual. The Steelers offense of the 1950s was so predictably dependent on straight-ahead runs by the fullback Fran Rogel that fans instituted a glum cheer before kickoffs: "Hi diddle diddle, Rogel up the middle." The defense was little better. Toward the end of a home loss to the Green Bay Packers, one fed-up Steelers fan jumped out of the stands and tackled the Packers' ball carrier himself. The fan was thrown out of the stadium; critics said the Steelers should have given him a uniform. The Steelers—and Pittsburgh—became a laughingstock. Even Johnny Carson chimed in: "One Pittsburgh Steeler says to another, 'Do you think we'll ever start winning again?' The second Steeler says, 'What's *winning?*'"

The Chief had five sons, and by the late 1960s the two eldest, Dan and Art Jr., were helping run the team. (There was no room for the other three, who went off to oversee the family's racetracks.) The young Rooneys brought to the Steelers an air of professionalism and meritocracy. In 1969 the Steelers hired a new head coach, thirty-seven-year-old Chuck Noll, an assistant in Baltimore who had reportedly turned down the top job in Oakland because he didn't want to work for Al Davis. Noll lacked the barroom color of the Chief's usual hires—he was fond of mathematical theory, gourmet cooking, and classical music—and he had different football views too. He understood the game as less a jumble of brute force and bad bounces than an exercise in leverage, cohesion, and, above all, athletic grace.

The first college player the Steelers drafted under Noll was an undervalued defensive tackle named Charles Edward Greene, soon known as Mean Joe Greene, a blend of speed, power, and a supernatural tenacity. "He was something new," one sportswriter would later comment, "like aluminum when it first came out." Greene anchored what would become the impregnable Steel Curtain defense. The following year Noll drafted Terry Bradshaw, a mouthy and unpolished but golden-armed quarterback from Louisiana. Although the Steelers kept losing (they went 1–13 in Noll's first year), they were amassing great young talent as Noll reshaped the team in his image.

Going into the 1972 draft, the Steelers argued over their top pick. Noll wanted Robert Newhouse, a stocky and speedy running back out of the University of Houston. Art Rooney Jr., the team's head scout, lobbied for a different running back, Franco Harris from Penn State. Harris was much bigger than Newhouse, six-foot-two and 225 pounds, and maybe even faster. But he was a mystery. Despite his size, Harris wasn't a bruiser. He had an unorthodox running style—running scared, some thought—darting and then cutting back, never letting tacklers get an angle on him.

Art Rooney Jr. drove up to Penn State several times to scout Harris. "He looked like a Greek god," Rooney recalled years later, "this beautiful nose straight down his face, a big guy, not black and not white." Harris was the son of an Italian mother and a black GI father who met near Pisa after the Allies liberated Italy. Franco, the third of their nine children, grew up near Fort Dix in southern New Jersey. He had an excellent sophomore season at Penn State and a very good junior year, but as a senior he was disappointing. Coach Joe Paterno benched Harris for the Cotton Bowl after he twice showed up late for practice. Word got around that Harris had been intentionally late, testing Paterno's authority. This hardly helped his murky reputation: he was lazy, he didn't play hurt, he lacked mental toughness. Art Rooney Jr. knew Harris wasn't a bad kid at all, just unusual, introspective and maybe a little iconoclastic—*an individualist,* the other scouts sneered.

Chuck Noll didn't want any individualists mucking up his meticulous new system. And though he was hardly a rah-rah coach, Noll only wanted players who were desperate to win. The Steelers' own scouting reports doubted Harris's desire: "Not a hustler. . . . Question his top competitiveness. . . . Could be a great pro but might not even be a good one."

Art Rooney Jr., however, was not only the Steelers' head scout but the owner's son, and so it was that on draft day the Steelers made Franco Harris their first-round choice. Noll phoned Harris with the news.

When he hung up, Noll turned to his assistant coaches. "He sounds like a dud," he said. "He's got no enthusiasm."

Steelers fans were also unhappy. They preferred their players rough and rugged, like themselves.

Franco Harris was the unhappiest of all. Pittsburgh was dead last on his wish list of pro teams. Having grown up in New Jersey and played college ball in the wintry wilds of central Pennsylvania, he was hoping to be drafted by a California team or the Miami Dolphins. Pittsburgh was cold and the Steelers were losers.

In training camp, Harris was thoroughly underwhelming. The veteran Steelers traded glances: *this* is our No. 1 pick? Harris was big, all right, but he had bird legs, no biceps, a roll of baby fat around his middle, and he never seemed to shift out of low gear.

The Steelers began the 1972 season with two losses and two wins. Harris barely played, and when he did he missed assignments or fumbled the ball. But he was given a chance in the fifth game, against the Houston Oilers. He broke out for 115 yards and scored his first touchdown. Maybe he wasn't a bust after all?

Two weeks later, in Buffalo, Harris ran for 131 yards and scored three touchdowns. "We didn't do anything to motivate him," Chuck Noll told reporters, "although it would be nice to take credit for it. It's all his. He put his mind to it."

Harris put his mind to it all season long. For six straight weeks he

ran for more than 100 yards, tying an NFL record set by the great Jim
Brown of Cleveland. Harris became only the second Steeler, after John
Henry Johnson, to gain 1,000 rushing yards in a season. John Henry
Johnson and Jim Brown: *they* were the kind of running backs that Steelers fans dreamed about. They ran hard and straight, plowing through
tacklers or dragging them along. Franco Harris, meanwhile, would
sooner scoot out of bounds than blast into a linebacker—which might
make sense to some people but not to the good people of Pittsburgh,
who expected their Steelers to walk away from each play concussed, if
they walked away at all.

But it turned out that Franco Harris and the good people of Pittsburgh had more in common than either had imagined. He was relentlessly down to earth: instead of blowing his rookie salary on some flashy
sports car, he took the bus to Three Rivers Stadium every morning. He
wasn't a chest-thumper: Harris never spiked the ball after a touchdown,
and when reporters swarmed him after a big game, he told them that,
Sure he played hard, but it was his blockers who were *really* busting
their tails out there, and they should get their pictures in the paper too.
Harris was polite to the press—he was polite to everyone, almost laugh-
ably so, especially to the kids who'd begun trailing him all around
town—but he hated calling attention to himself. He'd visit Children's
Hospital on his off day and get upset if it made the papers.

He was always in the papers. With his caramel skin, Roman features,
plush beard and Afro, his face was a sculpture. He was variously described as resembling a Moorish sheik or an Old Testament prophet.
People weren't sure what to make of his mixed ancestry. When he was
in college, all the pro teams had scouted him, including the Washington
Redskins and their coach, Vince Lombardi, who won five champi-
onships with the Green Bay Packers. "Hey, Coach, watch this guy run,"
said one of Lombardi's assistants who was studying film of Harris.
"He's half-black and half-Italian."

"Half-black and half-Italian—he's probably half a runner too!" Lombardi hollered, and walked on past the film room. Later, Lombardi relented. He took a look as Harris darted his way to one touchdown after
the next. "Goddamn!" he shouted. "Look at that Italian *run*!"

The Steelers' PR man now came to Harris's locker with a question: "The reporters want to know—are you black or are you Italian, or what are you?"

If it's got to be one or the other, Harris told him, say black. "In New Jersey we were always considered a black family—we couldn't get housing in white neighborhoods," he told one sportswriter. "I don't deny my Italian blood, I just never thought of myself as Italian. Mostly, I've thought of myself as being an individual."

But in Pittsburgh no one was just an individual. It was a city without a melting pot, and race mattered. The local amusement park offered Carpatho-Russian Day, Serbian Day, Italian Day, and Slovene Day, among many, many others. Black-white tension was particularly thick in Pittsburgh. In the name of urban renewal, thriving black neighborhoods had been bulldozed and dead-ended. The assassination of Martin Luther King Jr. had produced bloody riots; the only white people looking out for black men, it was said, were the Irish cops and the Vietnam draft boards. Slavs and Poles and Italians, meanwhile, held their own grievances. With the steel industry having peaked, high-paying mill jobs were scarce, while the corridors of true wealth and patronage—City Hall and the police, fire, and transit departments—were practically off-limits if you weren't Irish.

In 1903, the muckraker Lincoln Steffens, having witnessed Pittsburgh's nighttime constellation of mill-furnace fires, called the city "Hell with the lid off." Politically, he said, it was "Hell with the lid *on*." By the early 1970s the air wasn't so dirty—office workers no longer had to change their white shirts at midday—but the politics were. Factions begat factions. Everything was political, and all politics were personal, and there was nothing, absolutely nothing, that could unite Pittsburgh . . . or that was the theory at least, until the autumn of 1972.

On the back of Franco Harris, the Steelers won nine of their last ten games. After so much losing football in a football town, a winning team turned an army of factions into one big Steeler Nation. And no single Steeler was more celebrated than this strange, wonderful rookie.

Of course they all wanted their own piece of him. The Irish heard his name as Frank O'Harris. The Greeks fancied him Frank Oharis. He was claimed by black fans, to be sure, and rightfully. But it was the Italians, the city's largest ethnic clan, who planted their flag with the greatest vigor.

Tony Stagno and Al Vento, a baker and a pizza man, respectively, launched Franco's Italian Army, a fan club fueled by jug wine and absurdist theatrics. It began with a few handmade signs and prosciutto sandwiches. Soon the Army was distributing thousands of tiny Italian flags at Three Rivers Stadium; whenever their hero scored a touchdown, they waved salamis and staged a dress parade. As Harris's fame spread, the Army went national. Noted Italian-Americans, including Frank Sinatra and Henry Mancini, rushed to join. But the Army was nothing if not inclusive. It officially appended a Dutch Division, an Israeli Brigade, a canine corps, a nurses' unit, and Franco's Black American Army.

It was the same year that Hank Aaron, threatening Babe Ruth's home-run record, received a crop of racist hate mail. "Niggers are the same as apes and have the morals of an alley cat and are Parasites and the Scum of the Earth," read one letter. Pittsburgh, meanwhile, never known as a racially enlightened town, somehow united behind Franco Harris. "The spontaneous formation of fan clubs such as . . . Franco's Italian Army spiced the life of Pittsburgh," the *Pittsburgh Post-Gazette* editorialized at season's end. "The bi-racial characteristic of the Franco fan club in particular was a much needed tonic for our times."

Winning the Central Division of the American Football Conference was also a nice tonic. Now the upstart Steelers would face the dangerous Raiders on Saturday, December 23. If the Steelers prevailed they'd need just one more victory to make it to the Super Bowl.

Only forty years of football failure could have produced the frenzy that gripped Pittsburgh. "Meek ribbon clerks discourse learnedly on post patterns and zone defenses," reported the *Post-Gazette*. The night before the game, several hundred Steelers fans held a pep rally downtown. Once they were properly lubricated, they marched on the Hilton Hotel, where the Oakland Raiders were staying. They hurled their empty beer bottles at the Hilton as if it were the enemy itself. The police tried pushing them back. One man insisted on getting inside—he said he played for the Raiders—but the police chose to disbelieve him (or perhaps they did believe him but couldn't pass up the opportunity) and clubbed him on the head, a wound requiring six stitches for the man who was indeed Raiders tight end Bob Moore. (He would play the next day, ineffectively, his head bandaged.)

Saturday dawned cold and damp. The game fit the weather. It was a toe-to-toe defensive battle, which, like a pitchers' duel in baseball, is hailed by purists but leaves the typical fan—a nine-year-old boy, for instance, watching on television—more tense than excited.

By late in the game, the Steelers led 6–0. The stands began rumbling the roar of victory too long deferred. The Raiders had the ball but the Steelers defense had been so stingy, so canny and ferocious, that the lead seemed safe. Even when Dwight White, the Steelers' strapping defensive end, left the field with a pinched nerve, no one panicked: there was barely a minute left in the game.

But on the next play Kenny Stabler, the Raiders' quarterback, broke free and ran right past where White's fill-in should have been but wasn't, and although Stabler ran ugly, like an old man lugging groceries across an icy parking lot, he reached the end zone, which led the entire city of Pittsburgh to groan as if it had been kicked in the stomach.

The average Pittsburgher was known to suffer a well-earned inferiority complex. It was a city where, as a matter of course, the strong trounced the weak, expressed no regret, and demanded the weak accept the outcome, which they generally did. "I have always had one rule," a U.S. Steel executive famously said in 1901. "If a workman sticks up his head, hit it." The failed Whiskey Rebellion of 1794, the bloody Homestead Strike of 1892, even the Steelers' losing streak—they all proved that, without a miracle, Goliath beats David every time, and whether you're going up against George Washington's government or Andrew Carnegie's iron-and-steel empire or Al Davis's Oakland Raiders, you are bound, in the end, to lose.

On this day, Steelers fans had dismissed their history for nearly an entire football game. Kenny Stabler put them back in their place. They sat now in silent misery, which was unusual only in that it had been preceded by hope.

Trailing by one point, the Steelers got the ball back but couldn't move it. Time was about to expire. On the sidelines, their teammates were openly deflated. In the stands, sorrowful men stomped empty beer cups into splinters. On the fourth level of Three Rivers Stadium, Arthur J. Rooney shook the hand of the priest who'd watched the game with him, left his box, and rode the elevator down to the locker room to console his players.

Reaching the ground floor, the Chief heard a wild and unfamiliar clamor. Were the fans so fed up with losing that they had rioted? Had they perhaps murdered an Oakland Raider?

When the Chief's ride began, the Steelers were backed into their final corner—fourth down, 60 yards from the end zone, only twenty-two seconds left. In the huddle, Franco Harris listened as Terry Bradshaw called a play, the 66 Circle Option. Harris was upset. In the 66 Circle Option, Harris did nothing more than hang around the backfield and block for Bradshaw. It seemed a lousy, uneventful way to end his magical rookie season.

The Steelers broke their huddle. Bradshaw took the snap. Although the Raiders had most of their men back in pass coverage, he was immediately under assault. Harris, whose distaste for physical contact included blocking, wasn't much help. Bradshaw frantically dodged one Raiders rusher, then another. Just as he was about to be tackled, Bradshaw blindly unleashed a bullet pass. What happened next would have confused even Pythagoras.

The ball zipped downfield where it, one Steeler, and one Raider met with great force. Neither man, however, came close to catching the ball. It ricocheted free, seemingly destined to land on the turf and kill the Steelers' season. But the ball, instead of falling to the ground, had somehow remained aloft and now traveled in a wobbly arc back toward the line of scrimmage. Suddenly Franco Harris arrived at full gallop and, cradling his hands as if to rescue a baby tossed from a burning tenement, caught the ball at his shoetops. Never losing stride, he headed for the end zone, shoulders rising and falling in grand fashion, arms and legs pumping fluidly, a Giacometti come to life. The Raiders were by now realizing that Franco had caught the ball out of the air, and they pursued him, four of them and then three—Franco was flat outrunning them—two Raiders and then the last one, whom he stiff-armed, in a tightrope sprint now, his toes just inches from the sideline, and he crossed the goal line.

The clamor the Chief heard, stepping off the elevator, was other-worldly. It sounded as though fifty thousand people had been locked in a train bound for Hell and, when the doors opened, they found they had somehow been diverted to Heaven. Fans rushed the field; at least one man broke his leg jumping out of the stands. They hugged the Steelers and the Steelers hugged them back. Unbeknownst to all of them, the referee had not yet ruled the play a touchdown. He was on the phone with his supervisor in the press box, making sure the strange ricochet play was legal. After a few minutes' deliberation, he came back onto the field and signaled a touchdown—a call, the Raiders later protested, meant primarily to preserve the referee's life, for the exultant crowd indeed might have rioted otherwise. The party continued on the field and then throughout the city. It was the wildest celebration since Pittsburgh's other David-beats-Goliath moment, back in the final game of the 1960 World Series, when a coal miner's son named Bill Mazeroski hit a ninth-inning home run to lead the Pirates past the mighty New York Yankees. Now, in the locker rooms at Three Rivers Stadium, the Raiders wept like lost children while the Steelers took turns throwing their arms around a half-naked Franco Harris as he explained anew for each reporter how he had happened to make what many years hence would be declared the single greatest play in NFL history.

By midnight it had been given a name: the Immaculate Reception. The play's miraculous nature was ascribed to various sources:

Franco Harris's mother, the former Gina Parenti of Pietrasanta, Italy, revealed that, in the moments before the catch, she put on her favorite record, Beniamino Gigli's "Ave Maria," to encourage the Fates, or God, to guide her son's hand.

Art Rooney Jr., who had reason to gloat for having drafted Franco Harris in the first place, took pains to take no credit: "That catch wasn't good scouting," he said. "It wasn't good coaching, it wasn't good playing. It was seventy-two years of good Christian life on the part of my father."

The *Pittsburgh Press* put it this way: "The god of all the losers who have ever been smiled down through a ghostly gray sky yesterday, and in the last desperate seconds of a mean, bitterly fought football game did truly wondrous things."

As with any truly wondrous thing, any awe-inspiring event that announces itself on the spot as history, the Immaculate Reception would become a myth burdened by misinterpretations and lies. As with Woodstock, for instance, or the Virgin Mary's appearances at Fátima, untold thousands would falsely claim they had witnessed the Immaculate Reception in person. Millions more would say they had seen it on television—which, in Pittsburgh at least, was also a lie, for the NFL's blackout rules of that time prohibited the game from being broadcast within seventy-five miles.

BUT IT WASN'T blacked out in upstate New York, and I saw it, live, on WRGB-NBC, Channel 6, on our thirteen-inch black-and-white set with the broken volume knob that you needed a pliers to adjust, and I was overcome with a sort of joy that I hadn't known to exist.

Someone standing outside our living-room window might have been distressed at the sight: a smallish, messy-haired boy in knee-patched pants corkscrewing himself into the air, again and again, his mouth frozen open in a great "O" but no sound escaping it, leaping and leaping until collapsing onto the couch. I couldn't have articulated my joy then. I don't know if I can now. It was the fullest moment I'd ever lived through, brimming with unlikeliness and underdog-ness and, yes, miraculousness (though I would not have dared say that in my mother's presence). By this time I knew a few things about Franco Harris, though not nearly as much as I soon would. What I did know, as of that Saturday evening just before Christmas in the year I was nine years old, was that if Franco Harris had quit football the next day and announced that he was starting a circus, I would have run away to join it. An army? I would have enlisted. I would have picked rags with him or shucked corn. There were others who felt that way, I'm sure, at least on that night. There were others who, in the seasons to come, would get his autograph or shake his hand in a restaurant or scream his name from the cheap seats at Three Rivers Stadium. But I doubt there was anyone who would come to need him as much as I did.

4

A DISASTROUS DISTURBANCE
OF THE HEART

—————•◦❀◦•—————

THE FOLLOWING DECEMBER, nearly a year to the day of
the Immaculate Reception, my father died. Christmas was ruined, of course, that year and forever. The shame of it was that he had finally stuck his head up through a lifelong cloud of depression. But my
father was a common man, not so different from the miners and steelers
of Pittsburgh, and as soon as he stuck up his head somebody hit it.

His body had been just waiting to give out. If you poked a pin everywhere he had something wrong, he would have looked like a porcupine.
Appendicitis, high blood pressure, a bleeding ulcer, a hernia: all the gifts
of having swallowed too much sadness. He was a born optimist but his
brain produced sadness in vast quantities.

His mother, Gittel, died when he was fifteen and he never really re-
covered. She had been the source of all the warmth in their home, a
buffer between her six children and her stern, pious husband Shepsel.

My father silently blamed Shepsel for the death of his mother. Gittel
was only fifty-one and had been worked like a plow horse. It was she
who ran the family's little kosher restaurant and kept their home—
barely sleeping, rarely eating—while Shepsel piddled away time at the
synagogue.

Shepsel was determined that my father, with his good head for Torah and wonderful singing voice, become a rabbi or a cantor. To Shepsel, my father's interests—baseball and novels and swing music—were trash, American foolishness, *narishkeit*. While Gittel was alive, she kept a peace between her wanting-too-much son and her giving-too-little husband. After her death it became a bitter, wordless war.

My father was twenty-five and still under Shepsel's roof when the Japanese bombed Pearl Harbor. He enlisted immediately. Several months later, several thousand miles from home, he listened to an Army chaplain tell him, for the first time, about the Virgin Mary. He was enthralled. More than Jesus, it was Mary, a mother figure, who drew him into Catholicism. Mary, like Gittel, became his intercessor. His belief in her—his love for her—was absolute. From that moment forward, he wore a Blessed Mother scapular beneath his shirt, removing it only to shower.

When he met my mother, he treated her as Mary incarnate: flawless, precious, divine. He wrote poems comparing her virtues to Mary's (which embarrassed my mother, and thrilled her). After the war, having bought a diamond solitaire with his mustering-out pay, he carefully chose the holy day on which he would propose marriage: the Feast of the Immaculate Conception.

He found himself unable, however, to forge a life from any of his secular enthusiasms. Was his mother's death so crippling, or was he simply not talented enough? He wanted most to become a writer. The best he could manage was his low-paying, late-in-life job as a copy editor at a middling newspaper. I always assumed he'd been railroaded somehow. I always assumed that he wrote beautifully. But long after his death, I came across a sheaf of his papers, most of them essays or lyric poems praising the Virgin Mary. Reading them, I was dismayed. They were corny, earnest, meandering—everything that made him, as a person, lovable. They were love letters, really, trying in vain to paper over a deep, hard melancholy.

A doctor today would have treated him with antidepressants and bought the time to get his body back in order. The physical problems he held at bay with strength and humor. The depression, though, he couldn't beat. In the late 1950s he earned between $3,000 and $4,000 a year, working as a file clerk and bookkeeper. With six and then seven children, things were tight but passable. By the early 1960s, however, just before I was born, he made less than $1,000 a year. His depression was keeping him in bed for increasingly longer stretches.

I was a very young boy during the worst of it and was kept unaware. When I learned years later how hard my father fought, I wanted to applaud him, enshrine him, grant him the kind of glory that is too often wasted on people who happen to be rich or famous. My father fought without an audience. When a black mood encased him, he would lock himself in the bedroom because he didn't want us kids thinking he was angry. Over the years he tried vitamins, self-help groups, the talking cure; he let himself be strapped down for electric-shock treatment that left him forgetting the names of his own children. (Granted, there were a lot of us.)

Late at night, he would cry to my mother. "I've let you down," he'd say. "I've let the whole family down." She cradled his head and told him to not be ridiculous and to not worry about the money.

She meant it. My mother picked up and carried on her back the entire family. She specialized in thrift and moxie, and once she decided that the family would survive my father's sickness, there was no doubt. She nursed him and the rest of us through those lean and dark years that, because they were the only years I had known, didn't seem so bad at all.

I was the most junior member of a great rollicking rural fraternity, free to watch and learn. My brothers and sisters spoke their high-school French around the supper table, and I knew *"fermez la bouche!"* by the time I was four. I knew the life stories of all the saints we were named for. I knew to plant corn in a hill, never a row, and to fertilize it with a fish head (an old Indian trick, my mother said); I could pluck a chicken. I knew the infield-fly rule and the entire batting order of everyone's teams, and I even knew which sister paid whom to set the kitchen clock back so she could stay out late and still beat curfew.

I recognize now that all this joy hung like a sun behind a scrim of clouds, the scrim of my father's depression.

It was the Virgin Mary who finally helped him break through. It was she—as my father told anyone who would listen—whom he prayed to for guidance and who led him at last to a radical new prayer movement called the Charismatic Renewal. The movement was not an official part of the Catholic Church, and the Vatican was wary of it. Normally this would have scared off my parents but desperate disease is cured by desperate means or not at all, and my father's condition was by now desperate.

My parents attended their first Charismatic meetings in Albany, then started up their own group at Our Lady of Fátima. They met in the church hall, half the lights off to save power, the air smelling of gravy from past church suppers. These meetings were mystical and mysterious and, to me, terribly frightening. There were never more than a dozen adults. I was the only child. I would have rather stayed at home but I wasn't nearly brave enough to say so.

My mother would close her eyes and tilt her face heavenward. From her lips came a voice I had never heard, high-pitched and whispery, in a language that made no sense. But she at least was the same person. My father was transformed. His shoulders no longer slumped. The wattle under his chin stretched tight. His limbs were shot through as with lightning. He too spoke in tongues, a pained wall of sound that seemed to pass into him, not from him. He wasn't exorcising a *dybbuk*, he was swallowing one, and I sat for two hours in a hard metal chair staring at the floor and praying that I wouldn't also have to swallow, for it looked and sounded as if he were swallowing knives.

But afterward! He drove home with his arm around my mother, and from the backseat I stared at the outline of their heads and wondered who they were. They weren't the same people who had just shouted nonsense in the church hall, but neither were they the same parents I had arrived with. My mother, relaxed, rested her head against my father's shoulder. My father was serene, confident, whistling. They were people I didn't know in a place I'd never been: a *normal* place. On the drive home from those prayer meetings, my parents seemed like any other kid's parents, not the pinched, anxious, zealous, uneven, overexcited, underfunded, rule-bound, hidebound people I studied every day to try and fathom how one made his way through the world.

I CANNOT SAY for sure that the Charismatics did it. Maybe the chemicals in my father's brain somehow sloshed about, shifting him into a prolonged manic high. But like some long-slumbering fairy-tale giant, he roared back to life.

I had heard my brothers and sisters speak of a father I never knew, a playful and attentive and selfless father, and here he was. Even after a long shift at the newspaper he had all kinds of zest. He taught Peter to drive, and when a police car pulled them over he switched seats fast so Peter wouldn't get the ticket. He founded a family newspaper and installed me as roving correspondent (immediately and permanently convincing me to one day become a newspaperman). He took the older kids aside one at a time to talk about college or what kind of work they might like to do. He and I once went, alone, all the way to New York City to see my Orioles play the Yankees. I still remember the game and what we ate for breakfast and which shirt he wore and the Sen-Sen smell of his breath.

There wasn't nearly enough of him to go around and I wanted more than I was allowed. I deserved more; I had waited longer. I pouted when I couldn't get to him. In my diary, I wrote: *Who does he think he is to be so happy all the time?*

He had been forced to be needy and he'd hated it. Now he wanted only to give, give, give. That summer we grew far more corn than we could ever eat—those fish heads really worked—and he loaded up bushel baskets and left them on neighbors' porches at night. He started a church library and, in tribute to his rescuer, a chapter of the Legion of Mary. A few Saturdays, he took me to the VFW hall to visit the old men who drank whiskey and shot pool there. Mostly my father just listened to their war stories. One of them was in a wheelchair, and he had to cup his hands like a seal's flippers to hold his glass between the base of his palms. On the drive home, I asked my father why we had to go to the VFW. "We *don't* have to go," he said, cheerily. "We go because we want to spend a little time with some good men."

He had at long last become the man he was meant to be. He had always gone at life full tilt; it was life that failed to return his enthusiasm. Finally they were working in sync. On Christmas morning in 1972, just two days after the Immaculate Reception, my father sat at the tree in his baggy striped pajamas and a red-and-green crown made from construction paper, calling out presents like a carnival barker.

"Whoa-ho, another one for Stevie! Step right up, young man!" He gripped me around the waist and I collapsed happily into his warm, stubbly face. "What do we have here?" It was a big box and he shook it so hard the bow fell off. "Doesn't make much noise, does it? Shall we take a sniff?"

And so on and so on until I ripped it open and found a football, made of such a stiff, cheap plastic that, as I discovered later, it hurt too much to kick or catch. But I didn't care. My new love had been noted.

THE FOLLOWING YEAR, on the Sunday night after Thanksgiving, my father and mother drove into Albany for a Charismatic prayer meeting. Even though their own group was thriving, they were still fond of the Albany meeting, which drew a few hundred people. Albany was an hour's drive, so I didn't have to go.

My father was the first person to testify at the meeting. Then he closed his Bible, sat down, lowered his head, and experienced what doctors would later call "a disastrous disturbance of rhythm known as ventricular fibrillation precipitated by a heart attack." But no waving of the arms, no gurgled shouts: my father called no attention to his agony. He simply slumped over, didn't even fall off his chair. My mother rode in the back of the ambulance, reciting the Rosary. At the hospital, he first appeared to be dead but then showed signs of life and eventually stabilized.

My mother explained all this the morning after in a tone of grim exhaustion. It was a miracle that he'd survived, she told us. He was going to be all right, she told us. He was going to be home by Christmas, she told us.

The older kids visited him but I didn't. There was no use missing school, my mother said, since he'd be home soon. But that wasn't the real reason she didn't bring me to the hospital. The real reason, it turned out, was that my father's disastrous disturbance of rhythm and the resulting lack of oxygen had left him with an indeterminate degree of brain damage, and she didn't want me to see him like that.

But I believed my mother: he'd be all right and he'd be home soon. The Steelers would be playing the Oakland Raiders again in the playoffs this year, and I was hoping my father would watch with me.

The Raiders still felt they'd been cheated by the Immaculate Reception a year earlier. The two teams had by now cultivated a rivalry approaching hatred. The Raiders claimed that the Steelers spied on their practices. The Steelers said the Raiders offensive linemen greased their jerseys so the Steelers defenders couldn't get a grip on them. The Raiders accused the Steelers of watering the Raiders' sideline the night before a game so it would freeze. The Steelers said the Raiders sent in a mushy ball whenever the Steelers tried to kick a field goal. Jack "the Assassin" Tatum, a Raiders defensive back, started a competition with his teammates to see who could record the most "limp-offs" and "knockouts" of Steelers receivers. A Steelers fan was said to have planted a bomb for Tatum at the Oakland bus station.

This game, like the previous year's, fell on the Saturday before Christmas. On Friday, we were let out of school early for the holiday break. My mother wasn't home yet. After a while, I heard her car in the driveway. She came inside and asked me to find Beth and Dave, and I did, and then my mother told us that our father had died. She went upstairs to lie down, and Beth and Dave went upstairs too.

But she said he'd be home! In time for Christmas! It was obviously a mistake. Banks make mistakes, stores make mistakes, hospitals make mistakes. It's all right, I thought, if he doesn't come home until after Christmas. But just . . . fix the mistake!

The next day I watched the game alone. I don't remember where Beth and Dave and my mother were. This time the game was in Oakland. A Raiders fan held up a sign that read "Murder Franco." I was horrified; I hoped Franco hadn't seen it. He'd been injured all year, and the announcers said he still wasn't 100 percent. I saw him hobbling around on the sideline like an animal who'd just sprung his leg from a trap. Someone threw a chocolate ice-cream cone from the stands, and it hit one of the Steelers in the back of the head. Franco brought him a towel. The Steelers got slaughtered, 33–14. It was a terrible day. I didn't cry when my mother gave us the news about my father but I was crying now. I kept looking for a shot of Franco at the end of the game—was he crying too?—but they showed only the winners.

Apparently, concerning my father, there was no mistake. He really was gone.

His funeral Mass was held on Christmas Eve morning. I sat not with my family in the front pew but on the altar, cassocked, with Father DiPace. I was first and foremost a servant of God. Everyone who came in was handed a card that my mother had had printed up:

PAUL DUBNER

CHRISTIAN HUSBAND AND FATHER

BORN INTO THIS LIFE JULY 9, 1916

BORN INTO ETERNAL LIFE DECEMBER 21, 1973

After Mass, as I was pulling off my cassock, Father DiPace told me that I should rejoice about my father's Eternal Life. He explained that God would never take a father from a family with young children unless He loved that man so much that He couldn't bear to live without him in Heaven. That's why I should be rejoicing, because God loved my father so much. Later that day, my mother told me the same thing. It made me wonder if she and Father DiPace had talked beforehand to get their stories straight. She also told me how happy my father was in Heaven, meeting all the saints and whatnot.

So is he dead or isn't he? If he's just floating around and meeting people up in Heaven, why couldn't he stick around here and meet people?

The cemetery was frozen, so after the Mass they put his body in a stone building to wait for spring.

Back at the house, I heard my mother telling some of her friends that she was grateful that my father had finally found peace.

And I'm thinking . . . is she *nuts*? I wasn't grateful to anyone. Confused, yes. And embarrassed. (Your father wasn't supposed to die when you're a kid, everyone knew that.) Most of all, I was mad. I was mad at my father for dying, mad at my mother for being grateful, mad at God for orchestrating the whole thing.

But I didn't say anything. And still I didn't cry. Because, after all, I was supposed to be rejoicing.

WHEN THE AUTHOR Alexandre Dumas was four years old his father died, and he too was told that it was God's will. He grabbed his father's gun and ran into the attic to get close to God and shoot him.

I was too much of a coward to execute God. Instead I sentenced Him to life in prison. I would keep Him from committing further crimes. Perhaps someday I would spring Him free, or perhaps not.

I suppose my father said good-bye to me that night, before he went off to Albany, but the way things hummed around our house and with my mother always running late, who could be sure? Then he just disappeared.

There was nothing heroic about his death. In the storybooks I read, heroes died a stormy, bloody, noisy death. If a Norseman in ancient days was dying from natural causes, he carved himself up with a sword so he'd be received in Valhalla as a slain warrior. A dying old king was put out to sea in a slow-burning ship so he'd leave the earth in a blaze of glory. My father, meanwhile, a husk of depression and brain damage, expired in a hospital gown, waxy fingers clutching his Blessed Mother scapular, a houseful of children waiting for him to come home.

It may be true, as Freud said, that you cannot become a man until your father dies. But I wasn't asking to become a man yet. Freud also said that every son wishes to kill off his father and steal his mother's heart, and that may also be true. But not yet! Not like this! I killed mine off too soon, and too clumsily.

Now what?

A few weeks after my father died, I went snooping in my parents' room. I had never before done this. Their room was our Holy of Holies, the sanctum from which emanated all wisdom and judgment (and, though I was foggy as to the mechanics, all of us children). I don't know what I was looking for. Perhaps a sign that my father really did live on somehow. Instead I saw, rising from a pile of bills and unanswered mail, a file folder labeled "SPD Death." It likely held the death certificate, doctors' correspondence, and other documents pertaining to the death of Solomon Paul Dubner. I didn't open it; the label alone did the trick. For many years, I would think of my father as a man defined by his inevitable death, a person neatly reduced to a file folder, tucked away permanently from sight and use. Not SPD, but SPD Death.

He, after the death of his earthly mother, had reached out and found a heavenly mother to save him. I was not about to embrace the heavenly father who spirited my own father away. That would make me a collaborator. But I had to reach out for *someone*. A trapdoor had sprung open beneath me; the verities of my short life had been scrambled, and I was being asked to accept a story that made little sense and lent no comfort. So I reached out for someone sensible and comforting, someone concrete and capable, someone real enough to be true but strong enough to not die.

Soon after the death of my father I had this dream:

Franco Harris was coming to Albany to give a lecture at a VFW hall. I got myself there, waited until he had spoken and until everyone else had left, and then, practically choking on my shyness, invited him back to my house for supper. I had asked my mother to make spaghetti and meatballs—because he was half-Italian but also because her spaghetti and meatballs was better than most of her cooking. Franco agreed to come. We ate, and afterward he and I went out to the yard for a football game. It was dark now, pitch-dark, lit only by the one bulb on the barn. Franco and I were the Steelers. We played a long, hard game against another team—probably the Raiders, although it was hard to tell. Time was running out and the other team was ahead by one point. But we had the ball and we were driving. Franco took the handoff. His foot got caught in one of those cow hoofprints and he went down hard. He didn't cry out, but once the tacklers had unpiled he could barely stand. He limped back to the huddle. There was time left for only one more play. He handed me the ball and said, "Kid, you're going to have to take it from here yourself."

I had the very same dream the next night and the next, and nearly every night onward until I was no longer a child.

5

THE STEALTH MESSIAH

MY LIFE SO RESEMBLED HIS that I was certain fate had brought us together.

There were nine kids in his Catholic family, eight in mine. No one had much money and no one complained. When Franco was my age he shoveled driveways, bagged groceries, and shined shoes at his father's Army base; I baled hay, stocked shelves, mucked out barns. Franco joined a school group that raised money to buy food and toys for needy families; I went out with my mother collecting canned goods and used clothing for church. Franco's mother, like mine, wore the pants in the family; they both had dark hair, pretty faces, and a fondness for "Ave Maria." Our fathers were World War II veterans who worked hard all their lives to feed their families. Franco's father, whose name was Cadillac, had stayed on with the Army and was still stationed at Fort Dix—the very base from which my father was honorably discharged after the war. One difference, though: Franco's father was still alive.

We were also united by our abnormal ancestral conditions: Franco's was mixed-up and mine was murky. We were neither of us All-American boys. I imagine that if someone from church had bumped into my father buying gefilte fish at the Piggly Wiggly in Schenectady, that someone would have been confused. The Harris family was similarly confusing, with their brown faces and Italian names: Daniela, Mario, Franco, Marisa, Alvara, Luana, Piero, Giuseppe, and Michele.

Franco's condition, of course, was more obvious than mine. I had a friend named Tommy McNamara, a good kid, a Jets fan who knew how I felt about Franco. We played barn hockey, and our games often turned vicious. One day, when Tommy was getting the worse of it, he jammed me up in the corner and shouted, "Yeah, well, Franco Harris is a *mulatto!*" I didn't know what the word meant but I knew it wasn't good. And I knew that Franco must have suffered the slings and arrows of a great many Tommy McNamaras.

My family's condition was more mysterious. I only knew that, except for the strange food they ate and the gibberish they occasionally flung at each other (it turned out to be Yiddish), my parents had plastered over their beginnings. The unnamed relatives, the untold stories, the unwelcome questions: we plainly had *something* to hide.

But Franco couldn't hide. Not that he would have. He was proud of who he was because he took pride in himself. "I am what I am and I'm not ashamed of it," he told one sportswriter. "My physical body just happens to be part black and part Italian. But what's in my mind and inside of me comes from a lot of different experiences and a lot of different people."

I hated that reporters were always pestering him with questions—"I don't want anybody really nosing around, snooping into what I'm doing," he once said—but I loved having the answers. By the time I was twelve years old I had read everything to be found about Franco. There were, to the best of my knowledge, five books about him, all but one written for grade-schoolers. The fifth, simply called *Franco Harris*, by Don Kowet, was more comprehensive. It became a bible of sorts for me. Although it was only a clip job—one writer's pasting-together of dozens of newspaper and magazine articles—I didn't know that at the time, and I wouldn't have cared. It had all the biographical detail I could want and it ably distilled the nuanced, humane worldview that made my hero unique.

He didn't talk like other adults and certainly not like other ballplayers. He really thought about a question before he answered it. Most adults seemed to be reading from a script—a script written to keep you from knowing too much or from thinking about options they didn't want you thinking about. Franco, though, said what he believed. Sometimes it took forever—his friends called his slow pace Franco Standard Time— but you knew his answer was real. He wasn't mean, ever, but he wasn't scared of the truth either.

We didn't speak that way in my family. We lived behind a veil. We were taught to choke off negative thoughts. *(If you don't have something nice to say about somebody . . .)* We were also taught to beat back desire of every variety, to not expect too much from life, and to ask for even less, since—though I never saw a scrap of confirming evidence—the meek were supposed to inherit the earth.

Franco was humble but he wasn't meek. I was meek but not humble. Humility comes from confidence; meekness comes from a lack of it. Meekness is a frightened dog on a leash: *If it weren't for this leash,* he snarls, *I'd tear you apart.*

Franco didn't wear a leash. "You've got to be strong to stand as an individual," he told one reporter. "It's like a little poem which is very hip—a Muslim named Bama sings it on his album. It goes, 'If you're strong, you're within your right to be wrong.'" On a wall in his apartment, Franco was said to have hung a plaque with an American Indian saying: "There is nothing so strong as true gentleness."

I studied his words and watched his deeds. Other ballplayers talked tough all the time, as if you had to be a he-man to be a man. Franco came right out and said he didn't like getting tackled. He had the world, or at least Pittsburgh, at his feet, but he wouldn't bend his principles— no beer commercials, he told his agent, because kids watch television too. He protected his privacy but when he went for a bike ride and a bunch of kids followed him home, he asked them inside and made them hamburgers.

In the Dream, I had him all to myself. When I invited him home for spaghetti and meatballs, I could tell he had other things to do, but still he accepted. (I was taking advantage of the well-known fact that Franco had a hard time saying no.) And I could tell he didn't really want to go outside and play football, especially right after eating, but he followed me without a word. This was another trait we had in common, or appeared to: we were eager-to-pleasers. But he really was that way; I just acted eager to please, fearful of seeming otherwise.

The Dream always faded out at the crucial moment, with the clock running out, us trailing, Franco getting hurt, handing me the ball, and telling me I'd have to take it in myself. Every night I went to bed hoping for a different conclusion. I hoped that Franco would take the ball and blast through the line and carry me on his back to ... to ... to *what?*

In his second season with the Steelers, Franco bought a house on Pittsburgh's run-down North Side. I found a long magazine feature about it, at the library, in *Ebony* magazine. It was a big, old, red-brick house with fourteen-foot ceilings, stained-glass windows, wide-board floors, and a fireplace in every room. The windows were all boarded up when Franco first saw the place, but he fell in love with it and had it renovated from top to bottom. Friends laughed at him, asked why on earth he wanted such a house. "I ask myself that too," he said. "I just like the neighborhood. It has a character all to itself, you know. A lot of people I know are afraid to live on the North Side, but the neighborhood doesn't scare me off. I felt that things were going to get better there, and if I could help to make it better, fine."

So now we both lived in old houses too. From the pictures in *Ebony*, his neighborhood looked cramped and shabby. It reminded me of the streets I read about in *A Tree Grows in Brooklyn*. One picture showed Franco sitting on a stoop talking to an old white lady with a checkered dress and cat's-eye glasses. Franco was wearing a long-sleeve, button-down shirt tucked into his shorts. The effect was simultaneously square and hip. (I tried to copy it and succeeded only in looking square.) He told the *Ebony* reporter how much he liked listening to jazz. (I asked my brothers, and they loaned me some Chick Corea and Earl "Fatha" Hines records. Earl Hines was from Pittsburgh; I had started playing the piano, and now he became my favorite.) Other pictures showed Franco cooking, paying bills, stretching out on a recliner. "Having a home means a lot to me," he said. "I want this to be a place of privacy, but I also want it to be a place that's open and where people can feel free to walk in. I'm really going to enjoy the house. It just *feels* good."

A part of me wanted to live in that house. A part of me wanted to be his best friend, his little brother, his Boy Robin, his John the Baptist. But I never even wrote him a letter. We did that in my family, sent off glowing letters to ballplayers, asking for autographed pictures. But Franco wasn't like the others. He was my hero in a way that no other ballplayer or piano player or even astronaut could approach. He was special, but not because he was a football player. It was *him*. He was a great football player because he was special, not the other way around. He would never admit that, but I knew it to be true. I didn't worship him for what he did; I worshiped him for who he was.

I thought of him as dwelling somewhere between man and god, like the heroes of Greek mythology. They, I knew, had begun their lives as mortal men and women, walking the earth just as Franco now walked the earth, before their noble deeds elevated them to the mountaintop. What an opportunity I had, to get in on the ground floor of my hero's life, while he was still alive! Jesus, of course, was the heroic example with which I was most intimate. I liked Jesus, honestly I did, but I liked him a lot more as a generous, willful, free-thinking person than a bloodied God hanging on my bedroom wall. Once they turned him into a crucifix, he stopped being real to me. Franco was also generous and willful and free-thinking, but he was still real enough to watch on television and read about, real enough to cast my ailing present into his shining future.

The point of having such a hero, however, wasn't simply to pal around with him. Any hero with the time and inclination to pal around with a kid like me couldn't be much of a hero. Nor was the point to become a football player. Even if my school did have a team, the first hard tackle would have broken me in two. No, the point was neither to become Franco nor to befriend him. The point was to *attain* from him—to attain an equilibrium I lacked, a humility I faked, and a strength I had never known.

I THOUGHT IT had a nice ring to it: Franco Dubner. That was the name I began using on my school papers. I hoped my teachers would pick up on it and call me Franco when I raised my hand, which was all the time, but they didn't.

With my mother I was less bashful. I asked outright for an official change of name. In the past we had talked at length about my name. She instructed me to cherish it, for Saint Stephen was a true hero of our faith. Like my parents, Stephen was a Jew who found the Church of Jesus. He was "a man full of faith and of the Holy Ghost" who, assigned the lowly task of caring for widows and orphans, performed great miracles in the name of Jesus. The Jewish priests were so afraid of Stephen's sway that they hauled him in on blasphemy charges. Offered a chance to renege and save his neck, Stephen blasphemed all the louder. The story ends with Stephen being hustled outside the walls of Jerusalem and stoned to death, becoming the first Christian martyr.

Although martyrdom struck me as a dubious honor, I'd never had anything against Stephen. It was, I thought, a fine name. But, I now told my mother, meaning no disrespect to her or Saint Stephen or anyone, I would like to be called Franco.

She refused.

I pleaded with her. She told me I should be grateful for the name I had. I promised to not eat supper ever again until I got my new name. She said I would only be punishing myself. I threatened to run away. She said it would break her heart if I did.

At last she relented, in her measure. She said I could take Francis, as in Saint Francis of Assisi, for my confirmation name. But confirmation was five years away and Francis was not Franco.

I called the Schenectady County Courthouse to ask if I could legally change my name and they said, Of course you can, as long as you are eighteen years old, and I said, Oh, and they said, How old *are* you, and I said, Twelve.

Inspired by natural events around me, I subscribed by this time to a Theory of Mutability. In our falling-down chicken coop, I had watched sweet fuzzy chicks grow into savage roosters. I had seen muddy caterpillars become feathery butterflies. My own parents had shed the skins of their birth in some fashion, and for a time I believed (for reasons that remain unclear to this day) that every boy, myself included, turned into a girl at age sixteen (and, I suppose, vice versa, though I never gave that scenario much thought). My Theory of Mutability held that no chrysalis was impossible, that no one was immune to conversion, and that I was entitled, at the very least, to wear the name of my hero.

Cassius Clay had turned into Muhammad Ali. Superman regularly became Clark Kent. My own family had changed names like clothes. When my oldest sister, Mary, went away to college, she shrugged off the holy weight of her name and became Mona. Neither of my parents went by the names they were born with. My mother, who started out as Florence Greenglass, had buried her birth name entirely. Her first hero was Madame Asta Souvorina, an iron-fisted, Roman Catholic, Russian émigré ballet teacher. Until she met Madame, my mother had evinced little passion or direction but ballet became her lifeblood, and Madame her deliverer from an otherwise drab middle-class future. At some point the two of them decided that, as a ballerina's name, Greenglass was too . . . *Brooklyn*, so my mother went to court and adopted Winters instead. (This paid unexpected dividends several years later, when her cousin Ethel Greenglass, who had married Julius Rosenberg, was arrested as an atomic spy; the Greenglass name became poison but my mother no longer bore it.) My mother then fell so completely under Madame's influence that she followed her into Catholicism. When she was baptized, she traded Florence for Veronica, in honor of the woman who swabbed Jesus' face as he stumbled under his cross through Jerusalem. The mother named on my birth certificate, therefore, was Veronica Winters, not Florence Greenglass, and it seemed patently unfair that a woman of such fabricated nomenclature now forbade me to become Franco Dubner.

She thought it was just a childish crush but I couldn't tell her the truth. I didn't dare tell her that Franco visited me nightly while I slept. My feelings for him represented a blasphemy as bold as Saint Stephen's. I had neither the courage nor the vocabulary to express this blasphemy, particularly to the one person I now depended upon for survival. It was a primitive arithmetic I carried out in my head: my mother worships Jesus, and if I am to stay in her good graces (the only graces available to me), I had better appear to worship him as well. I never spoke against

Jesus; I never cursed him; I would serve as an altar boy until leaving for college.

But he did not live in my heart. It was Franco Harris who lived in my heart. I wore Franco as my father wore his Blessed Mother scapular. He was my rock and my redeemer, my protector and my inspiration, my stealth messiah. Though they refused to grant me his name, they could not pry his spirit from me.

6

A Mother Is Not a Man

••◄◖∽◗►••

M Y MOTHER, I now have no doubt, tried to be everything
to me at once: mother and father, guardian and role model,
teacher and friend. But this was a barren new world in which we found
ourselves, absent of landmarks.

Just a few years earlier, she was the queen of a hive thrumming with
life; now she was a widow home alone with her youngest son. With Beth
and Dave gone off to college, I was suddenly an only child stranded
with a pious, headstrong, depleted mother. Neither of us was prepared
for a one-on-one encounter. I did as I was told and what was expected of
me. We didn't have much to talk about; we rarely mentioned my father.
We lived as if in an interlude. When would the action resume? But the
world we knew had ended. It became clear that my mother had never
been the heart of our family. She may have been its engine, its anchor,
the giver of life and maker of rules, but my father was the heart.

My mother excelled at getting things done. It was she who had long
ago engineered the family's leaving Brooklyn for the countryside, where
she could raise good Catholic children and stuff them with fresh air and
vegetables. She mastered the arts of organic farming and chicken-
slaughtering, vitamin-taking and tourniquet-tying, church activism and,

above all, God-love, none of which she had known as a child. She seemed to possess an infinite supply of energy.

For a quarter-century, that energy had gone toward sustaining our family. Now it found a new outlet: the Right-to-Life movement. My mother was spiritually and physically disgusted by abortion. She began with prayer vigils and petition-gathering; before long she was marching on Albany and then Washington.

When abortion was legalized in New York State a few years before the 1973 *Roe v. Wade* decision, my mother wrote stern letters to our assemblywoman: "I agree that there are many problems to be considered when unplanned pregnancies take place. This solution is just as stupid in our day as it was when G. K. Chesterton pointed out that when there aren't enough hats to go around, the problem isn't solved by cutting off some heads."

She wrote to the Speaker of the Assembly, to Governor Rockefeller, and, eventually, to President Nixon:

> To demand an end to the life of an innocent, unborn human being so that his or her mother may have her "right to privacy" is the most twisted of reasoning imaginable. Since when does the right to *privacy* of one human being take precedence over the right to *life* of another human being?
>
> Something is very wrong with the values put forth by the Supreme Court's majority decision. It brings to mind the beginnings of the *legal* elimination of the mentally ill in Germany (a policy which Hitler then found so useful in ridding his country of those he considered undesirable) and the legal mass eliminations (murders) of Jews, Catholics, the crippled, the elderly, the ill and, yes, the unborn human beings. . . .
>
> Where is our country heading? Are we now to have such a ruthless, barbaric law, basing our decisions on utilitarian motives and convenience? Capital punishment, now no longer used for most convicted criminals, is reserved for innocent and defenseless babies!
>
> Since you have gone on record as being opposed to abortion-on-demand, President Nixon, I would greatly appreciate hearing your

views on this matter, and any thoughts you have on what can now be done to protect the lives of the unborn children of our country.

My mother enrolled me in her crusade. I stuffed envelopes, drew up "Abortion Is Murder" posters, biked to the library to look up politicians' addresses. I didn't even consider not helping. I was an obedient son and altar boy, "a soldier in God's Army," as my mother put it, and saving babies seemed like a perfectly noble cause. But her passion for unborn children seemed to outstrip her passion for those already born. Sometimes, working into the summer night alongside my mother at the kitchen table, clammy forearms sticking to the plastic tablecloth, I caught myself thinking: *saving all these babies is well and good, but what about* me?

FOR MY THIRTEENTH BIRTHDAY, my mother took me to the Van Dyck supper club in Schenectady to see Earl "Fatha" Hines perform. It was the summer of 1976. My mother had arranged it all. She knew I loved Hines's records and she knew that Mrs. Memmereth, the mother of a girl I went to school with, worked as a hostess at the Van Dyck.

The club was situated in an old house on an old city street. Its wallpaper was faded and its carpet worn but the place was elegant, not shabby like our house, the way an old car with big humpy bumpers was elegant. We arrived just past dusk. People were smoking. Mrs. Memmereth greeted my mother and me at the door, as if she'd been waiting for us. She didn't ask if I was looking forward to the eighth grade in the fall or how our corn was coming in, which I appreciated.

"Would you like to go straight to your table or have a drink at the bar?" she asked.

"The table, please," my mother said.

As we followed Mrs. Memmereth, sliding between the tables, I was rendered breathless. The men wore suit jackets and shined shoes, and they swirled their cocktail glasses. The women wore necklaces and leaned forward as they spoke, their bare shoulders gleaming in the bluish stage lights. The women didn't swirl their glasses but picked them up delicately, sipped, put them down, their thin fingers leaving

whorls in the condensation. The room was noisy but not noisy, a blanket
of mumbles.

We were led to a table directly in front of the piano. Mrs. Memmereth
picked up the RESERVED sign and smiled at me, a firm quiet smile: *Yes, it
is an important night.* I smiled back. It was a rare moment of true rapport
with an adult, and I enjoyed it. Mrs. Memmereth held out the chair for
my mother, which made me wish I had thought of it first. I considered
sidling up to Mrs. Memmereth, taking advantage of our rapport, and
telling her (politely, of course) that if my mother had cooked up some
birthday treat—a cake and singing waiters or some such—that thanks
very much but I'd rather not. I had always been shy, but since my father's
death the shyness had worsened, from a sprain to a compound fracture.

The moment passed, however, and Mrs. Memmereth returned to the
front of the club. We had eaten dinner at home to save money, so when
the waiter came we ordered only ginger ales. My mother unfurled her
napkin, laid it gracefully into her lap, and surveyed the room. She
looked as if she'd been coming to nightclubs forever. I knew that a thousand years ago, during the war and before she met my father, she had
performed as a ballerina in clubs, but I hadn't expected this. She was
wearing beet-red lipstick and small, glittery earrings, and I beheld her
suddenly in a different light.

I was shocked when she suggested we come here. A nightclub shel-
tered nearly every vice my mother opposed: drinking, smoking, low
lighting, the suggestion of sex, and music that was distinctly unhymnal.
Yet here she sat, fixed with a placid smile and no trace of judgment.

I saw that the piano was positioned at an angle on the bandstand,
which further elevated my mother's stock. It was just as she had counseled me to angle the piano before my school's talent show: about fifteen
degrees off perpendicular with the front of the stage. "You need to let
them see your hands," she'd said. "But they have to see your face too. If
you were an accompanist it wouldn't matter. But you're a *soloist.*" She
gave the word a prideful, practiced emphasis. "And don't forget: smile!"

In the talent show I played a hepped-up blues in C, part Earl Hines
and part Otis Spann. My mother had also suggested I use a candelabra,
à la Liberace. I couldn't tell my mother how tacky this idea was. Instead

I lied. The stage manager, I told her, wouldn't allow live candles—a fire hazard. My mother was disappointed. Her ballet training had given her a rather pronounced show-biz sense: big smiles, high kicks, flashy endings. But *she had a show-biz sense*, my mother did, which set her apart from all the other mothers of Duanesburg, the farmers' and plumbers' and mechanics' wives, and which at this moment, viewing the angled piano at the Van Dyck supper club in Schenectady on my thirteenth birthday, I thought was extraordinarily cool.

All of a sudden Earl Hines was standing right before me. He was ancient. He gave the crowd a little half-bow, sat down, counted off with the drummer, then tucked into "St. Louis Blues," and I felt myself slip right inside his fingertips. The song moved on its own, as if it were being released from Hines rather than manufactured by him. It resembled the music I played in the way a cloud resembles a cotton ball. He wore a silky patterned jacket, a white shirt, and a burgundy ascot. His fingers each moved with startling independence, his left foot beating out an indecipherable pattern on the carpeted bandstand. The other musicians—drummer, bassist, and reed player—were, like Hines, black, but thirty or forty years younger.

After a five-minute medley, Hines stood up and with a great flourish introduced his vocalist, Marva Josie. As she claimed the stage, the first thing you noticed was her hair. It wandered well past her elbows and was perfectly straight, dark brown with a few pale streaks. Her dress was shiny green, very long and very tight; her lips smiled but her eyes did not. As she raised the microphone to her mouth, you saw the fingernails: they were monstrous. Six inches long, each of them, painted with light and dark stripes, curling about like snakes. I hated snakes; they scared me terribly; if one appeared while I was mowing the lawn I would give chase and chop it up. Marva Josie sang "The Man I Love" and "Chicken Shack Boogie" and "Honeysuckle Rose." After each song she ungripped the microphone, slowly extracting one finger at a time, letting each snaky nail creep free, and when she was finished she dramatically held her hand aloft, the stage lights lapping at her nails like the Fires of Hell. She stirred inside me a fearful quivering in the stomach as well as a solemn throbbing a few inches to the south. Then the quartet began a new song, a song I recognized from the opening riff, and I froze.

Marva Josie sang: *I don't want you to be no slave . . .*

I concentrated on the music. I could not bring my eyes to Marva Josie, and I surely could not bring them to my mother.

I don't want you to work all day . . .

I studied Hines's fingers like a final exam. Anything to appear oblivious to the words. He sure takes this song slow, I said to myself, not the way the Rolling Stones blitz through it.

I don't want you to be true . . .

I took a sip of ginger ale through the thin red straw, casual, as if I hung out here all the time with my mother, listening to dirty songs.

I just wanna make . . .

Ugh.

LOVE to you, baby, LOVE to you . . .

It was the longest rendition of the horniest song in the history of mankind. They sped up, thrashed about a bit, went through all the verses again, then Marva Josie wailed for a while—*LOVE to you, baby, LOVE to you*—and by the time they were done my neck had gone prickly along with my lap, and I was sure the entire Van Dyck was watching to see if my mother was going to box my ears or simply cover them.

But she clapped along with everyone. She didn't hoot or whistle like some of the men did, but neither did she grab my arm and storm out. Full of surprises, my mother.

The first set was over. The band had left the stage when Mrs. Memmereth rushed up and touched Hines's elbow. She said something and he smiled, a forced smile, raised his old eyebrows and nodded, quickly, as if pretending to remember something he'd hoped had been forgotten. He seemed to look at me. He returned to the stage.

"Ladies and gentlemen," he said, "may I have your attention? A young man is celebrating his birthday this evening, and I am told that he plays some piano."

The crowd chuckled, clapped a bit, relaxed. I felt my sphincter tighten.

"I wonder if I might ask him to join me onstage for your listening pleasure?" Earl Hines looked down at me and held out his hand.

I turned to my mother. She wore a look of badly feigned surprise, her brows dancing up toward her widow's peak, her lips both pursed and smiling, as if caught in mid-kiss.

This was ridiculous. I couldn't play piano with Earl Hines.

His hand remained outstretched as the audience began clapping in awkward, white-people rhythm.

"What's the kid's name?" someone shouted.

Hines kept his smile afloat until Mrs. Memmereth leaned into his ear.

"Master Stephen," he pronounced. "Master Stephen is the young man's name."

"Let's go, Stevie! Let's get it on!"

They were riled up now, the way people get when someone else is suddenly wedged into a situation in which they wouldn't be caught dead.

What could I do? I considered pretending I was deaf, or maybe blind, but how long could I keep that up? I thought about just leaving, running off through the kitchen door, but I didn't feel as if my legs would carry me. I could demur but I didn't know how to demur. I felt myself climbing stiffly onto the bandstand. The clapping died down and I heard Hines ask me gruffly, "Top or bottom?"

I didn't know what he meant and I was too shy to ask.

"Bottom," I said.

He sat down on the right-hand side of the bench, leaving me the bottom half of the keyboard. "What shall we?" he asked.

I didn't say anything. I knew a few of the songs he'd played—knew them as in *was able to identify them*—but it wasn't as if I had a repertoire. What was my mother thinking? I genuinely didn't have a single song in my fingers or mind . . . other than the Hines-Spann thing I'd been calling "Talent Show Blues," a mid-tempo boogie-woogie in C, the only key I could really play in. The crowd had grown quiet by now and Hines was staring at me.

"Or shall we make it up as we go along?" he asked.

"Let's just do a blues, mid-tempo," I said.

"A blues it is. Key?"

"How about C?"

"A man after my own heart."

Even though he was on top, he started things off. It sounded great, his two big hands working the treble keys, like a boogie-woogie record sped up. Finally I jumped aboard. But I couldn't get in sync; I was flapping, drowning. He sensed it. First he loosened up what he was doing so I wouldn't sound lost. As we finished one twelve-bar pattern he slowed down the next one so I could jump on, like a merry-go-round. Then we got into a sweet little groove, me and Fatha Hines, and once I had the bottom nailed down he started doing nifty things up top. He played short, flighty runs that sounded like giggling girls. He bracketed my changes with staccato hammerings, like a bunch of chattering birds. He started rolling his shoulders back and forth, bumping into me with a sloppy smile, nudging me to get rolling for myself, and I did. Too scared to look into the crowd, I watched Hines. I saw the sweat beading on his temple. His skin was an ashy black. He was, I realized, the first black man I'd ever sat beside. I could see his teeth down to the gum and they were yellow; he smelled of cigarettes and something I now know to be dry-cleaning fluid. He smelled also of liquor. He smelled especially of lilac, a lady's perfume. I'd gotten the idea that he and Marva Josie had something going on, and now I was sure of it. Fatha Hines was a hoot but he wasn't very fatherly.

We finished just as I was starting to enjoy myself. I heard the clapping as Hines swallowed up my right hand in both of his—they were as big as baseball mitts—and then he disappeared offstage.

At our table, my mother patted my hand as a parade of men stopped on their way to the rest room to whack my back. Someone sent over a drink, which my mother sniffed and pushed aside. Then she asked if I wanted to stay for the second set. It was a question tinted with advice: leave them wanting more. So I did. This time I came around and held the chair for her.

MY MOTHER, I now have no doubt, always did what she thought was best for me. Sometimes it made me chafe; occasionally it was a rocket

ride. At the Van Dyck she hit both marks. At the Van Dyck she managed to give me the thrill of a lifetime and to shame me within an inch of
my life.

My mother was not familiar with the concept of shame. (How else
could she phone up the Van Dyck and arrange for her novice-piano-
player son to sit in with a jazz king?) She conducted her life with a
surety that suffered no doubts, no fools, and no shame. I, however, carried a big sack of shame on my back, I wore it on my face, and that was
the shame of being fatherless.

Nothing good comes of being fatherless. People feel sorry for you
(and their pity is suffocating). They hold you responsible for his dying
(they deny this but you know it is true). They blather on about how he
smiles down on you from Heaven (to which there is no proper response
but muted rage).

You, meanwhile, are frozen in time. You move through the grades at
school and you might even get good marks, play sports, edit the paper.
But at your core you remain frozen at the time of his death. This is a
strategy. You hope that you will someday have a chance to replay the
event and reverse the outcome, just as you lie awake after striking out in
the ninth inning and continuously replay the at-bat until, in your head,
you drive in the winning run. So you keep yourself locked down at the
time of the dying. Your life goes on but you don't always go with it. You
find yourself not hearing what others hear and seeing things they don't.
You think about how life could be different but you can't even guess how
those differences should feel. Because you have been taught to carry
yourself in a civil manner, in a holy manner, you throw a blanket over
your anger. But when no one is around, you catch a frog and stick fire-
crackers in his mouth and let him have it. Whenever someone asks you if
you are all right, if you need a hand, if you want to talk, you say, No no no
no, everything's fine. This is a big lie. You know what you are looking
for. At church and the diner and Wolfe's Market, you find yourself staring at men who are your father's age. You are searching their faces for a
spark of assurance, that almost arrogant look that passes from a father to
his son, born of the son's desperation as much as the father's desire, a
look that says, Yes, I am here to save you. It says, Go ahead and reach for

something beyond your grasp, for I will pick you up if you fall. But you never find that look—at least not directed at you. So you begin to wall yourself off. You refuse all help, all advice; you avoid risk and lower your expectations. You become afraid to venture outside your own skin, and your world grows smaller and darker.

Your mother does what she can but she suffers one irreducible flaw: she is not a man. She is also, you now realize, mortal. Whenever you are home alone at night, you imagine that she has been killed in a car accident. You put away money in a peach can under the bed; you are endlessly calculating how much you could earn from your various odd jobs if you had to survive without her.

She, meanwhile, brings men to you, Mr. Duszkiewicz and Mr. Uvegas and Mr. Nespor, dropping them off at your doorstep the way a cat drops off mice. They take you for "outings"—fishing on Warner Lake, a demolition derby over in Schoharie, a semi-pro baseball game in Schenectady. You can't think of anything to say that would interest them, and you have to go to the bathroom too often. You feel like a charity case. You feel like you should be wearing a sign around your neck: FATHERLESS SON ON OUTING WITH SOMEONE ELSE'S FATHER. One of them even brings you to a father-son church supper—he took his own kids earlier in the day—and as soon as you arrive you pretend to have a stomachache so you can go home.

Their eyes are full of effort—they are so nice, these men, and they try so hard, buying you ice cream and filling up their chatter with "life's little lessons"—but there is no inspiration there. When they look at you, they can see only what you *are:* a boy with no father. You are searching for someone who sees what you *want*, what you *can be.*

There is only one man with such a look in his eyes. It doesn't matter that you have never met him, that he lives far away, that he is half-hidden beneath a football helmet. Every night in your dreams he pays you a visit and you go forth every morning with another shred of confidence that, despite your obvious handicap, someone *is* watching out for you.

7

A BIRGer Binge

—◦◦❈◦◦—

I T IS TEMPTING to believe that my relationship with Franco
would have flourished even if he had been a one-season wonder,
even if the Steelers had retreated to their losing ways. But I doubt it. In
sports, winning really is everything. A losing streak may be ennobling
but only in retrospect, once it has been broken. (Ask any fan of the
Boston Red Sox or Chicago Cubs if he feels remotely ennobled.) It is the
winning, not merely the cessation of losing, that brings redemption.

In this regard, sport is more redemptive than life itself. If, in life itself,
you finally win after losing too long, the win is tainted. The politician
who runs in election after election until he finally wins one is considered
less an enthusiast than an egomaniac. But in sports, a victory of the
proper magnitude washes away all previous losses like a hard rain.

For the athlete, the bounty of victory is obvious: money and glory.
This has long been the case. In the Roman Republic, a charioteer named
Diocles amassed career earnings of thirty-five million sesterces, as
against the one thousand sesterces per year the average Roman family
of four lived on. Then as now, critics warned that athletes were ob-
scenely overpaid. "Decent men groan," said one, "to see [Diocles] earn
an income that is one hundred times that of the entire Roman Senate."

In ancient Greece, glory was heaped upon athletes by no less a personage than the great poet Pindar. When he wasn't busy chronicling Greek military conquests, Pindar wrote lengthy lyric tributes to Olympic champions. This makes him one of our earliest sportswriters, and while his praise was easily as purple as that of the scribes covering, say, Joe DiMaggio's hitting streak, he had better reason: Pindar's poems were commissioned by the athlete's family. When Diagoras of Rhodes won the boxing competition of 464 BCE, Pindar wrote:

O father Zeus, you who rule Atabyrion's slopes, honor the hymn
    ordained for an Olympic victory
and the man who has won success at boxing, and grant him respectful
    favor
from both townsmen and foreigners, for he travels straight down a road
that abhors insolence, having clearly learned what an upright mind
    inherited from noble forebears declared to him.

Although purchased, such praise was hardly empty. In the days of the Greek city-state, the athlete—who was usually a warrior as well—was literally a representative of his fans. Today, once you get past high-school sports and the Olympics, that is not the case. The modern athlete is overtly mercenary.

And yet we don't much care. We root as if our Cubbies or our Steelers were truly *ours*—a remnant, some psychologists believe, of the time when warriors were actual genetic representatives of their tribe. Even today, we can share in the athletes' glory (if not their money). Recent psychological studies show that a devout fan's moods rise and fall substantially with his team's fortunes. A big victory can buffer depression; the fan might feel more optimistic and confident, even more sexually attractive. In the academic literature, this phenomenon is known as Basking in Reflected Glory, or BIRGing, which has a short-term, hormonal component (a surge in testosterone) and a long-term, psychological one.

During the 1994 World Cup in Atlanta, a social psychologist from Georgia State University conducted saliva tests on some serious BIRGers: male soccer fans from Brazil and Italy. Their teams met in the championship match. Brazil won. Afterward, the tests showed, the

Brazilian fans' testosterone levels had risen 28 percent; the Italians' fell 27 percent.

All too often, a BIRGer's team will lose, leaving him without sufficient Glory in which to Bask. This has been known to produce legitimate psychic damage. (Again, talk to those Red Sox and Cubs fans.) Such a BIRGer might, in time, become a CORFer, abandoning his losing team in order to Cut Off Reflected Failure. A particularly fair-weather BIRGer, anticipating that his winning team has run out of steam, may even start COFFing—Cutting Off Future Failure.

I had suffered a jolt of bad luck, it is true, in losing my father at a too-young age. But not all my luck was bad. Having stumbled upon Franco Harris and the Pittsburgh Steelers in the early 1970s, I also stumbled upon one of the greatest BIRGer binges in the history of sports.

AFTER WINNING the Immaculate Reception game in 1972, the year before my father died, the Steelers only had to beat the Miami Dolphins, at Three Rivers Stadium, to go to their first Super Bowl.

My best friend, Richard LaPoint, was a Dolphins fan. On the surface Richard and I were not compatible. His family didn't go to church; he wasn't particularly school-smart; he had a red-faced, blondish look and an unnerving hardness about him. He didn't smile much and whenever another kid did something foolish, Richard said so. "Fool!" he'd shout. "You damn fool!"

It was a strange thing, such an adult holler coming from the mouth of a kid. Richard's parents fought a lot—they got divorced later on—and I imagine that's where his yelling came from. But beneath that hard layer was an honest and decent kid with whom I had one defining equivalence: the need for sports.

Even in Little League, Richard was so big and strong and fast as to seem a different species of boy. He also couldn't stand losing. Richard was the first kid chosen up for any game, and I was second. We therefore always played on opposing teams, and his always won. I wasn't all that bothered. In fact—although it makes me unhappy to report this—I took comfort in the inevitability. Losing to anyone else would have irked me but I never expected to beat Richard and, deep down, didn't hope to. That was my family's way. "Enough is as good as a feast," my mother was always saying. This mentality imprisoned and infected me. I could not muster Richard's killer instinct because I felt undeserving, and without it I was bound to lose.

But if I could not directly defeat Richard LaPoint, I had a proxy: the Pittsburgh Steelers. Their beating his Dolphins would be the perfect payback.

In the days before the big game, I did little else but march around our house with the hard plastic football I'd just gotten for Christmas. I re-enacted the Immaculate Reception in the kitchen, in the living room, and, after my mother booted me outside, in the crusty snow drifting over the front porch. Like the truest Steelers fans, I believed that Franco's catch had been at least approved, if not choreographed, by God. I also believed, therefore, that a victory against Miami was fore-ordained. (Franco's Italian Army, taking no chances, hired a plane to drop leaflets reading "Surrender!" on the Dolphins' hotel.)

Miami had been to the Super Bowl the previous year and was unde-feated this season. They led the conference in both offense and defense. They had not one but two 1,000-yard rushers, Larry Csonka and Mer-cury Morris. Csonka, a hairy bull of a man, was Richard LaPoint's fa-vorite player.

"Csonka's the *man*," he told me. "Can't you see that? And Franco's a *pussy*. Always running out of bounds like a scaredy-cat."

Against the Dolphins, the oddsmakers had the Steelers as slight un-derdogs. But after the Immaculate Reception the previous week, the Steelers had a miracle in their pocket and momentum on their side. Fur-thermore, a few days before the game a Harvard mathematician deliv-ered a paper to the American Association for the Advancement of Science in which he announced his foolproof formula for rating every football team in the league. Mathematically speaking, he concluded, the Steelers were the very best.

The mathematician, it turned out, was a Pittsburgh native. He was also, it turned out, wrong. The Steelers played well, Franco included, but nothing miraculous happened, and the Dolphins won 21–17.

"It was not to be," wrote the editorialists of the *Post-Gazette*. "Yet when all is said and done, we are certain the 1972 Steelers season will live in the annals of Pittsburgh for that incredible last-minute reversal in the division playoff on Dec. 23 with the Oakland Raiders. . . . Even though the string of miracles ran out at Three Rivers Stadium yesterday, they'll never take the thrill of that one away from us."

I was less sanguine. I had prayed for a victory and, although my mother had long told me that prayer was a question, not an answer, I felt betrayed.

The Dolphins went on to win the Super Bowl. Richard LaPoint wore his Dolphins ski cap to school every day, on into spring and summer. Richard wasn't a big talker; he didn't gloat with his mouth, only the hat. It was aqua and orange with a white pom-pom. Only the toughest kid in school could have gotten away with a pom-pom hat.

Double-crossed by prayer, I took refuge in the clichés that *Sports Illustrated* taught me. Now, I told myself, the Steelers knew what big-time victory—and defeat—tasted like. After coming so close, I told myself, they would be even hungrier next year.

THE 1973 STEELERS' SEASON, which would end one day after the death of my father, was a rocky one. The Steelers won eight of their first nine games, but Franco was often hurt: bruised ribs, a strained thigh, a tender knee, a bad big toe. He was said to be depressed when he didn't play and frightened when he did—that a tackler would target his knee and crush it.

The sportswriters and Steelers fans started riding Franco. Maybe he only had rookie's luck last year, they said. Maybe he wasn't tough enough for the NFL. Maybe he should have trained harder during the off-season, they said, instead of taking all those speaking engagements at a thousand dollars a pop.

Cheap shot! Most of his lectures, I had read, were for charity. And he *did* train hard—running and rope-jumping and all kinds of strange flexibility drills he'd dreamed up. He even kneaded Play-Doh to get his hands stronger so he wouldn't fumble. Couldn't they see how much he was hurting? He had to hold a Dixie cup of ice on his knee for an hour after practice. What right did they have to challenge his desire? Just because defensive ends and linebackers played with broken bones didn't mean anything. Franco was different—he ran with feeling, the way Earl Hines played the piano. He wasn't about brute force; he was an artist.

Toward season's end, between the time of my father's disastrous disturbance and his death, the Steelers went on a losing streak. Franco caught a lot of blame. The Italian Army virtually abandoned him.

Every attack on Franco went straight to my heart. I felt compelled to locate the flaws in his critics' arguments. Eventually I found one. Sometimes they blamed Franco for the Steelers' losing streak—this year's team, after all, was the same as last year's except for his output. And sometimes they said that Franco wasn't very good to start with. But, I reasoned with myself, if he wasn't very good, then the Steelers should have been able to win without him; and if the losing streak *was* his fault, then he must have been the team's savior after all. I had caught his critics in a contradiction, a lie! One of their charges could be true but not both. As far as I was concerned, they canceled each other out, making any future criticism of Franco Harris, either directly or indirectly, by parties known or unknown, utterly null and void.

Against the Dolphins in Miami on *Monday Night Football*, the Steelers had fallen behind 30–3 by halftime, when my mother made me go to bed. In the *Schenectady Gazette* the next morning I read that Franco scored a touchdown in the second half, but then he got the dry heaves. On the school bus, Richard LaPoint reminded me that Franco was a pussy.

The Steelers squeaked into the playoffs, playing the Raiders in Oakland. I was sure that Franco would redeem himself.

But he didn't. My father's funeral Mass was two days later, on the morning of Christmas Eve. And then we had Christmas, although I don't remember anything about it—the tree, the presents, the Nativity set on the piano. Maybe we didn't do any of that. What I do remember is the Super Bowl a few weeks later. The Miami Dolphins won it again, 24–7 over the Minnesota Vikings. Larry Csonka ran through the Vikings like a train through a picket fence. Like Richard LaPoint through me. Csonka set the Super Bowl record for rushing yardage and was voted the game's Most Valuable Player. Maybe Richard was right: Csonka was the man and Franco was a pussy. The world, I was learning, was an unforgiving place run by strong men and heartless gods.

BY THE AUTUMN of 1974, the first season of my fatherlessness, I looked forward to Sunday afternoons with desperation, the way my mother looked forward to Sunday mornings.

The Steelers opened with a win and a tie, but then were shut out—shut out!—by the Raiders, and Franco sprained his ankle. They won their next few games but fell into disarray. Franco was ineffective, and Chuck Noll began playing musical chairs with his quarterbacks. He benched Terry Bradshaw in favor of Joe Gilliam, who subsequently made the cover of *Sports Illustrated* as the league's only black starting quarterback. Gilliam had a great arm but he tended to use it too often. He threw fifty times in one game, more than double Bradshaw's average. Watching on television, I spent what felt like hours waiting for Franco to get the ball. Bradshaw was reinstated, benched again, then brought back for good.

By then Franco was healthy, and the Steelers turned the ball over to him. He responded gallantly, leading them to the division title. The sportswriters again swarmed him; they demanded the secret of his success.

If I were him, I thought, I'd hold a grudge for all the bad press they'd written since last season. But Franco was bigger than that. He was as polite—and honest—as ever. And he made it sound so easy! "When I'm running," he explained, "I see numbers, not faces. When I see the big numbers, that means big linemen. I try to stay away from them. The little numbers mean defensive backs. I know I have a better chance of running over them. Besides, just to think of some of those big guys catching me is enough incentive to run faster. In those situations, it's funny how much speed suddenly just makes itself available."

By playoff time, Franco and the Steelers were deep in a groove. In their first-round game, against the Buffalo Bills, Franco outrushed O. J. Simpson and scored three touchdowns, a playoff record. Against the Raiders in the conference championship game, he ran for 111 yards and two more touchdowns.

The Steelers were finally going to the Super Bowl. And all of Pittsburgh had fallen in love again with Franco Harris.

This time he didn't love them back quite as much. I didn't blame him. As a rookie, he met their ardor with bashful appreciation. Now he knew their praise to be conditional. He refused to mistake their backslapping for genuine feeling. "I really don't like that instant intimacy very much," he told reporters. He could barely go out in public anymore, but he was unwilling to cordon himself off. "I think this enforced isolation has affected a lot of famous people in a lot of ways," he explained. "They turn to other things—drugs, alcohol, weird habits, weirder lifestyles—to escape from the utter isolation that often goes along with utter success." He made it plain that he was a plain man who happened to play football for a living, and that some of the idolatry went a bit far. "Because we're so highly visible," he said, "people sometimes feel that we're special, as opposed, say, to being a plumber. But if network TV followed the plumber into your home, instead of the football player onto the field, fans would be keeping records of the time it took one plumber to fix a leak compared to another plumber."

I knew he wasn't complaining about me. Our relationship was different. That was clear from the Dream, from the look on his face when he agreed to come back to my house—not as if it were an *obligation*, not as if I were a mere *fan*. I was a part of him. He had come to find me, racing across time and trouble as one soul races across the cosmos to find another.

Franco didn't admit it until after the Super Bowl, but in the week leading up to the game he had such a bad head cold he didn't think he would play. The Steelers' opponent was the Minnesota Vikings, who wore purple and white; they were led by a fearsome, oversized defensive line and a savvy, undersized quarterback, Fran Tarkenton. The Vikings had twice been to the Super Bowl and, although they lost both times, that experience was thought to give them the edge. The *Schenectady Gazette* ran a column headlined "Purple People-Eaters Will Pummel Pittsburgh Patsies," which I dismissed as immature and ill-informed.

By game time Franco was feeling better. He spent his final minutes in the locker room snapping pictures of his teammates. Three hours later he was back in the locker room drenched in champagne. On the biggest stage of his life, he had played his greatest game. The Steelers won the Super Bowl, and Franco Harris, running for 158 yards and breaking Larry Csonka's record, was voted its Most Valuable Player.

I couldn't wait to see Richard LaPoint in school on Monday.

When seventy-four-year-old Arthur J. Rooney, the Chief, who had waited more than four decades for this victory, stepped up to claim his trophy, everybody in the locker room—every Steeler and reporter and NFL official and towel boy—wept along with him.

THE LEGEND GOES like this. In the summer of 1936, the Chief traveled to New York for a weekend of horseplaying. He was not yet a rich man. He was in fact deep in debt to his bookies, and the football team he'd founded in Pittsburgh three years earlier was in trouble.

He was the son of a saloon-keeper, the grandson of miners and steelers. He had been a boxer and a baseball player, but his truest love was gambling. In New York he planned to settle his debts and take one last shot at the horses who had led him to this low point.

First at the Empire City racetrack in Yonkers and then at Saratoga, the Chief embarked on what would come to be known as the greatest performance in the history of American horseplaying. He won early and often, as many as eleven races in a row. At Empire City he parleyed $300 into $10,000, which at Saratoga he turned into $256,000 or $380,000 or $500,000, depending on who tells the story. Thus was born the Rooney family fortune. In Depression-era Pittsburgh, even $256,000 would go a very long way. (His football team had only cost $2,500.)

He transported the money back to Pittsburgh in an armored car and immediately began shelling it out. He had never been accused of not being generous, and never would be. He gave to Father Dan, his priest brother in China, and a multitude of other churchmen. He gave to any man with a thirst, be it literal or metaphysical. He paid Byron "Whizzer" White, the All-America tailback and future Supreme Court justice, a gargantuan $15,800 to play one season for the Steelers. At the Roosevelt Hotel in downtown Pittsburgh, where the Chief kept his office and where a group of nuns often ate lunch, it was a standing rule that no nun would ever touch a check as long as Mr. Rooney was alive.

Over the decades, the legend of the Chief's jackpot became skewed. People said he used those horse winnings for the original purchase of the Steelers, and he let them think it, for a team midwifed by such good fortune would certainly win again one day.

No one, least of all the Chief, imagined that day to be so distant. He had five sons, whom he loved but treated roughly, and a sixth child, the Steelers, whom he treated like the daughter he never had. He doted on her, worried about her, spoiled her a bit, and prayed she would find her destiny. As he adored her, the football-mad people of Pittsburgh grew to adore the Chief—though never more so than in 1974, when he finally brought the Super Bowl trophy home to Pittsburgh. The Steeler Nation rose up in ecstasy.

So did I. Would there ever be another year as sweet as 1974? It was the year that I—and the Steelers—tasted the subtle rapture of a postponed power.

THE SARATOGA RACE COURSE LAY ONLY thirty miles from Duanesburg. Although I'd never been there, I cherished this connection, however tenuous, to the Steelers' success. I too had bet on a horse, and now he had come in. Franco Harris was ascendant. As the Super Bowl MVP, he was given a luncheon at the Plaza Hotel in New York, to which he brought his parents, Gina and Cadillac. In addition to the MVP trophy, he received a free car, a green station wagon worth $7,800. (He asked if he was eligible for the $500 manufacturer's rebate, which everyone laughed at but I thought was a good idea.) He appeared on *The Mike Douglas Show* and got to sing with the Fifth Dimension. (I didn't see it. He was reportedly a terrible singer but enjoyed himself immensely.)

The NFL was thrilled to have in the spotlight a player of Franco's character and charm. He was, in jock parlance, "a real class act." No one worried about Franco punching out a reporter or getting coked up or being caught with a pair of hookers in his hotel room. "The thing that makes me proudest about Franco is that he's never changed through all this success," Cad Harris told reporters at the Plaza. "He's still the down-to-earth kid he's always been. The only difference is that now he's bigger."

I approved of all the nice things everyone was saying about Franco, but I appreciated him on a deeper level. He was owned by no one. He thought for himself, upended expectations, bowed to no pressures other than those he generated. In a person with an evil inclination, such independence could be dangerous. But Franco was a force for the good. He was a sensitive man who triumphed in a brute's game, an honest and gentle man who swam through the deceit and harshness of the modern world and emerged whole, clean, and happy.

He led me to think I might do the same. He gave me permission to begin thinking for myself, to believe in and for myself, and I was a boy who needed permission for the slightest thing.

Bit by bit, I began to shed my resignation and my feeling-sorry-for-myself-ness. You are who you choose to be, Franco said, and if you let others judge you, all you get is sad and bitter and paranoid. I began to see the future not as a preexisting grid onto which I would plop myself down in the sole permitted quadrant—the Angry Fatherless Catholic Boy Quadrant—but as a wide-open expanse through which I was free to skip, stumble, or sprint.

Then again, it may have been the testosterone. I was BIRGing mightily. Studies have shown that it is the fan with the lowest self-esteem who receives the greatest psychological boost when his team wins, and I would have to think I qualified. In the weeks following that Super Bowl, which fell just after the first anniversary of my father's death, I tripped in and out of a rambunctious high. The slightest trigger—writing "Franco Dubner" on a math quiz, passing Richard La-Point in the hallway—sent me looping. I could have climbed a mountain barefoot, swum the ocean with strength to spare. Mornings, I woke up fortified by the Dream. (I still wished I could change the ending and make Franco slash across the yard for the winning touchdown the way he slashed through the Vikings.)

And this was a high that wouldn't subside. The Steelers won the Super Bowl again the following year, and just missed the season after that. In 1977, when I was fourteen, they had an off year, but came back to win the Super Bowl again in 1978 and 1979. Before Franco arrived, the Steelers had never made the playoffs; they hadn't missed since, and they'd become the first team ever to win three (and then four) Super Bowls. *Sports Illustrated* started saying they might be the best football team in history. The longer they won, the more often they appeared on television, and the more rabidly my life revolved around Franco and Pittsburgh.

There was a newsstand in Schenectady that carried out-of-town papers. I had my mother buy me the *Pittsburgh Post-Gazette* whenever she went into the city. (I was by now boycotting the *Schenectady Gazette* for its anti-Steelers bias.) I may have been the only person alive to regard the city of Pittsburgh with unmitigated enchantment.

I identified with it. Like my family, Pittsburgh had been greatly dissipated of late. The culprits in my case were the death of a father and the natural dispersion of grown siblings. Pittsburgh was suffering a death of its own: Big Steel's. Just as the Steelers finally rose after decades of loss, the real-life steelers began losing jobs by the tens of thousands. A lot of them moved away. Some bought Steelers tickets with unemployment checks. For them, as for me, the Steelers became much more than a football team. "You can't put a price tag on how valuable they were to the human spirit here," Myron Cope, the dean of Pittsburgh sportscasters, said years later. "Wherever people gathered, the Steelers were the dominant topic. They were winning, and winning huge, and it gave people something pleasant to talk about for a change instead of, 'Where the hell am I going to get work?'"

This desperation was attractive to me. So was Pittsburgh's work ethic, its desire to carve a fierce arc of triumph across a sky exhausted by soot and loss. In my ninth-grade history class, I asked the teacher if I could write my term paper about Pittsburgh instead of Africa, as he'd assigned. Even when he laughed at me, my enchantment went undiminished.

I read that the North Side, Franco's neighborhood, lay in a river flat ringed by seven hills, just like ancient Rome. (No wonder Franco felt so at home there!) I learned that Pittsburgh was 50 percent Catholic, and that priests had had to triple up their Saturday-night Mass schedules since Sundays were now set aside for the Steelers. Chuck Noll and several of his players—Jack Lambert and Jack Ham and Rocky Bleier, but not Franco—were Saturday-night regulars at Our Lady of Grace, where Father John Marcucci wore a black-and-gold stole with the Steelers' logo. Father Marcucci liked to compare the Super Bowl to Heaven— they were both the ultimate prize, he'd preach, requiring single-mindedness and sacrifice. He pointed out that Saint Paul had preached likewise, comparing a Corinthian athlete's crown of holly to "the imperishable crown" of Heaven.

"Paul was using the athletics of the town as a backdrop for preaching the religious direction," Father Marcucci explained. "So I'm standing on solid ground, even though Saint Paul didn't have a Steelers stole or anything."

I mentioned the Steelers priest to my mother. I said that, since it was just the two of us at home now, Pittsburgh might be a nice place to live.

She said she'd "give it serious thought." That's what she said whenever the answer was no but she wanted to let you down easy. I told her that Mr. Rooney went to Mass every morning. I told her they called Chuck Noll "the Pope" (but didn't tell her why: he was so aloof as to consider himself infallible).

Aside from a vague desire to live in Pittsburgh, my future goals were murky. Franco always talked about goal-setting, but I couldn't seem to follow his lead.

I did toy with becoming an NFL placekicker, the only position I had the size for, and I practiced for a few months in the yard but never really got the ball airborne. (Once it smacked my dog, Toby, right in the muzzle, and he bled all over the grass.)

I thought I might still become a priest, if only to satisfy my mother, but my feelings about God calcified one afternoon when my mother's friend Mrs. Burke called. I answered the phone, hollered downstairs for my mother and, instead of hanging up the extension, only pretended to hang up. I heard Mrs. Burke say that Patrick, her youngest son and a good friend of mine, had just been hit by a car and killed. At the funeral the Burkes passed out Mass cards: "We thank you Father for giving us so many friends to help us rejoice in the rebirth of our Pat into your heavenly kingdom." And I was so tired of being asked to jump for joy every time someone died that I vowed to not only not become a priest but, as soon as it was feasible—when I finally went off to college, that is—to quit church entirely.

I did not like the idea of staying in Duanesburg any longer than necessary. I did like the idea of writing my way through life, especially since that had been my father's dream. I would have loved to cover the Steelers for *Sports Illustrated*, but I didn't know how to make that leap from the high-school paper.

There was talk suddenly of reinstating the military draft, and so, in the tenth grade, I became a preemptive Conscientious Objector. My father had volunteered during World War II, as had Franco's father, but Franco didn't serve and neither would I. During high school, Franco had considered following his father into the Army, even thought about attending West Point. But as sentiment against the Vietnam War deepened, he changed his mind. During his freshman year at Penn State in 1968, he found that sentiment all the more compelling. "Kent State, I think, was the most tragic thing in the history of our country," he told a sportswriter years later. "I couldn't believe our own countrymen shooting and killing." He said that antiwar groups at Penn State tried to pressure him into helping destabilize the university. "But I still was kind of a punky kid from New Jersey," he said, "and I didn't want anybody to tell me what to do, especially college kids."

No, I told myself, I don't want anybody telling me what to do either. Nor will I fight for a country that kills its own.

ONLY HINDSIGHT ALLOWS ME to see this irony: I had come to consider myself a free thinker while borrowing my every thought from a professional football player. My worldview, such as it was, had been received intact from a man I never met and who didn't know of my existence.

Perhaps this is not so different from believing in God and following His laws. Perhaps it is a natural inclination, especially among the small and weak, to attach ourselves to something large and great—and distant, the better to preserve that perception of largeness and greatness—in the hopes of saving ourselves. Perhaps we are hardwired for hero worship.

Hindsight affords me a further irony: this hero of mine had much in common with my own mother. I would have furiously denied this back then, but now I see it is true. They each strove for decency even when surrounded by the opposite. They built their own consciences from the ground up and plotted their own courses, immune to prevailing attitudes and cheap fixes.

And they were both stronger than I was. Together, one of them near and one far, they lifted me out of a pit and set me on solid ground.

I FEAR THAT this portrait of my younger self may be too dark. I was never a miserable or morose boy, and though my father's death certainly tossed me into a storm, I did inherit his optimism. My brothers and sisters, if you asked them today, would tell you that I was a happy little boy, and much of the time I was. I didn't brood (too often) or act out (too much) or even complain (ever, for criticizing the shape of my world meant criticizing my mother, and I was nothing if not reverent toward her). What I did do was hope—for a future full of new beginnings and bold experiences.

MY MOTHER AND I, it turned out, wearied of our old lives at the same time. We were both ready to shake off the hangover of my father's death. She put the house up for sale, and I folded my last two years of high school into one. She was a fifty-eight-year-old Right-to-Life widow and I was a sixteen-year-old Conscientious Objector who had finally, just recently, stopped dreaming every night about his boyhood hero.

The Steelers won their fourth and final Super Bowl the year I finished high school. Franco had just turned thirty. He was in peak form. All that criticism about being a wimp for dodging tacklers, about going slow in practice—he'd shut everyone up. He saved himself for when it mattered, and when it mattered there was no one better. He still wasn't a chest-thumper, still deflected all the attention he could. I followed him right up to the end. When his father died, the summer I was leaving home, I thought about sending a condolence card but never got around to it.

I certainly did not plan on forgetting Franco so fast. But a change of scenery will do that. I wound up in the piney mountains of North Carolina, at a college called Appalachian State University. I stopped watching football entirely. I outgrew him without even noticing. There were pianos to play, stories to write, girls to chase. No one knew me there; I was at last unburdened and unfettered. I no longer had to lug around my dead father or my family's piety or the mystery of our lineage.

There may exist in this world some circumstance sweeter than a second chance, but I have yet to find it.

Book Two

A HERO IN THE FLESH

8

REUNITED

———◆◁∞▷◆———

I SPENT MOST OF the flight trying not to vomit. Across the aisle a slender, yellow-faced businessman—he looked like a wilted vegetable—was doing just that, again and again and loudly. The stewardess collected each airsick bag he filled. She'd hand him a new one and pat him on the shoulder. I fingered my own bag—was it the same kind they use for coffee beans?—and then snapped it open. It was a small plane, flying through the core of a spring thunderstorm, on a route notoriously choppy for its mountain updrafts. The pilot said the turbulence would last only ten more minutes. He said this every fifteen minutes. I stopped believing him over Altoona. It was the eighth of April, 1999. Beyond the turbulence, my stomach was churning under its own power, for I had set out on the most beguiling and foolhardy journey known to man: I was going to meet my hero.

I wore a new sweater (deep navy, merino wool, too expensive), pressed trousers, shined shoes. I had even had my hair cut to minimize the Shaggy Writer look. I knew that Franco was casual, but I wanted to show respect. Because stepping off an airplane with dried vomit on oneself is not a sign of respect, I attempted now to distract my nausea.

I stowed the thick sheaf of magazine and newspaper articles I'd been reading. (I didn't want to vomit on them either.) I closed my eyes and, like a lawyer about to make his opening statement, began rehearsing the raft of facts I knew to be true concerning the life of Franco Harris.

He had one child, a son named Dok, who scored a perfect 1600 on his SATs and was now a sophomore at Princeton. Dok was short for Franco Dokmanovich Harris Jr., Dokmanovich being the maiden name of Franco's wife, Dana (his common-law wife, technically, since they never actually married). Franco and Dana, who is white, met at Penn State— she majored in home economics, he in food service and administration—and by now they'd been together for the better part of thirty years. Until Dok was born, in 1979, Dana worked as a stewardess for Eastern Airlines. Franco last played football in 1984, the year I was graduated from college.

His long career ended abruptly and bitterly, after a contract dispute with the Steelers. But he stayed on in Pittsburgh and wound up running a company called Super Bakery, which made nutritious baked goods. Doughnuts mostly, "healthy" doughnuts. It was a niche business, selling mainly to schools and hospitals, but Super Bakery reportedly did $10 million in annual sales.

He had recently bought another company, Parks Sausage of Baltimore. He remembered the company's slogan—"More Parks sausages, Mom. Please!"—from when he was a kid and hoped to revive it, along with the company's market share. Parks, the first black-owned company in America to have its stock publicly traded, had fallen into bankruptcy. (The previous CEO had taken to unscrewing half the lightbulbs to cut his electricity bills.) When Franco stepped in, he was received as the savior of a venerable, dying company. "I'm delighted to see you, sir!" the bankruptcy judge had said, and Franco received a standing ovation in the courtroom. Beyond its legacy, Parks provided hundreds of inner-city jobs, while its brand-new factory anchored an otherwise dicey Baltimore neighborhood.

It was the Parks deal that landed Franco on the cover of the *Black Enterprise* magazine I saw in Times Square, the magazine that triggered my hero-worshiping memories of the man who shepherded me through a fatherless boyhood.

When my visit home, to the sex club now known as the House of

Dreams, didn't turn out as expected, I decided to write Franco a letter. I told him I became an "immediate and lifelong fan" upon witnessing the Immaculate Reception when I was nine years old. "But," I wrote,

> you were more than a football hero to me; you were a role model as well. There were plenty of great football players but very few who projected the image that you did: hard-working, generous, self-effacing, respectful.

I never stopped admiring the values he embodied, I told him. And although I lost track of him for nearly twenty years, I wasn't surprised now to read that his post-football life seemed to revolve around the same values:

> When I read that you were trying to save Parks Sausage, I thought, *Well of course—that's exactly the kind of thing that Franco Harris would do.* But that's not really why I'm writing you. I'm writing because it's very rare that someone's childhood hero—whether an athlete or movie star or astronaut—turns out to truly be a role model several years down the road. Especially in this age when athletes are worshiped beyond all proportion, it's heartening to see that the man I admired as an athlete has become a businessman and citizen who clearly exemplifies the kind of excellence that makes this country great.
>
> I'd very much like the opportunity to meet with you with an eye toward writing about you and your various successes.

Two weeks later my phone rang. "This is Franco Harris," he said, matter-of-factly.

"Hello!" I mumbled something to the effect of, "Did you receive the letter I sent?"—which he obviously had, since here he was on the phone.

"As a matter of fact, I just read it this afternoon," he said.

"Well, I hope you'll see your way to inviting me down to Pittsburgh."

The next several weeks were bad, he said, lots of business travel, but we made a date for the second Thursday in April. I hung up stunned and giddy.

I began assembling a dossier on him. Hundreds of old sports articles and whatever business-press coverage I could find on Super Bakery and Parks. I hunted down used copies of the children's books about Franco I'd read long ago. I also began reading up on the philosophical and psychological motives of hero-worship. I wanted to be as prepared as possible for our reunion.

Yes, a reunion. Just as meeting a long-lost relative is a reunion even though it is your first meeting. Franco and I shared a past; we had been buoyed and bruised by the same timeline; our intimacy had been real.

But what shook me now, as the airplane bashed its way through yet another cloud bank, was the thought of consummation. Would he like me? Would I like him? I felt horribly overcommitted all of a sudden, like a man approaching the altar to marry a mail-order bride, purchased sight unseen. *What, exactly, am I doing here?* My mouth turned dry and metallic. I tried to lower my expectations—which, sadly, wasn't hard: I pictured Franco letting me buy him a cup of coffee in an airport lounge, chatting about the glory days for fifteen minutes, and sending me on my way.

He had said he would meet me at the gate, but I wasn't counting on it. Franco Standard Time was said to run anywhere from two hours to two days slow. I had rented a car, just in case, and booked a hotel near the airport.

Thirty miles outside of Pittsburgh, the plane finally settled down. The fields below were starting to green up; the trees stood silvery and bare. "We're looking at clear skies and sixty-two degrees," the pilot said, all chipper, as if the turbulence never happened. The fields soon gave way to a carpet of sharp-peaked roofs, red and rusty and gray, huddled together on hillsides like runaway children. We flew over a burned-out warehouse, a pair of rivers, a train sitting idle on the track, and suddenly we were parked at the gate. Was Franco?

On shaky legs, I spotted him immediately, talking with two other men.

"Franco!" I said, shouted really, before I meant to, still ten yards away.

He stood up, made his way toward me, and offered his hand. "Hey, Steve, how are you?" No one called me Steve anymore—I'd been Stephen

since college—but I liked it. We shook. His hand was big but soft, like
well-tenderized meat. "Good to meet you," he said, easy, looking me in
the eye. The other men had followed. "Dave, Ron, this is Steve."

I shook their hands. Dave was tall, lumbery, quiet. Ron was shorter,
peppier. Franco was . . . well, Franco was *standing in front of me*. His
hair had thinned a bit, and he wore a red flannel shirt, khakis, and
brown loafers—he brought to mind a contractor out bidding for a
kitchen remodeling job—but *he looked just like Franco Harris*. He was a
big shiny magnet, and I, even though I was full-grown by now, with a
new wife and a writing career and a Manhattan address, I was a scrap
of iron filing.

I stood there beaming until Ron finally said, "Well!" and Franco
asked me if the flight was all right.

"Fine," I said. "A little bumpy but no problem."

Just then the yellow-faced businessman trudged past, his necktie still
flung over his shoulder. Franco, Ron, and Dave watched him weave
through the terminal.

"Feel like a doughnut?" Franco asked.

It so happened that Super Bakery, trying to break out of its institu-
tional niche, was test-marketing some retail product at the airport.
That's why Ron and Dave had come along. Ron was Super Bakery's
marketing man; Dave headed up the retail project. Franco led us over to
a kiosk, one of its glass cases freshly stocked with Super Donuts, glazed
and powdered and sprinkled.

"They're a first-generation batch," Franco said.

"Prototypes," Ron said.

The doughnuts were corpulent, slightly oblong, and, after my flight,
deeply unappetizing. *Prototypes.*

"I'll have a glazed, thanks."

I bit in—it was good, chewier than your average doughnut, sweet
and nice. "*MMM-mm*," I said, meaningfully. The three of them looked at
me, then one another, then back to me.

"How about a, um, a, um, a juice or a water?" Franco asked. *Franco
Harris has a stammer.* Slight but noticeable. It was the first I'd ever heard
him speak, really—live, unedited, in-person. It was also the first I'd ever

seen him jingle coins in his pocket or stroke his eyebrow with the point of his index finger.

No thanks, I said, but he pulled a water bottle from the cooler anyway. When I took out my wallet, Franco waved me off. *He's buying. I'm eating Franco Harris's doughnut, and he's buying me a bottle of water.*

"You've got to try this one too," he said. "This one's a Super Bun." It was chocolate-coated, the size of a smashed softball. Franco suggested we all sit down to talk. Ron, Dave, and I picked out a table while Franco paid for my water.

Ron started to grill me, in a nice way. (Dave wasn't interested. Franco had stayed behind at the kiosk and was rearranging his doughnuts in the case; Dave seemed to be considering whether he should help.) Ron said Franco mentioned that I was a writer from New York, but that was it. Ron wanted to know what I'd written, whether I was on staff or freelance, and what on earth I was doing in Pittsburgh.

I left the last question to molder. I told Ron that, for the past few years, I'd been a writer and editor at the *New York Times Magazine* but was now leaning toward free agency. I said my first book had recently been published, about my once-Jewish parents' embrace of Catholicism and my own excavation of that buried past.

"Wait a minute," Ron said. "I read something like that in *USA Today*. That wasn't your book, was it? Was that you?"

Yes it was, I told him, and Ron perked up even further. I did too. I took a bite of Super Donut, a sip of water, a bite of Super Bun. The first wave of sugar rush set my scalp tingling. I was liking Pittsburgh.

I watched Franco approach our table, deliberately. Even in his prime he walked gingerly, as if worried that his fleshy torso would crush his spindly legs.

"Hey, Franco, Steve just wrote a book," Ron said. "I read about it in *USA Today*. His family has a wild story. His parents were both Jewish, but before they met each other they became Roman Catholics. . . ."

Ron went on for a bit, with surprisingly pinpoint recall. I would have liked to hug him. He made me sound so *interesting.* Finally Ron turned to me. "But wait a minute," he said. "*What* did you say you're doing in Pittsburgh?"

I had planned on having this talk one-on-one with Franco. But Ron forced my hand. I said I wanted to write a book about, about, about—well, about a boy and his hero.

"You know, I never have cooperated with a writer before," Franco said.

"I know," I said. "The Don Kowet book and the one by the Hahns, all those books, they were just clip jobs." For all Franco had been written about, he was never *examined*. Not properly anyway.

I laid out my vision: a book about a football player and the kid who loved him, the two of them never meeting until years later, whereupon the childhood infatuation blooms into a mature conversation about sport and life and hero worship.

Franco was a good listener; you could tell he took things in. He smiled sheepishly when I talked about how the Immaculate Reception came to mean so much to me, stuck on a ramshackle farm in Duanesburg, New York. As I spoke, I met his eyes (noncommittal), then Ron's (rapt), then Dave's (bored), then back to Franco. I tried to lay off the schmaltz. I tried to sound sane. I didn't dwell on my father's dying, and I certainly didn't say that Franco became a sort of messiah for me. Nor did I mention that I was carrying on my person a dozen typed pages of interview questions and a ten-point Franco Wish List. I also made sure to leave out, for now, the Dream. *Do not tell him the Dream, do not tell him the Dream, do not tell him the Dream, for if you do Franco Harris will freak out and unfold his long legs from his red plastic airport chair and walk away, and he would be right to do so.* I did admit that I called myself Franco Dubner for a time, that I was captivated and inspired by him—I was careful not to say "obsessed"—and that, all these years later, the sight of him on the cover of *Black Enterprise* sent my mind sprawling and drove me to seek him out.

I had no doubt that I made a most professional and balanced impression.

"So you were really, like, *obsessed*," Ron said.

"Oh, *yeah*," I said.

Then I told them the Dream.

When I got to the end—Franco handing me the ball and saying, "Kid, you're going to have to take it from here yourself"—I watched his face. At first he seemed mildly distressed, like someone expecting to taste chocolate ice cream and getting pineapple instead. Then he grinned. It was a beautiful grin, lips closed at first but then all teeth, his eyes crinkling. He didn't say anything right away, but he didn't pick up and leave either. Then he asked if I was ready for another Super Donut.

HE LOADED my bag into his trunk, which was jammed with tennis gear. *So he still plays tennis.* He had to scrunch down to get behind the wheel. *He's put on some weight, but not much; he's just a big guy.* His car, a red 1994 Volkswagen Passat, had 97,000 miles on it. *So typical—nothing flashy for Franco.* The radio was tuned to lite jazz. *Not my taste, but . . . I wonder if he'll like the Joshua Redman CD I brought him—just a little present.* He slowly shifted into gear, slowly backed out, slowly dug into his wallet at the parking-lot booth. Although Franco Harris had been a football player, and although football is famous as a contest of controlled violence, I had never in my life felt less in the presence of violence.

He didn't say where we were going, and I didn't ask. We pulled onto a freeway.

"Mind if I turn on a tape recorder?" I asked.

"No sir," he said.

Because I'd already spilled the Dream, I thought it best to abstain from further sports-fantasy-stalker talk. Instead I asked how Parks Sausage was coming along.

"So-so," he said. The company's fancy new factory had turned out to be an albatross. It cost too much to operate, he told me, and its sausage-making equipment was ancient. "It just seemed like whatever could go wrong did go wrong," he said. "We'd have a big promotion on this one product, and then *that* machine would break down, you know? We didn't have the money to really invest in new machinery. And if we can't be great, why even be in it? Money kept having to go into the building, so we couldn't spend it on marketing and advertising. I said, 'I want to build a *brand*, I don't want to spend all my money on the *building*.' They say volume can cure a lot of ills, but we were never able to get to that volume."

So he sold the factory. Now, he explained, he was running Parks as a virtual corporation, just like Super Bakery, outsourcing the manufacturing and distribution while saving his own energies for product development and marketing.

He really *is* a businessman, I realized as I listened to him, not one of those ex-ballplayers who buys a company so he can have a corner office. I thought to ask whether his selling the Parks factory meant he hadn't saved all those inner-city jobs after all. But I didn't.

"So it seems like you had an interesting background," he said, out of nowhere. He spoke so softly I had to lean in to hear him. He smelled good—not all cologned-up, but good. If he were a wine, I would have said he had heavy notes of berry and currant, with men's-club undertones. "It sounds like you were dealing with a lot of different things," he was saying, "questions like, 'Who am I?'"

I was taken aback—he wanted to know about *me*? I took it for an accident, a onetime gesture of politeness.

"Right," I said. "It's like that story from when you were a kid, walking on the boardwalk, and an old black guy looks at you and says, 'I don't get it—you've got Roman features but you're black. What's the deal?' And that was the first time *you* ever really thought about *your* background."

He didn't say anything. I wondered if he didn't remember the story.

"Anyway," I said. "That's sort of the way it was for me as a kid. I knew there was something strange in my background, but I didn't understand it. At the time I didn't know the story of my parents' conversions and how they were cut off from their families."

"You know what—with a lot of parents in our parents' generation, they just *did not talk* about their problems," he said. "Like my mom, what she went through with the war over in Europe, I never knew until the last ten or so years. She just never talked about it. And my father never talked about the war, never talked about growing up in Mississippi. I bet that was tough."

"And I'm sure serving as a black man in the Army at that time was no picnic," I said.

"Yep, but you know what? They did not want their kids to know all their hardships."

"What did your dad do in the Army?" I asked.

"I don't know what his function really was. He got to the rank of sergeant, then when I was sixteen he kind of retired, got a civil-servant job working in the kitchen at the Army hospital. But you know, he really couldn't read or write. My mom, she only went up to the third or fourth grade in Italy, but she can read and write both Italian and English. Finding that out about my dad, that was a shocker."

"Did you ever talk to him about it?"

"Not really. I remember one time we had to do a commercial together—"

"Wait, don't tell me," I said. "For Peter Paul Powerhouse candy bar, right?"

"Yeah, right. And it was kind of tough because—"

"Because he had to read cue cards?"

"Right. Yeah, that was kind of tough. But you know, he was a great provider. He worked two jobs, and he was home *every* night, you know what I mean? He provided for nine kids. I mean, *nine kids*. And you had a lot in your family, huh?"

"Yeah, eight. Are all your brothers and sisters alive and well?"

"Yep," he said. "We're very, very lucky. So, in your book, with your parents becoming Catholic, then you were raised Catholic?"

"I was raised *very* Catholic," I said. "I mean, I was an altar boy—"

"No way, were you?"

"Oh, yeah, practically from the time I could walk."

"Are you still Catholic?" he asked.

"No," I said. He really *did* seem curious about my life. So I explained. "I became lapsed pretty fast when I went to college, and a few years afterward, when I moved to New York, I started looking into my parents' Jewish history. I wasn't thinking, Hey, maybe *I* should return to Judaism. But when I started tracking down my father's relatives and got to know them, the whole tradition resonated for me—in part, I'm sure, because my entire family, for centuries and centuries, had been Jewish. So I began to study in earnest, to learn about the history and the religion and the culture. After a while, it got to the point where I realized that as much as I was going to be religious—and I'm not an overwhelmingly religious person—that I was going to be Jewish. So that's what I did, I began to live my life as a Jew."

"Huh, no kidding," he said. "That's really interesting."

"Well, it's caused some major friction with my mom. She is one Catholic lady. I gather she could give your mom a run for the money." I was thinking of the story about Franco's mother playing "Ave Maria" just before the Immaculate Reception.

"No, my mom is not overwhelmingly religious," he said. "I mean, she was raised Catholic and all that. But no, she doesn't agree with the Church about everything."

"So obviously your mom is alive."

"She's seventy-two, and thank God, she's doing great."

"Does she still live up in—"

"New Jersey."

"In Mount Holly? The same house?"

"Yep. I was just home for Easter."

I T W A S , I thought as we drove along, the best car ride ever. I had arrived in Pittsburgh unable to visualize our reunion; I had arrived in a tight spiral, runaway desire twisted around the fear of a letdown. I am guessing this is how Emily feels in *Our Town* when, from the grave, she is allowed to revisit one day from her childhood. How can she resist? And yet how can she fail to be disappointed?

But riding around in Franco's car, I felt remarkably at ease. Exhilarated, yes, but the sort of exhilaration you feel after being away from home and you return to find everything just as you remembered it, just as you liked it.

Most reunions are spent grasping for the slender threads that once held you close. If Richard LaPoint and I were to meet up today, I don't know if we could generate ten minutes of conversation. But Franco and I had more in common now than ever. Back then, I was a kid and he was a superstar. Back then, he was thirteen years older than I—*thirteen years older*, twice my age. Now he was . . . *only thirteen years older than I*. We belonged, technically, to the same generation. Our war-veteran fathers were both dead; his mother was actually younger than mine. We both paid taxes and had wives. We were both moderate Democrats (he had twice campaigned with Bill Clinton, and I twice voted for him).

It turned out that Franco was giving me a tour of Pittsburgh. After twenty minutes on the freeway, traffic slowed. "This is the Fort Pitt Tunnel," he said. "I just want to say, I do think this is one of the most beautiful entrances of any city."

He wasn't kidding. The freeway had been perfectly ordinary, slicing through brand-new shopping strips and fading neighborhoods. But the Fort Pitt Tunnel plunged us suddenly into a mountain. (It is a point of pride in Pittsburgh, I later learned, that this road was built through the mountain and not around or over it, as a more dainty city might have done.) The tunnel, dark and smoky, delivered us onto a blindingly bright perch, high on a bridge above a wide river. The scene below, in panoramic miniature, was startling. It seemed as if we had climbed atop a stepladder to survey a vast diorama built by a gang of slightly loony nine-year-olds. There were bridges everywhere, painted yellow. One big river flowed into another and became a third. Packed onto the hillsides were the old neighborhoods, a mosaic of clapboard and chimney and church steeple straight out of a Grandma Moses painting. A many-spired Philip Johnson tower gleamed gaudily from a herd of downtown skyscrapers. And over to the left, squatting on the riverside like a giant gray ashtray—but a wonderful ashtray—was Three Rivers Stadium.

"Wow!" I said.

"Yeah," said Franco. "Like, *voilà.*"

We crossed the bridge in silence.

"They're going to tear Three Rivers down and build two new stadiums," he said.

"How do you feel about that?"

"Well, history and tradition are great, but I like progress too. And I don't want those things to hold back progress. If it's *good* progress." He said this in a tone indicating that the Three Rivers scenario was indeed good progress. "So, do you still root for the Steelers?"

"No, not really," I said. "Not since you retired." Which was a slight fib, since I had lost interest even before he retired, as soon as I left for college.

"You follow the Giants?" he asked.

"I do, but not devoutly. I watch more football than I should—and baseball and basketball—but I'm not wrapped up the way I was as a kid. How about you?"

"Oh, I still pull for the Steelers," he said, as if surprised there would be any question.

We drove through downtown, slowly, office buildings and cafeterias and wig shops, the lunchtime bustle just starting. A bike messenger sped past: "Hey, Fran-*co!*"

"You still get it pretty regularly, huh?"

"Now and then," he said.

We looped back across the river over another bridge, then drove up a steep incline. "This is called Mount Washington," Franco said. He parked at an observation deck and we got out, leaned over the rail. The entire city lay below, silent and glistening. It had turned into a sterling spring day.

"Which river is which?" I asked.

He had to think for a minute. "This is the Monongahela, that's the Allegheny, and right over there they become the Ohio. Um, I've got to make a call."

"Sure."

He strolled to the other end of the observatory as he dialed. I did my best to not overhear. It wasn't very interesting anyway—just setting up a business meeting. He put the phone in his pocket and walked back.

"I'm probably one of the worst tour guides in the city," he said, "but I'm doing my best here."

"Are you kidding? This is fantastic. It's a beautiful city."

"You know what, as I travel and I meet people, they say, 'Oh, *Pitts*-burgh,' and I say, 'You've never been there, right?' They say, 'No.' I say, 'Okay, because if you'd ever been there, you would never make that face.' Because Pittsburgh will definitely surprise you."

We drove back off Mount Washington and over another bridge into a flat, bright, ragged neighborhood. "This is the North Side, where I used to live," he said.

"You moved?"

"Yeah, out to Sewickley, about twelve miles out." *Sewickley.* I liked the sound of that. "I still own the house here, though. When I first came to town, I was riding down this street, I knew nothing about Pittsburgh—"

"Franco! Franco!" It was an old lady, beating a rug on her stoop.

He waved. "Boy, she's still here?"

"An old neighbor?" I asked.

"Yep, a *long* time ago. Anyway, this house coming up here on the corner was all boarded up. *All* these houses were boarded up—this was 1973 now, you have to understand—and I was dumb enough to buy it. Just something about it I loved." He paused. "So, where do you live?"

In the West Fifties of Manhattan, I told him, near Carnegie Hall. We drove slowly past his house. I remembered it well from the long-ago article in *Ebony.* It was brick, handsome but not quite stately, on a shaded corner lot, three stories with bay windows and a wrought-iron fence. The gate had an "FH" laid into the ironwork, six inches high but painted black like the rest, nothing tacky about it.

"I could walk to the stadium from here, maybe fifteen minutes," he said.

"Is it true you didn't own a car your rookie year?"

"Well, halfway through the season someone let me use a car, but I just told myself I wasn't going to buy one. Matter of fact, I was walking across this bridge right here, and these little kids come up to me, said, 'Franco, where's your car?' I said, 'I don't have a car.' They said, 'Oh, come on, where's your Cadillac, where's your Cadillac?' And it just really pissed me off, that they thought I should have a Cadillac, that they thought *that's* what it was all about. So I just said, I am *not* going to buy a car. It made it tough, though, because I lived out on the east side of town that year, and I had to hitchhike or catch a bus into the stadium every day."

His voice had a recitative quality to it. He may have told the no-car story before. (Who was I kidding?—he'd probably told it a thousand times.) But I didn't care. His very presence was making me happy. *My* voice, meanwhile, kept rising up in my throat, the voice of a twelve-year-old boy, damp with excitement.

"So I've got a personal question for you," I said.

I was only joking—exaggerating, really—but Franco looked as if I'd jabbed him with a hot needle. "A personal question?"

"That scar on your hand," I said, "is that the one from the lightbulb?" It was a long, straight, paper-thin scar, running from the base of his middle finger to the outside of his wrist.

"Um, no, no, that's from a helmet. I did hit a lightbulb once"—he held aloft his other hand—"I think it might have been this one, or this one. One of these."

"But that one's a helmet—you remember whose?"

"Uh-uhn. No, everybody's hands get all scarred up." He drove on a bit. "Hey, do you want to think about a bite, get some lunch?"

Yes, I said. I wanted to get some lunch. Dinner too. I wanted to move to Pittsburgh.

He asked if Italian was all right, and I said yes it was.

The restaurant, Piccolo Mondo, occupied the ground floor of an office building that sat atop a hill. The tablecloths were pink, the crowd suit-and-tie. The owner gave Franco a big hello, as did the waitress, whose name was Judy. She asked after Franco's mother and one of his brothers. I sat back to survey the place. What I saw was an entire roomful of eyes sweep onto Franco and then, satisfied, back to their tables, a tribe of aging businessmen whose fortunes and families may have continued to grow but for whom the last truly great time was the 1970s, when Franco Harris and the Pittsburgh Steelers made all of them world champions. They looked appreciative but also smug, I thought, as if Franco were a mascot. *My* appreciation, I assured myself, was purer than that.

Judy brought us menus. As we had driven up to the restaurant, I thought of the spaghetti and meatballs Franco and I ate in the Dream, and how good it would be to finally do so now. But, having *told* him the Dream, I decided this wasn't a good idea. I decided to not sabotage our reunion by staging a reenactment that even a disinterested party might consider creepy. Instead I ordered gnocchi stuffed with asparagus. Franco ordered angel hair with shrimp and scallops in a vodka sauce, plus peppers stuffed with veal and pignoli, plus a green salad with extra blue cheese on top. When we finished with the menus Franco reached over and straightened them, squaring their edges with the table corner. It was an odd gesture; I wondered: polite or obsessive-compulsive?

Franco asked Judy for a glass of chianti, and then I did too. She hurried them right over.

"*Salute,*" Franco said, raising his glass.

"*Salute,*" I said. "Thanks for the tour."

We each took a sip, then he raised his glass again. "Um, what do you say, *le-hime?*"

"Yeah, *l'chaim.*" We clinked our glasses.

His cell phone rang. It was a sausage conversation, and he chopped at the table, like a football coach, to make his points: "That stuff'll be pretty lean, right? . . . So, are we going to have 100 percent fulfillment on those orders? Because there's no reason not to."

But after that call he was all mine. He told me how he was living his dream—that he loved playing sports as a kid, but what he always wanted to be was a businessman. He told me that, growing up, he hadn't known any college graduates. His whole family was shocked when Franco's older brother won a football scholarship. "I couldn't believe it," he said. "I mean, all you have to do is play football and you can go to *college,* and you can go to college *for free?* I'd never *heard* of a scholarship. I'd never thought about college before. But the following year, I made high-school All-American."

"You had a little added incentive?" I asked.

"A-yep."

His family, like mine, never went to restaurants, never took vacations, never traveled at all. (Even if you had the money, how do you fit ten people in the car? My family had to go to Mass in two shifts.) But by his senior year of high school, Franco was being recruited by colleges all over the country. "I loved it," he said. "*Loved* it. I visited about nine different colleges—some I went to twice. If you can believe this, it was the first time I ever went west of Philadelphia. It was the first time I saw lobster. It was the first time I saw people eat steak rare. It was my first airplane ride, to Columbus, Ohio. It was like, *man!*"

I told him about my first airplane ride, when I was thirteen, and my mother saved up enough to visit my brother the Air Force pilot in Arizona.

"A fighter pilot?" Franco said. "Wow, he came a long way."

The bond between us was just as I'd imagined. We were like two trees who'd grown in the same soil. "It sounds like your childhood and mine were pretty similar," I said, "in that you were living in your world and you made yourself happy in it because you didn't know what you were missing."

"Hey, listen, I had a great childhood, I loved it. But I loved getting out into the big world too."

"And your football career must have been fantastic."

"I've been very lucky, very blessed. I mean, every stage of my life has been wonderful. I *loved* playing football, and to me, I played with the best guys ever, and I was on the best team ever, and it was one decade of *un*believable joy. And I love what I'm doing now. I mean, it's great people, we have fun, we work hard, and we have a great, bright future. I *love* it." He pushed a plate toward me. "Here, Steve, make sure you have one of these stuffed peppers."

When our entrées came, I described in further detail the book I wanted to write. "Some of it is certainly your biography," I said, "and some of it is my story. But I'm also interested in the whole idea of the hero, of the role model. I'm interested in the relationship between a hero and a hero-worshiper. I'm interested in how a hero lives through the spotlight and what he does with his life after the spotlight has been turned off."

It took him a minute to respond. "Coming from that perspective," he said, "I think it would be interesting. And I guess I have no problem with that, going from the angle you're talking about. As a matter of fact, I like that."

He paused, or maybe trailed off.

"Is there a *but* here?" I asked.

Another pause. "I guess I'm picturing that the focus goes mostly on you," he said. "Which is good—good for me."

I didn't quite understand this last fillip. And I chose, essentially, to ignore it.

Our conversation resumed. His words traveled across the table and melted into mine. I was overwhelmed by contentment, by the rare feeling that, at this moment, I was exactly where I ought to have been.

We talked politics, we talked Pittsburgh, we talked family. Franco said he still couldn't believe that Dok, studying politics at Princeton, was such a brain. Our mothers, we decided, were birds of a feather—and we were still their little boys, try as we might to shake free. Franco was upset that, as we spoke, NATO planes were bombing Serbia and Slobodan Milosevic into submission. "I'm probably a little biased," he said, "because Dana's family is Serbian. Still, I find it hard to believe in this day and age that people in so many parts of the world are killing one another. Sometimes I think if you put people in the same room just doing something, they get along fine, but as soon as someone with power comes along and says, 'Well, this is the way it should be,' everybody starts to fight. I mean, in the Middle East and Africa, what they've been doing to one another, *sheesh*."

I agreed with him. "It really does make you look at the U.S. and say, My God, for all the problems that we've had and have, it's an amazing country."

"Oh yeah," he said. "The thing is, having hope is so important, and where is there greater hope than in the United States? When you have every class and every race and every nationality feel that they can go to the greatest height, then everybody keeps trying to reach that. That's why we have to make sure that we *maintain* that sort of thing in this country. Because no matter what, there's always that sliver of hope. Always. For anybody. I mean, it's just incredible. And that's what makes this country great."

He stopped, shook his head as if he'd gone on too long. "Well, at least that's what I think."

We clinked our glasses again.

All right, so neither of us was Henry Kissinger. But here we were, two men, two free men, talking from the gut about our country and our mothers like a pair of long-lost comrades. He was a child of slavery on his father's side and Fascism on his mother's, both of them poor. I was the grandson of four immigrants, also poor, who endured the customary immigrant trouble and, prior to that, trouble that was customary only to the Jews. His parents and mine had to save their pennies to feed their children. Yet here we sat in a hilltop restaurant with starched pink tablecloths in Pittsburgh, Pennsylvania, the hard land of Andrew Carnegie and workmen who got their skulls bashed in, our bellies full and our glasses empty, having outlasted all those suit-and-tie men, having a wonderful conversation—at least *I* thought it was wonderful—about nothing and everything.

We were champions of our own destinies—and maybe, I thought, even friends.

BACK IN THE CAR, Franco said he had a tennis lesson at 5:00 P.M.

"Can I come along?" I asked.

"I guess so. Have you booked a hotel room yet?"

Yes, I told him, back at the airport. I was hoping he'd offer me a bed at his house in Sewickley, wherever that was. Instead, he said we should find me a hotel closer to town. We pulled in first to a Holiday Inn. A room cost $114. Franco shook his head, said we could do better. A nearby Marriott charged the same. The Hampton Inn turned out to be $80. If I'd been visiting a friend, even a relative, I wouldn't have wanted to trouble them with finding a better deal. But it pleased me that Franco had offered.

He said he had some things to take care of before his tennis lesson, so he dropped me off at the Hampton Inn. He'd pick me up, he said, at four-thirty.

I spread out on the bed and made sure my tape recorder had captured our morning tour and lunch. It had. The cassettes were my first evidence of time spent with Franco. They were magnificently real. I felt as if I had snuck into some little Italian church and broken the toes off a saint.

I looked over my pages of interview questions. I reviewed my Franco Wish List:

1. Walk through Three Rivers Stadium with Franco
2. Meet Dana and Dok
3. Spend time at his house
4. Watch tape of Immaculate Reception with him
5. Throw around a football
6. Tell him about "Franco Dubner"
7. Eat spaghetti and meatballs
8. Visit a Super Bakery plant
9. Go on a Super Bakery sales call
10. See Franco naked

I knew I couldn't do it all on my first visit. So far, I had accomplished No. 6 but balked at No. 7. No. 10 wasn't a sexual thing. Honest. I just wanted to *see*, the way a car hound wants to see under the hood. No working athlete is as fully clothed as a football player. He spent all those years wrapped up in black and gold, a few dozen pieces of cotton and leather and molded plastic. Even on his elbows he wore pads. All you could see were his forearms, his hands, and the whites of his eyes. I wanted to see the rest. I wanted to behold his proportions and angles as one beholds Michelangelo's David. Franco's head, like David's, was said to be too large. At Penn State, he had to wear a custom-made helmet. Lynn Swann, a friend and former teammate, once joked that Franco's election into pro football's Hall of Fame was keeping Swann out: "That big old bust they made of Franco's head, it takes up two spaces, so there's no room for the next Steeler that comes along."

No. 10 was, I realized, the most unlikely item on my list. But the whole day had been unlikely, hadn't it, and it was only half over.

9

THE URGE TO MERGE

———◆◆◆◆◆◆◆———

BUT WHAT DID I want from Franco? What *was* I doing here?
Was I merely hoping to fulfill a childhood fantasy?

I had arrived in Pittsburgh with two acute desires: to spend time
with Franco Harris and to write about him. The desire to write made
perfect sense. Writing has always been my natural reaction to a nagging
curiosity; it is the means by which I puzzle out a mystery, whether the
mystery is a man or a crime or a moral dilemma.

Often, though, the true puzzle is figuring out *why* the curiosity is
such a nag—to figure out, in this case, why I felt such a need to spend
time with Franco.

It was serendipity, I realized, that reintroduced me to him. Until that
morning in Times Square, I had never heard of *Black Enterprise*, much
less bought a copy. But serendipity alone hadn't led me to Pittsburgh.
My father had a hand in that. My father had the temerity to die; my father left a gash in me that never healed.

For years I told myself that it *had* healed, that I was fine, that everyone's father dies just like everyone gets chicken pox, and at least I got
mine over with early.

The only benefit of my father's premature death was that I lost him
before I could turn against him. I am unable to picture the teenager I

would have become had my father lived. I do know that my mother and I were bound to each other as only a mother and her baby boy can be, and I have read enough Freud to suspect that, for a time at least, my ailing father would have come to stand in the way.

A different boy, a more brazen one, might have luxuriated in the freedom granted by his father's death. "My luck was to belong to a dead man," Jean-Paul Sartre once wrote. "Had my father lived, he would have lain on me at full length and would have crushed me. As luck had it, he died young."

Those were not remotely my feelings. And yet, after a youth circumscribed by loss and frugality and prohibition, I charged off in greedy pursuit of their opposites. During freshman year of college I started up a rock band, which left little time for studies and none for church. I never went longer than a week or two without a steady girlfriend; I read books by the bushel and wrote stories and songs on every scrap of paper. I graduated, kept writing, quit the band, moved to New York City, went to graduate school, got married, wrote some more, got divorced, wrote some more until I wrote my way to the *Times*, and figured I had surpassed my frozen boyhood.

I had *certainly* surpassed my father's death. Or so I thought.

I had spent thirty-some years assembling myself, piecing together a self-portrait the way we all do. A shard of this, a glimmer of that; reflections, projections, inventions. But one piece, I finally realized, always went missing. I could never manage to make myself feel whole. *He* held the piece; my father had absconded with it. And I was left to hunt for that piece. I had become a writer because that was his dream, and because my dream was him.

I remember the moment of realization: an editorial meeting at the *Times Magazine*, a gray Thursday morning, too muggy for October, rain dribbling down the windows. Times Square stood ragged and silent eight floors below. Jack Rosenthal, the editor-in-chief, was in his early sixties, as wise and decent as they come. He wore round eyeglasses and kept his hair neatly combed, his tie knotted judiciously. He had a soft voice, authoritative but not harsh; even in a state of high agitation it never frightened.

As Jack opened the meeting, ticking off some routine business, I felt abruptly as if I were about to cry. I was struck mute and wobbly and small. This terrible feeling had visited me for years, but I had never identified it until this day: it was me at twelve years old. It was me, scanning the faces of the men at the church supper, hoping for that fatherly spark to pass from one of them to me. Hoping to steal that spark.

I had caught myself scanning Jack's face for that same look. Still hoping to steal the spark. Still wanting to blurt out: *Take me, lead me, teach me, protect me, give me permission.*

Ever since leaving home, I had made my way along an unbroken chain of older men. Professors and bosses and girlfriends' fathers: one hairy hand after the next I sought to grasp. Some of them didn't seem to notice; others were kind and generous beyond reason. But none could grant me that missing piece of myself.

That, I had come to see, lay buried with my father, a father I'd barely known. And so I set out to resurrect him.

I began with a visit to my mother, who had by now moved to Florida. Tell me of his character, I said, of his likes and dislikes, but tell me especially of his past.

The conversation with my mother became a long one, stretching for years, and in the end it became a book. But she was never really able to answer the questions about my father.

This was because she only knew half of him, the Catholic half. By the time they met, at a Manhattan church during the war, they were each deep in the bosom of a spiritual tempest. Their common background as Brooklyn Jews was less meaningful than their common future as Catholic pilgrims. As they hurled themselves toward Heaven and each other, they consigned their unhappy pasts to a locked drawer. My mother fell in love with a Catholic soldier named Paul Dubner, home on furlough from his medic post in the South Pacific. She never knew Solomon Dubner, who grew up a few neighborhoods away from her, in Little Jerusalem.

Frustrated by my mother's ignorance, I began seeking out my father's relatives—my relatives—first in New York, then in more distant precincts, England and Argentina and Israel. I made quite the nuisance of myself. Tell me tell me tell me, I'd say, What do you remember of him? I read the books he read as a young man; I dissected his wartime letters home. I tromped through the village in Poland where his parents had come from, where his aunts and uncles and cousins stayed behind and were killed by the Nazis.

Beneath an August sky as flat as glass and again in the slanting rain of November, I would stand over his grave in Duanesburg. *Why am I even here?* I would ask. *Why does this dead body exert a greater influence than all the living ones?* The whole notion of human burial struck me as prehistoric and unnecessary. To say nothing of a waste of real estate. Sometimes, flying into LaGuardia over the endless acres of cemetery in Queens, I'd think, *People should be* living *here.* And yet there I stood over my father's grave, and there I wept. I did everything short of digging him up and shaking apart his bones and begging him to tell me who he was and why he'd left me and how to proceed without him.

My efforts did not go entirely unrewarded. It was while searching for my father that I found my way into Judaism, which proved a more comfortable home than Catholicism. I also began to dream of my father, albeit rarely and fleetingly, dreams in which he didn't say or do much. In my waking hours, I would occasionally conjure his laugh—though never his speaking voice—and believe that I had indeed reclaimed him. But the next day I might find myself unable to summon even the shape of his face. For all I learned about him, he remained a beloved cipher. And he never did surrender that missing piece.

It was just as I concluded that I knew my father as well as I ever would (which was none too well) that I happened upon Franco Harris on the cover of *Black Enterprise.* He was flipping a Parks Sausage hard hat into the air, smiling his earnest smile.

Franco Harris! My memory went galloping backward, to our yard and his nightly visitation. And my mind flew to a bizarre conclusion: even now, I knew more about Franco Harris than I knew about my father, far more, despite having spent five years searching for the latter and twenty hardly thinking of the former.

He was easily the truest hero I ever had. He also offered the huge advantage of not being dead.

IN THE CLASSICAL SENSE, there is no such thing as a living hero. Greek and Roman heroes were, by definition, dead, just as a saint must be dead, just as water must be wet.

But that definition has been expanded upon for centuries. There are in fact few words as variously interpreted, as fluid and arbitrary, as *hero*. It comes from the Greek *heros*, which has been defined as "an embodiment of composite ideals." Perhaps that is why it has been so broadly interpreted—because it is a composite to start with, a hodgepodge, but worse yet, a hodgepodge of *ideals*, which can be so subjective as to seem imaginary. (As Bertrand Russell once said, the essence of the ideal is to be *not* real.) My brother Peter, in an unconscious nod to the word's original definition, keeps what he calls a Composite Hero, a sort of ultimate role model comprising the attributes of several people he knows: the grace-under-pressure of a certain lifelong friend, the communication skills of a former boss, the self-assuredness of his own twelve-year-old daughter.

So what is hero worship? Is it the tragic grandeur of Homer's *Odyssey*? Is it the perpetually bent knee of an obedient Catholic? Is it the waiting outside a stage door to collect some actress's scrawl or the sifting-through of Bob Dylan's garbage? Is it the five-year-old boy trailing his father around the house as if he were God? Is it my brother Peter's handpicked assemblage of worthy traits?

Yes and yes and yes and yes and yes.

And who is a hero? The philosopher Sidney Hook—who, like my father, grew up the poor son of immigrant Jews in Brooklyn—once wrote that "whoever saves us is a hero." Hook may have written this with a jaundiced eye (for he was no hero-worshiper), but his definition seems to me as true as any.

Franco Harris surely saved me. His nightly visitation, beginning in the wake of my father's death, was so sustaining that it felt divinely inspired. I sometimes wondered if he had been designated to watch over me, as Odysseus, setting off for war in Troy, left behind Mentor to watch over his son Telemachus. And had a deity then inhabited Franco, s the gray-eyed Athena inhabited Mentor, to ensure the prosperity of her young charge?

And I . . . was I a complete *meshuggener* for thinking such thoughts?

Maybe not. In the psychological literature I read before flying to Pittsburgh, I learned that my brand of hero-worshiping was not so rare. It arose from a need known in some psychological circles as the Urge to Merge.

There are at least three separate phenomena fueled by the Urge: religious faith, love, and hero worship. These three fierce attachments have much in common. Above all, each satisfies a compelling human need: to connect with something larger than, greater than, and beyond ourselves.

Ten people will offer ten different reasons for the Urge's existence. A theologian might argue that we reach out, to Whomever, in an unconscious effort to reestablish our relationship with the Creator. John Dewey, the champion of Pragmatism, believed that man constantly seeks higher connections because he distrusts his own nature. Psychologists say we must project our own fantasies onto a God or lover or hero before we can digest and internalize them. To a biologist, the Urge to Merge is a purely chemical reaction; to a small band of modern cultural anthropologists who study "terror management," the Urge is our need to enlist another being in the daily struggle to live on while acknowledging, as no other animal does, that we must also die.

For whatever reason, this is what we do: latch onto Another to save or sustain us, inspire or protect us, to bring us legitimacy or clarity.

The Urge to Merge has many phases, of course, many shapes and colors. A child's feeling for God is rarely the same as an adult's, just as a hero-worshiping child (which is common) and a hero-worshiping adult (which is less so) see their hero differently (or so we should hope). A father may love his teenage daughter and she may love him, and she may also love a boy named Zack, but those three loves are so discrete that we should at least coin some new words to describe them.

Still, when the Urge strikes, it is always the same. Its first stage is marked by what psychologists call intrusive thinking. (It used to be called infatuation.) To the teenager in love with Zack, to my young parents newly in love with Jesus, nothing really matters beyond Zack or Jesus. The earth might stop rotating and, if they happened to notice, they wouldn't much care.

In the early going, faith and love and hero worship are states of pure emotion. Reason has no role; rational criticism is suspended. We direct our energies toward marveling at the absolute perfection of our God or lover or hero (and congratulating ourselves for having chosen so well). We turn a blind eye to their flaws and remake their foibles into "eccentricities." We ignore their paradoxes. Even an all-loving God has to smite down a city now and then, we tell ourselves, just to keep up His chops.

The Urge to Merge is a need, not a want. (We don't have to be taught, for instance, to fall in love.) The Urge is primal and it is timeless; it seems to predate even God. "The idea of God," wrote Carl Jung, "is an absolutely necessary psychological function of an irrational nature, which has nothing whatever to do with the question of God's existence." Freud too believed that God was a construction, dating back to prehuman times. In his view, a tribe would select a leader, probably the strongest or fastest among them, and come to depend on him, love him, fear him—and, after he died, worship Him.

My father was, I suppose, that idea incarnate, even in his diminished state. While he was alive, he was everything to me: God, father, hero. The stubby editor's pencil he kept stashed above his ear was the most magic of wands. From it he created smudges, words, entire stories, all out of nothingness.

A child psychologist would say this is exactly as it should be, as it has always been. To a child, a parent is all-knowing and all-powerful, the producer of every joy and the solution to every problem. No other animal is as helplessly dependent as the human child; no other animal, therefore, is regarded with such awe as the human parent.

These days of awe, however, do not last. Just as the Urge to Merge is a symptom of the human condition, so is the Urge to Diverge. There is a little Oedipus in all of us. (Fortunately it doesn't always lead to patricide, incest, and war.) The once-flawless parent suddenly appears quite full of flaws. The perfect hero comes to seem a fake. And how, we'd like to know, could an all-loving God allow such atrocities on His watch? We might evade reality by "splitting"—separating the "bad" parent or hero or God from the "good" one in order to preserve the latter—or we might decide to leave them behind entirely.

Because my father died before the Urge to Diverge set in, I was blessedly excused from making such a choice. As a result, my love for him was frozen in time; it remained the love of a ten-year-old boy, tender and immature.

With Franco too I was blessed. He served me well and faithfully, and then, before the time came to turn against him, I simply outgrew him. This happened when I was sixteen, which is typical. Hero worship, according to psychologists who study it, tends to peak in the mid to late teens. Boys and girls shed their heroes in favor of the opposite sex, the head-rush of college or career, the first protracted views of the great, gaping world that lies beyond the family walls. And I had gone in for all of that.

But had my love for Franco, like the love for my father, also been frozen in time? It seemed so.

It further seemed that this frozen love had led my moderately competent adult self to contact Franco, persuade him to meet with me, and get myself to Pittsburgh, where I hoped to satisfy any number of pressing desires. Like a boy, I simply wanted to be in his presence, to moon over him. I also wanted to thank him for his long-ago inspiration. But I wanted his approval too, the way even a middle-aged man wants his father's approval; I thought Franco might appreciate how I, like him, came from humble beginnings and fought to live a dream. I wanted him to think I was special, just as I thought he was special. I even wanted, still, his guidance. Although my brain should have known better, a different reckoning system inside me hoped that *he* would somehow offer up that missing piece of me.

Yes, that was why I had come: in the hope that Franco Harris might complete me.

AT FOUR-THIRTY, I waited outside the Hampton Inn for Franco to pick me up for his tennis lesson. And waited and waited. Had he abandoned me?

I wouldn't have been shocked if he hadn't shown up at the airport that morning. I had been prepared for that. But he did show up and, instead of the fifteen-minute cup of coffee I feared, we had bonded; we meshed; we celebrated. Which was why my heart now mourned as four-thirty came and went, and four-forty-five, and four-fifty-five—and why it swooped when I spotted his red Passat at last. I nearly sprinted for it. Inside, we shook hands all over again. Was he happy to see me? I couldn't tell. He steered the car along Iron Drive.

I asked Franco how he felt when his football career ended so abruptly.

"I remember sitting down for about twenty minutes, just pondering," he said. "My thinking was, I've got nobody to call anymore, I won't have anything to do, I have all this time on my hands. So I got up and said, Well, I might as well get busy. I don't care what it is. I don't care if I work at a fast-food restaurant."

Franco had made good money in football. As a rookie in 1972 he was paid about $30,000, triple the average steelworker's salary and about ten times what his father earned working two jobs. By the early 1980s the Steelers were paying Franco well over $300,000 a year (to say nothing of endorsements and speaking engagements), and he put away a great deal of it.

But when he retired at thirty-four, he wasn't interesting in living off his savings. Nor did he want to stick his name on some pasta joint and grow fat in the back booth. He wanted to follow his childhood dream and build a business. To him, that meant starting from the ground floor.

He went looking for a product he could sell, a product he could stand behind, and he found it in Frozfruit juice bars. "They were delicious," he told me now as he drove, "and all-natural." He started out buying three pallets of Frozfruit bars. With his own hands, he loaded them into his Toyota hatchback, packed it with dry ice, and hit the road. Franco Harris, former Super Bowl MVP, became a familiar face in the convenience stores and supermarkets of western Pennsylvania, West Virginia, Ohio, Michigan, and Indiana.

He was, it turned out, a good salesman. His success prompted a call from a company in Cleveland looking for a partner to help sell a new-fangled doughnut.

"I told them, 'I'm not sure a doughnut is a food I want to be associated with,'" Franco said. "I didn't want to be involved in a food that I feel I can't tell a kid to eat."

But this was a nutritional doughnut, the men from Cleveland told him, engineered to deliver extra protein, minerals, and vitamins to schoolchildren and nursing-home patients.

We pulled into the tennis club. Franco cut the engine. "I said to myself, Well, I can either not do it, or I can try to change the standard of the doughnut."

He signed on. A few years later, he said, he bought the company and renamed it Super Bakery. It had grown, slowly but surely, ever since.

Walking through the parking lot, Franco stopped, bent to the ground, straightened. "Man, that's the second dime I found today," he said.

I followed him inside and downstairs to a locker room. It was freshly carpeted, brightly lit, and empty. I stood awkwardly as Franco unbuttoned his flannel shirt and slowly wriggled out of it. His chest was hairy, not very muscular but nicely toned.

I fell speechless. I'd had no inkling I might accomplish No. 10 on my Franco Wish List so soon. He reached for his belt. He pulled the tongue, passed it through the buckle.

Be grateful, I told myself. *This is what I hoped for. Be calm.*

But I wasn't calm. Like an anxious lover hoping to forestall climax, I sent my mind to wandering. It turned, somehow, to the boxer. A boxer stands in the ring nearly naked; he battles another nearly naked man until one of them falls. No wonder we have made such an idol of the boxer: we know every square inch of him. Enough to feel we own him. Such a ticklish issue, the naked athlete, especially when the color of the skin has a history. After a pro football game, a reporter stands in the locker room. The team owner, inevitably an older white man, strolls through his stable of exhausted, sweaty, naked men, most of them black, patting them on the rumps, and although these men are well-paid and free, a sane reporter cannot help but think of a plantation owner strolling through his slave quarters to appraise his chattel. But the reporter is also there for a look. He wishes to appraise the muscle and sinew and bone that produces such art.

The racehorse too stands naked. Maybe, I thought, it is no coincidence that the racehorse and the boxer, champions of nakedness both, are the two athletes whom sportswriters of the past century turned into icons. The racehorse is thought by some writers to possess human qualities—courage, intelligence, sorrow—more finely wrought than any human's. (The horse is also conveniently absent of human failings: he cannot give a damning quote or be caught in bed with another horse's wife.) In 1938, the knobby-kneed, valiant Seabiscuit gleaned more press attention than Roosevelt, Hitler, or Mussolini. Secretariat, after winning the Triple Crown in 1973, had his name entered into the *Congressional Record* as "Rex Americanus Equinas." When he died, a *New York Times* editorial called him "not a horse but the archetype of the horse."

"He was a cocky horse," said Secretariat's owner, "but not egotistical."

Franco had by now removed his loafers, his socks, his khakis. He was down to his briefs, which were white. They gleamed against his tawny skin, circling him as a celestial band circles the great Jupiter.

He stood up, about to strip down, about to stand before me as naked as Secretariat.

I fled.

"I have to use the head," I told Franco. *The head?* Was I suddenly a sailor? Never in my life had I called a bathroom "the head."

I bolted myself into a stall. So much for No. 10. Franco had plainly been nonplussed. How many hundreds of reporters, after all, had come before me? But I was apparently not ready to see my hero undressed. I put down the toilet cover and sat, fully clothed. I realized: I had never seen my father naked either.

I waited until I had heard a good deal of rustling. When I returned, Franco was safely lacing up his sneakers. He wore green shorts, a white Super Bakery T-shirt, and two wristbands, one pink and one baby blue.

Upstairs, the club pro was late. The receptionist wasn't sure if the pro even knew about Franco's lesson. Franco was unhappy. We sat down to wait in a lounge overlooking the courts.

"I wish I had sneakers," I said. "I'd hit with you."

"You play?"

"Badly," I said, which was true. Truth be told, I was glad I wasn't wearing sneakers. As eager as I was for some kind of athletic interaction with Franco, I wanted to save it for a sport I was good at.

"If you're bad," he said, "we'd be a good match."

I thought it would be nice to sit and talk some more. Instead, Franco asked a threesome if he could warm up with them until their fourth arrived. He did, and then the pro came, and Franco had his lesson. I watched from the lounge, through a glass wall. Forehands, backhands, lobs, ably executed. Franco wasn't built for tennis, but he always seemed to get to the ball. Sweat bloomed on his shirt in the shape of a rose.

When the lesson was over he waved up at me, pointed to the locker room. I let him shower alone. After fifteen minutes he came upstairs.

"See," he said, "things always work out all right."

FOR THE SECOND TIME in six hours we broke bread. Franco's suggestion. I asked if Dana didn't mind. "Oh, no," he said, "I told her." We went to a Chinese restaurant in an old train station across the river from downtown.

There is no meal more satisfying than the meal earned by exertion, and although Franco alone had exerted himself, I shared in his hunger. We downed three pitchers of ice water. We ordered enough food for four men—he was willing to forgo pork and shellfish in deference to me— and would devour every scrap, every grain of rice.

"So I'll keep asking questions, if that's all right," I said.

"Yessir."

"I really want to know about your first season in Pittsburgh," I said. "I want to know how you improved so much and so fast from college. It seems like once the Steelers drafted you, something just clicked. Was it that you took the draft as a vote of confidence and that you were going to do your utmost to fulfill it?"

No, Franco said. The turnaround had come a few months earlier, before the draft. It happened in Mobile, Alabama, at the Senior Bowl, where pro scouts get their last look at college players.

"I saw all these athletes that accomplished all these great things, with press clippings a mile long, and I didn't have any of that," he said. "All-Americans and this and that kind of stuff. And I said, Man, I think I'm a better athlete than most of those guys. How did they accomplish these things that I didn't? And that really bothered me. And then I guess the money motivated me a little bit, because if you got to be offensive MVP of the game, you got a bonus of fifteen hundred bucks! I was like, *Wow!* I said, I'm gonna try for it, you know what I mean? And I tried for it, and should have had it, but didn't get it. The other running back got it. And I just said, Franco, from now on, you can't give 'em a choice. I said, If you're going to play this game, you can't give people a *choice* about who's the best."

"Where's that motivation come from—your mother, your father?"

"I mean, not really, it's something that just happened that one week. If it wasn't for that one week in Mobile, Alabama, my *career* probably wouldn't have happened. It's just a reflection of yourself, how you look at yourself."

"Now this was after Joe Paterno benched you for Penn State's bowl game, right, because you came to practice late?"

"Right."

"You two didn't really get along."

"I think that was blown out of proportion. I mean, everybody thinks I was trying to challenge Joe, and you know, we both can be hardheaded at times, but I don't think I was trying to challenge him. I was just late, okay, I went to get taped, and me and Joe still don't see eye to eye on that. I was pissed, yeah, but still, Joe's a great coach, he has great values, and he does a great job. Handling young men eighteen to twenty-two years old, that's a tough job."

"Did you see him as a sort of father figure?"

Franco stopped eating, a vegetable dumpling dangling midair. He stared as if he'd just come across a most unusual animal at the zoo, but then checked himself, knowing it was impolite to stare.

"No," he said.

"Were you pretty close with your dad?"

"Not real close. I mean, my dad was a real quiet guy. But a good father, and a good person. He was just very quiet. But when he said something, that was it, you know what I mean? The complete opposite of my mom."

"Because she could be talked into something?"

"Well, she was talkable, definitely talkable."

"Moms are a softer touch," I said.

"Oh, yeah, especially with her *boys*. 'M'*boys!*' But no, my dad was a good man, and he would not do anything wrong. And he was home *every night*." Franco had said the same thing earlier in the day; it struck me as odd and faint praise, as if being home was somehow a chore.

"What kind of father are you?" I asked.

Franco stopped, as if he'd been accused. "How do you even answer that question?"

"I mean, do you see some of your father in yourself, in terms of discipline and whatnot? What sort of encouragement do you give your son, that sort of thing."

"Well, I've always promoted him to be a freethinker. I guess I really wouldn't know how to describe fatherly behavior."

"Do you feel you're closer with Dok than you were with your dad?"

"Uh-huh, yeah. He really surprised me, though. People always told me he was smart, and I would just kind of brush it off. A lot of our family has always been smart. I mean, I got A's in school. My younger brother, when he was coming out of high school, was in the top 5 percent of the country, and my one sister is now a lawyer. But Dok—"

"He took it to the next level?" I interrupted, eager to pay a compliment, eager to make amends for what seemed to have been an accusation.

"That's right," he said. "I finally saw him in junior high school at this math thing, where they bring the two hundred top math kids from western Pennsylvania to a competition, and he made the top ten. They were flashing these problems up on the board, all these letters to the second power, over the q's and m's, and they were hitting the buttons before I got done reading the problem. I said, My kid *knows* this stuff? First of all, I've got to say, it was kind of weird that the first competition

I'm seeing him perform in was a math competition and not an athletic competition. And then to see him *do* that stuff! Then during high school he was on the science team, so I would go every year to the science bowl and watch him compete. You know what? All four years, I did not know *one* answer!" Franco laughed at himself, hard.

"Is he liking Princeton?"

"Oh, yeah. I guess he won't be selling doughnuts and sausages anyway. That's how I used to scare him. I'd say, 'If you don't do well, you'll have to come sell doughnuts with your old man.'"

"What about when you were younger, who did you look up to? I remember reading about Walter Conti, the guy who gave you a restaurant job in college."

"Oh, yeah, Walter Conti, in a couple of ways. He's a great restaurateur and also a great person. And being around him had a great effect on me. I thought, Well, here's a very successful restaurateur, and you can still treat people right and help people and try to do the right thing."

"Were you ever not like that in your life?" I had never considered that Franco was anything less than sublimely considerate.

"I would like not to think so, but—well, at some point we all fail."

We talked for another ninety minutes, but it wasn't quite an interview, at least not like any interview I'd ever conducted. This was largely my doing, for I had abandoned all critical faculties. I could not turn off my adoration any more easily than the Tower of Pisa could hoist itself upright.

I asked Franco to tell stories I already knew just to hear him talk. I interrupted chronically, often spouting some detail to prove just how much I knew about him. Then, for long stretches I turned cloyingly confessional. I found myself telling him about my mother's failing health—she had a heart condition that was killing her slowly—and how hard it was to envision a world without her in it. I told him about my father's death; I spoke about Ellen, my wife, in a way I would only speak with a close friend. He didn't share any such intimacies with me although I hoped that, during future conversations, he would.

Critical faculties aren't everything, of course. I certainly wasn't out to challenge Franco or entrap him. I have never admired "gotcha" journalism and I don't practice it, but neither had I ever so completely turned myself over to someone I wanted to write about. Then again, my mission to Pittsburgh was not exactly journalistic. I had come with no assignment other than a heart-tug. I had been unwilling to subject Franco to the ruthless whims of a magazine editor—a ruthlessness I knew from having been one—who might find him neither sexy nor rich nor fabulous enough, to say nothing of au courant. I could just hear an editor saying: "A forty-nine-year-old doughnut salesman? From *Pittsburgh?*"

But Franco, to be honest, was also to blame. As he had done earlier in the day, he asked as many questions as he answered—about my work in journalism, about living in New York. Was he genuinely interested or merely evasive? I couldn't tell. And when he did take my questions, his every response felt measured, as if he were accorded a certain quota of words for the day. He didn't reject any of my questions, but he did hesitate after each one and often sighed before answering. The only enthusiasm he showed all night was for his doughnuts. "At the American Dietetic Association show," he said at one point, "we had a sugar-free doughnut with sugar-free *icing*. It was fan*tas*tic!" (So he *did* change the standard of the doughnut.)

But even the doughnut talk could be complicated. When I cited an article about Super Bakery I'd read in an academic journal—the company wasn't widely covered in the mainstream business press—Franco looked spooked, as if he'd picked up a hitchhiker and suddenly recognized him from *America's Most Wanted*. Did he think I was an industrial spy, sent by some rogue doughnut concern out of New York?

Toward the end of our dinner, I asked if I could call a few other people in his orbit. Perhaps his mother and Walter Conti and a few business partners. "Um, no," he said, "I don't think it's a good time for that."

All told, Franco seemed allergic to flattery, disdainful of self-congratulation, and extra-protective of his privacy. He spoke as he once ran with the ball: starting slow, stutter-stepping, briefly bursting forth, then easing out of bounds. Was he, then as now, considerate? Absolutely. He used to help his blockers off the turf, say "Nice hit" to his tackler. But protective? Absolutely. Once, when a Dallas Cowboy linebacker gave Terry Bradshaw an extra lick, Franco demanded the ball on the next play and ran straight through the linebacker.

Later, listening to the tapes, I found his reticence frustrating but also, somehow, charming. And perhaps justifiable. We tend to lump together the various species of modern celebrity—athletes, entertainers, politicians, Donald Trumps—into one big glossy creature. But the athlete may indeed warrant special consideration. The rest of them, after all, actively set out to court fame. An actress wants to be adored, a politician esteemed, a Donald Trump envied. They do what they do not in spite of the attention but *because* of it. Their careers couldn't survive without it. Only when the lights grow too hot—or when they make a misstep—do they demand privacy. Even serial killers save their press clippings. A federal prosecutor I know insists that the greatest crime-fighting tool of the past thirty years was *The Godfather*, for it so glamorized a fictional mafia that the real mafioso, in scrambling to live up to their new image, turned sloppy enough to be caught. For celebrities, the image is everything. Which is why we love to dissect their private lives: it is a natural curiosity to measure the reality against the image.

But for an athlete, the reality, not the image, is paramount. If Kobe Bryant, in all his poof-headed, slacker-sexy, hyper-endorsed glory, misses a last-second shot that would have won the championship, all he is—today at least; do not discount the redemptive power of sport—is a poof-head who missed the winning shot.

Nor did the athlete arrive begging for our attention. In the beginning he simply wanted to beat the other kids on his block. And he did beat them, all the way into the harshest spotlight imaginable—which proves a distraction, not a joy, an unsought byproduct of a winning streak that began twenty years earlier on the playground. Yes, he may have wanted glory or riches from the beginning, but that was not why he played. He played because he wanted to win. The glory and riches are the hole; the winning is the doughnut.

There will, of course, always be loudmouths and chest-thumpers and self-aggrandizers in sports. Muhammad Ali ensured that. Perhaps such behavior is even a subset—a minor one, I hope—of greatness. But I prefer Franco's way.

WE ATE our fortune cookies without reading the fortunes. Franco reached for the check. "This is on me, since you got lunch," he said. The restaurant had emptied; the waiter was stacking chairs.

On the drive back to my hotel, clumping over bridges in the dark, Franco grew quiet. His big hands steered the car lightly. He didn't mention tomorrow. Apparently we had no plans.

I wanted the ride to not end; I felt myself fall when the Hampton Inn sign came into view.

"I thank you very much," I said. "It was a great day for me, and I'll be in touch soon, all right?"

He didn't answer right away. Then he said, "I'll be on the road quite a bit."

The road? The road was fine with me. He might need me there. Don Quixote needed Sancho Panza. John Steinbeck needed Charley, who was only a poodle.

"Think you might ever let me come along on a sales call?" I asked.

He laughed. "I don't know—can you sell?"

"I'll learn."

We were parked at the hotel by now. We sat in the dark laughing for a minute.

"I'll tell you right now," I said, "I'm real eager to just keep at this. Whatever form it can take."

"Well, like I said, I think your part is more interesting than me, you know what I mean?"

"Sure."

"But, I mean, we'll work it out," he said.

We'll work it out. I had no doubt. Franco Harris was clearly a man of his word.

"Okay," I said. "We'll take it as it comes. It was a good day. I thank you very much."

"Travel safely," he said.

I called Ellen from my room.

"How'd it go?" she asked.

"He's wonderful," I said.

"So what's wrong?"

"What do you mean?"

"I hear it in your voice. What's wrong?"

I smiled to myself. This is what a wife knows.

"I wanted more," I said.

"Well, you know, that's the way you were on our first date too," she said. "You know what you want and you hang in there until you get it."

In the morning, the sky was an ominous royal blue, thick with storm clouds. The plane took off through a misty rain. I recognized a few of the bridges we'd crossed and the neighborhoods we drove through. From the air, the visual cacophony of the place was all the more pronounced—the sudden jumble of hills and rivers, ravines and skyscrapers, yellow bridges and gray football stadium. It looked, frankly, a little magical, the kind of place where you'd set a fairy tale.

And then, as we flew up into the cloud layer, it all disappeared.

10

DEATH, PRO AND CON

———————·•‹❦›•·———————

•

T HE CRITICS WERE wrong, all of them!
"There are few worse mistakes than the close-up inspection
of one's heroes," the sharp-witted journalist Murray Kempton once
wrote.

"Every hero becomes a bore at last," observed Ralph Waldo Emerson, whom I had always found otherwise sensible.

As early as the seventeenth century, a similar slander was put forth:
"No man is a hero to his valet."

To which I now said: *Feh*. Let the cynics prattle away; let them choke
on their own dyspepsia. What did they know of heroes? Had they com-
muned, as I had, with the hero in his lair?

I had journeyed to a distant land, returned with more than seven
hours of recorded conversation, and transcribed the tapes with the fer-
vor of a scientist on the brink of a great cure. I noted, but did not care,
that my hero was sometimes—well, bland. I noted that what had
seemed revelatory in the moment was often in fact rote, his voice created by the hundreds of interviews he'd given in the past. But none of
that mattered. Words, I realized, were not his medium. What the tapes
did reveal was a man as earnest as I but devoid of self-doubt, impatient
with irony and bitterness, a purveyor of hope and goodwill. A man who,

on close-up inspection, was exactly what he seemed from afar: a mensch of the highest order.

What I most admired about Franco, and considered the greatest testament to his strength of character, was his transition to life after football stardom. He simply put away his helmet and got to work. He did not try to squeeze out an extra season or use the autograph circuit to boost his ego and bank account. He did not take refuge on the golf course or in the ghetto of the sportscasting booth. He did not court self-destruction or death.

It has been said that every athlete dies twice. The first death is the end of his career, when his immortality is betrayed by his muscles. The rest of us are at least permitted to carry on in a straight line. It is acceptable to be an old king, an old accountant, an old writer, even an old pop singer.

F. Scott Fitzgerald's moldy dictum—that there are no second acts in American lives—has by now been proved so false that I wonder why anyone still cites it. Americans *specialize* in second (and third and fourth and fifth) acts. Except the professional athlete. The athlete is forced to renounce his lifelong pursuit at an age when most of us are just working out the kinks. He is generally ill-prepared to do anything else. Because he has been so conditioned by adulation, his every path clear-cut by boosters and fans, he enters a state akin to detoxification. He views his new realm, the realm of mortals, with dismay and shock. "The transition from the sports world," wrote the daughter of Hall of Fame quarterback Y. A. Tittle, "was, for all of us, a bit like going from the Himalayas to the parking lot."

I remember, when I first became a football fan, a gigantic but nimble offensive lineman named Jim Tyrer. He was an All-Pro, playing for fourteen seasons, mostly with the Kansas City Chiefs. And I remember what happened to him.

Kansas City, like Pittsburgh and Green Bay, is the kind of town where the football players are gods—a hard-working city with a winning tradition, and small enough that you might run into your quarterback at the A&P. In 1969, the Chiefs won the Super Bowl and Tyrer was much beloved. He was strong and dignified, articulate and generous. He'd speak to the Cub Scouts or the Rotary Club or even the Garden Club, and he wouldn't take a dime. Football paid him plenty, he explained. Tyrer especially watched out for his comrades. As the Chiefs' union representative, he helped negotiate a better pension plan. "Most athletes," he told a reporter, "live in a sort of euphoria that retirement is never going to happen to them."

It happened to Tyrer in 1975. He first tried marketing NFL paraphernalia but was ahead of his time. Next he tried selling insurance, then car tires. Finally he and his wife signed on with Amway. Nothing was working; off the field, Tyrer found he no longer knew how to win. His confidence deserted him.

Five years after retiring, Tyrer took a .38-caliber revolver and, in the bedroom of his Kansas City home, killed himself and his wife. Their children, who were asleep when they heard the gunshots, thought the house was being robbed and hid under their beds.

Jason Tyrer, the youngest of the four Tyrer children, was twelve when his parents died, barely old enough to remember his father's glory days. I decided to track him down. He would be in his early thirties by now, just a bit younger than me. When I found his phone number, I called and asked what his childhood was like in the years between his father's retirement and his death.

"Oh, it was great," he said. "We always had anything we wanted. We went to private schools, had the best of everything, a nice house in a nice neighborhood." But, Jason told me, they also had a foot-high pile of bills. His father, it turned out, hadn't been willing to downgrade the lifestyle that football had given his family. How does an All-Pro strongman admit that civilian life has beat him up?

"The guy was too proud to talk to anyone," said a former teammate of Tyrer's just after the murder-suicide. "He wouldn't ask anyone for help. Jim Tyrer would have been better off if he never played one lick of football."

These days, it's easy to assume that every professional athlete is set for life, at least financially, when he's done playing. That's hardly true. Yes, the marquee players in every sport earn enough to rival the GDPs of some small nations, but most athletes don't make the marquee. Most athletes don't even make it to the big leagues (about one of every eleven minor-league baseball players, for instance). If they do, they stand to earn a few hundred thousand dollars a year (nice money, sure), but only for a few seasons (the average NFL career lasts just over three years), and with no guarantees.

Jason Tyrer told me that his father earned $60,000 in his final season, 1974, the cusp of the big-money era. At the beginning of his career, he probably made about $5,000 a year. In Jim Tyrer and Y. A. Tittle's day, most athletes held an off-season job to get by. Even Frank Gifford, the New York Giants' golden boy, sold insurance over the winter.

By Franco's era, football paid well enough that most players didn't work during the off-season, but few of them left the game with retirement money. So at the age of twenty-eight or thirty-one or, in extreme cases like Franco's, thirty-four—he was blessed with good health and a long career—they had to climb down from the mountaintop and start all over.

"There's too many failures in that transition," Franco had told me over Chinese food, shaking his head. "Especially among minority ballplayers. I blame the ballplayers and I blame the fans."

"Why blame the fans?" I asked.

"The fan pressure, or maybe the people pressure, people's expectations. Somebody came up to me one time and said, 'Hey, you know so-and-so, played for the Cleveland Browns? Well, I saw him working as a *bellhop* at a *hotel.*' And I say to myself, If this guy has an honest, decent job, why are you smirking and saying *ha ha ha*? So, because of things like that, a lot of ballplayers won't take certain jobs, and that really upsets me. Because you have to start someplace. But ballplayers expect too much. They feel they can't, or won't, take something at the bottom. So they end up doing nothing. Their family falls apart and they fall apart. But why not just do *anything*? Because if they have the same drive and determination that made them a great football player, they can make it in *anything.*"

It's a bit easier, of course, when you've got four Super Bowl rings. For Franco and his Steelers teammates, those rings were talismans that kept working long after retirement. Many of them stayed on in Pittsburgh, where the rings did the most good, and as a group they have been tremendously successful. This may also be due in part to their coach, Chuck Noll, who constantly reminded them that football was a temp job. "One day," he was always telling his players, "you'll have to get on with your life's work." Some former Steelers did stay on in football jobs (Mean Joe Greene and Donnie Shell), and others became sportscasters (Terry Bradshaw and Lynn Swann), but most built new careers entirely—Jack Ham as a coal broker, Andy Russell and Dwight White as investment bankers, Rocky Bleier as a motivational speaker, Mel Blount as the overseer of a home for troubled boys. And Franco as the doughnut king.

The thing was, Franco loved the view from the Himalayas but he seemed just as happy in the parking lot. He loved flying down to meet with the Memphis school board, persuading them to feed their students his nutritional doughnuts. He'd visit nursing-home administrators and hospital boards in California and Florida and Ohio, and, once they were through taking pictures with him, he'd tell them about the new Super Bakery products that helped fight osteoporosis.

I could not see Joe DiMaggio talking shop with a bunch of nursing-home bureaucrats. Or Muhammad Ali or, God forbid, Michael Jordan. For all his happy-face TV commercials, Michael Jordan has been known to shirk the little people, even when the little people are seven feet tall. Immediately after leading the Chicago Bulls to their sixth championship, Jordan was approached in the locker room by Joe Kleine, the Bulls' third-string center. Kleine, happy beyond words, wanted a hug. "Why are you crying?" Jordan asked him. "I did it all."

For ballplayers like Jordan and DiMaggio, the athletic afterlife is just that—an echo of the previous life, which wasn't quite real to start with. The athlete in the stadium is, like the priest on the altar, half-man and half-god, suspended in timeless ritual. Remove either of them from their ritual and you remove their immortality as well.

One night when I was a boy, during a snowstorm, Father DiPace was giving me a ride home, and his car got stuck in a drift. We found a lit-up house and knocked on the door. A family was having dinner, pot roast, and invited us to join them. Afterward, Father DiPace accepted a tumbler of brandy; he took off his shoes and socks in front of the fire; he played poker. Before my eyes, he turned mortal.

It wasn't his fault, of course, any more than it is the athlete's fault that he seems suddenly mortal when he retires. We are the ones who tell him he is immortal in the first place. We lay the hero's laurel on the athlete's brow and the moment he leaves the stadium, we whisk it away. There is only one way for the sports hero to achieve true immortality and that is to actually die—not just leave the game—near the peak of his powers. "The hero dead," Robert Penn Warren once wrote, "is safe, more or less, from envy and detraction."

Death is the capstone of the hero's legend. If a death is spectacular enough, the legend may last forever. "If Jesus were to return to earth," one biblical scholar has predicted, "the first thing we would do is crucify him again." The most incandescent heroes die with their boots on: Abraham Lincoln, John Henry, Amelia Earhart, Lou Gehrig, John F. Kennedy, Martin Luther King Jr., Dale Earnhardt. When Bob Dylan was a teenager in Hibbing, Minnesota, he had three heroes: Buddy Holly, Hank Williams, and James Dean, each of whom was dead before turning thirty.

Especially in the quasi-religious realm of sports, death packs an awesomely transformative punch. Death removes all blemishes; it forgives all transgressions. In a famous piece of sportswriting called "Brownsville Bum," W. C. Heinz assessed the life of a boxer named Bummy Davis, who was a hothead, a low-blow artist, and a general no-goodnik. Davis was shot and killed in a bar when, not atypically, he punched out a man, one of a group of four, all of whom had guns. Heinz's story begins like this: "People will hate a guy all his life for what he is, but the minute he dies for it they make him out a hero and they go around saying that maybe he wasn't such a bad guy after all because he sure was willing to go the distance for whatever he believed or whatever he was."

In Pittsburgh, if you didn't know better, you might assume that Roberto Clemente was a freedom fighter or a steel baron or a bishop. His name turns up on streets, bridges, parks, charities. A simple utterance of the name—three syllables rising, then three more falling in perfect counterpoint—provokes a meaningful hush in any quarter. He is hero, legend, and saint.

Before he was all that, Clemente was an outfielder for the Pittsburgh Pirates. After the 1972 season, he died in a plane crash while delivering relief supplies to Nicaragua, where an earthquake had just killed thousands. Pittsburgh was already despondent when the news about Clemente broke, for it was only a day earlier that the Steelers had squandered their Immaculate Reception victory by losing to the Miami Dolphins. Clemente's death threw the city deep into mourning. There was only one way to climb out: by turning the outfielder into a martyr. And so it was done. Calls went out to the statue-makers, the Hall of Fame, the White House.

"Clemente was a great baseball player," one member of Pittsburgh's sporting establishment told me, "but he was a prick. Don't get me wrong—he would have been a Hall of Famer, no question. But he was a malingerer, aloof. Clemente was not well-liked. Willie Stargell was much more popular with the fans. It's only because the way Clemente died that the legend grew. The other thing is, Stargell was much more productive than Clemente. Clemente was selfish—always hit for average, never drove in a lot of runs. But boy oh boy, he sure knew how to die."

FRANCO, MEANWHILE, seemed to be thriving without the benefit of a dramatic death. He was, however, as hard to reach as a dead man.

Whenever I called, his secretary said he was traveling. The secretary's name was Jackie, and she seemed to take pains to be unhelpful. She was always vague as to his return date. Could it be that Jackie didn't want me to know when he'd be back? Or maybe *Jackie* didn't know—a failure of reverence toward Franco that was even more disturbing. She said she gave him my messages but I had a hard time believing her. Why wouldn't he call me back? I also had a hard time asking for him when I called. It felt too formal, and generic, to ask for "Mr. Harris." But "Franco" seemed too familiar. His name still had a whiff of the holy about it. My dilemma was similar to that of the observant Jew who believes that God is too great to be named directly. So he writes "G–d willing" and gives Him a raft of pseudonyms, including *Adonai* ("my lord"), *Shaddai* ("almighty"), and my favorite—it calls to mind a Secret Service formulation—*ha-Shem* ("the name"). With Jackie, I finally arrived upon a comfortable phrasing: "Is Franco Harris there, please?"

Finally, one day in July, he was. Three months had passed since my visit. We reconnected beautifully; we went right back to where we'd been at the Italian restaurant, at the Chinese restaurant. We talked sports a bit. We asked about each other's families. I asked about business.

"It's going pretty well," he said. "It looks like we might get our doughnuts in with DreamWorks."

I had told Franco about the week I recently spent at DreamWorks, Steven Spielberg's company in Los Angeles, while writing an article about Spielberg. I was tickled that he remembered.

"I've been out there twice now," he was saying. "I didn't meet with Steven Spielberg or anything, but I did meet with the chef. The campus is amazing and the food is great. All the employees eat for free. Stir-fry and fried rice, chili and dumplings, all kinds of Asian stuff."

"And Super Donuts," I said.

"Well, soon, I hope," he said.

I told him I was eager to get back to Pittsburgh and see him.

"Well," he said, "I'll have to look at the calendar."

"Do you think we could do that now?"

"I guess so," he said. He put the phone down, came back in about three minutes. "How about August twentieth?"

"August twentieth"—my calendar was wide open but I pretended to check—"sure, that's great." I hung up, quickly, before he could change his mind.

A few days later, Jackie called to tell me that August twentieth wouldn't work after all. "Franco will call you," she said, "to reschedule."

MY MOTHER REMEMBERED Franco Harris well. When I was a kid, she bought me a Franco jersey that I wore until it disintegrated. "Pittsburgh Steelers," she said, "number 32."

"That's right," I said.

"A good guy," she said. "Handsome too, nice features."

"Right again."

"And Catholic," she said, proudly and preeningly, as if she remembered and I hadn't. As if his being Catholic is what made him a good guy.

I was telling her about my visit to Pittsburgh as I massaged Tiger Balm into her lower back. She leaned forward in a powder-blue recliner, a crocheted pillow under her feet. She had an oxygen tube curling into her nostrils, and her ankles were purple and bloated. But otherwise she was exactly herself. Her hair was still black, her kisses still noisy, her wit and wits intact. One night recently she fell out of bed, around 3:00 A.M., and had to ring a bell for help. My sister Marthe rushed downstairs. Lying on her back, my mother said, "I guess there's no way the Army will take me now."

She had just moved in with Marthe's family near Syracuse, in upstate New York. For the last fifteen years my mother had lived on her own in Florida. There, she went for a swim every morning and then to a Byzantine-rite Mass. (Vatican II had loosened things up too much for my mother; she liked her Catholicism straight and strong.) Afternoons, she brought groceries to homebound neighbors. About once a week she stood under a palm tree outside an abortion clinic and, in a cheery, singsong voice, chanted, "Respect life!" My mother was not a punisher; she didn't hate. You were entitled to your own opinion as long as you realized that hers was the right one.

She was seventy-eight years old, and if it weren't for her damned heart she would have been fine. But its muscle walls were swelling, shrinking the pumping chambers; she literally had too much heart for her own good. It got to the point where she couldn't climb her stairs, much less swim laps or picket the abortion clinics.

In shifts, my sisters flew down to Florida to start packing her up. The final shift was mine. I would shut down my mother's apartment and fly with her to Syracuse.

This was the same apartment where I had interviewed her so many times, where we found out things about each other that should have brought us closer. But my abandonment of Catholicism and subsequent march toward Judaism—a "reversion," my mother called it—disappointed her on many levels. She was disappointed that she failed to make a priest out of me. She was disappointed that I reverted to a religion that, although she barely knew it—her family was determinedly secular—she considered antiquated.

Her greatest disappointment was a mother's deep hurt. She believed in a Heaven where she hoped to go when she died. A Heaven where she would be reunited with her husband and, one after the next, her eight children. A Heaven that only admitted Catholics. Even though some of my siblings were severely lapsed—at last count only three of the eight were practicing Catholics—there was at least a chance they would return. I, however, had left Catholicism entirely. I had, in my mother's view, *voluntarily precluded myself from entering Heaven*, which meant that we would never see each other again once she died. To her, my choice was inane, unnecessary, and cruel.

For a few years we feuded, silently and then with hard words. But in the end my mother's love proved even stronger than her faith. She softened; and I, still her baby in my eyes and hers, could not resist her embrace. By the time I came to Florida to help her move, we were learning to be simply mother and son again, not always Catholic and Jew.

The night before we flew north, I made dinner for the two of us, lamb chops and string beans and baked potatoes. As we sat down, I was thinking about a blessing over the meal. In the past few years, this had been a tender issue. She had her blessing, I had mine. We were each too stubborn to work out some kind of compromise. Usually, I would sit with my hands in my lap while she crossed herself and recited her prayer.

But now, at long last, things were different. Now we were at peace. There were additional factors: her failing health, the occasion of her last meal in her own home. I decided, therefore, to defer to the *minhag*—the religious custom—of the house and simply ask my mother if she wanted to say a blessing.

"Of course," she said, and made the sign of the cross.

I was fully prepared to hear my mother recite the blessing I had heard her recite thousands of times, the blessing I had recited *with* her thousands of times: "Bless us, O Lord, and these Thy gifts, which we are about to receive from Thy bounty, through Christ, our Lord, Amen."

Instead, my mother, seventy-eight-year-old Florence Veronica Green-glass Winters Dubner, bowed her head and said: *"Baruch atah Adonai, Elo-heinu melech ha-olam, ha-motzi lechem min ha-aretz."* They were the first Hebrew words I ever heard her speak.

She crossed herself again. "Amen," we both said.

On the flight to Syracuse, she fell asleep and her head found my shoulder. I didn't twitch for two hours.

She had settled in nicely at Marthe's house. She wasn't well enough to travel to Manhattan for my wedding, so Ellen and I drove up afterward with a videotape. She and Ellen got on well. We all watched the tape together.

"A real Jewish wedding," my mother said, not unhappily.

Her room was a circus. On any given weekend, three or four of us kids would be visiting, plus the hospice nurse and grandkids and pets. The dog kept tripping over the oxygen tube, disconnecting it from the tank. Squeamish about the more bodily chores that my sisters handled, I duct-taped it to the floor, happy to have something to do.

"The next time you see Franco," my mother told me, "remind him about your art project."

"What art project?"

"You don't remember?"

"I don't remember."

She described a painting I made in the fifth grade, a life-size self-portrait on stiff brown paper. I had painted myself wearing Franco's jersey, she said. And one other thing: Franco's beard.

At visit's end, when my sisters were out of earshot, my mother sat me down. "Next time," she said solemnly, "bring maybe a little chopped liver. And *pastrami.* They get some here, but it's not very good." She also wanted a bottle of Manischewitz on hand, blackberry, even though she didn't drink. She was getting ready for the trip home. You can apparently take the Jewish girl out of Brooklyn (and make her a Catholic), but you can't take the Brooklyn Jew out of the girl.

She would tell us old jokes with Yiddish punch lines:

"So a young girl goes to the doctor," she began. "She's got this *huge* mouth." (To demonstrate, my mother cratered open her own mouth, down to the tonsils.) "'*DOC*-tuh, *DOC*-tuh,' she says. 'My *MOUTH* is so *HUGE*. Is there anything you can *DO*?' The doctor tells her, 'Every night, stand in front of your mirror and say "prunes" one hundred times, like this.'" (My mother again demonstrated, arching her eyebrows and elegantly rolling the "r": *prrrunes, prrrunes.*) "So the girl comes back a week later. '*DOC*-tuh, *DOC*-tuh,' she says. 'My *MOUTH* got even *MORE HUGE*!' 'Did you do your exercises?' the doctor asks. 'Yes!' she says. 'One hundred times?' he asks. 'YES!' she says. 'Would you mind showing me how you did them?'"

Here my mother paused, made an overly straight face, and roared the word that by now we all knew meant "prunes" in Yiddish: "'*FLAU-men, FLAU-men.*'"

One Friday afternoon in October, my sister Mona called: Mom's heart, she said, was starting to fail. She might last a few more weeks and she might not. Arrangements were being made. The funeral Mass would be held back at Our Lady of Fátima; Mom had already picked out the prayers she wanted said. Peter would give the eulogy.

"And Mom thought it would be good," Mona said, "if you wrote the obituary. Is that all right?"

This made some sense. I had literally written the book on my mother's life; although she would have preferred to be the mother of a priest than of a Jewish author, she was proud of my writing.

"Sure, fine," I said.

But I would do no such thing. Not while she was alive. Ellen and I drove up to Marthe's the next morning. My mother had rallied. When I walked in, she was rouging up her cheeks.

"A little powder and paint," she said, "makes a girl what she ain't."

"Hi, Mom." We kissed.

"I remembered something else about Franco," she said. "I think his mother was Italian." This was no small thing. To my mother, who had never left the United States, a Catholic from Italy was the real deal, like a bialy from Bialystok.

She didn't seem all that sick. Or I wasn't willing to face it. I was thinking she'd live to see my children not only born but graduating from college.

A few weeks later I was in Chicago when my cell phone rang. This time it was Marthe. This time, she said, it was for real.

I made a flight to Syracuse and arrived at half-past midnight.

"Wait a minute," Marthe said. "Don't go in yet."

I imagined a doctor was inside. I imagined my mother dead, waxy and blue. Instead she had put on a pair of Groucho Marx gag eyeglasses. From beneath bushy eyebrows and a bulbous nose, she pretended to waggle a cigar at me.

"I'm feeling a little better," she said. "Too bad you came running all the way from Chicago. I guess I'm the mama who cried wolf."

The third call came late on a Saturday morning in November. I was home in New York, just about to leave for the airport. I was due to give a lecture about my book that night in Buffalo, where my sister Beth lives with her family.

After calling Buffalo to cancel, I set out with Ellen for Marthe's house. At the same time, I later learned, Beth got in her car in Buffalo, also heading for Marthe's. On the radio, Beth heard an announcement: that evening's lecture at the Jewish Community Center was canceled owing to the death of the speaker's mother. Someone had gotten ahead of himself, but Beth didn't know that. She drove on expecting to be too late. I drove on expecting another false alarm. We were both wrong.

Marthe's husband, Gary, met our car outside. Darkness was just settling. The porch lights gleamed yellow over the crusty snow. "You'd better go right inside," Gary said.

My mother lay back in the powder-blue recliner. All four of my sisters were gathered around her, a wordless hive of teary sniffles, hugging themselves and each other. One dim lamp burned. Its glow seemed to fall on my mother's face alone. My sisters were a quivery, shadowy mass, while she, motionless, radiated from its center, as if painted by Caravaggio. As if she, not the lamp, were the source of light. I did not know if she was alive. Something was certainly different. The oxygen tube, I realized, was gone. I had become accustomed to it. She looked so unencumbered without it, rejuvenated, like a middle-aged man who shaves off his mustache.

My sisters and I hugged, one by one.

"Mom was asking for you," Marthe said.

Was asking. I knelt at her chair. I should have driven faster, I thought. We shouldn't have stopped to eat, I thought, but Ellen had been feeling queasy.

My mother was breathing. I took her hands, which lay in her lap, cool, clasping a set of rosary beads. Mostly she remained still. Then her face flickered and her lips moved, but her eyes did not open. She breathed out a stream of short, sharp words: "Going home . . . going home . . . going *home!*" And then: "Quick!" Then she was silent again.

Her face lay open before me. I inspected it, read it like a map. One afternoon soon after my father died, my mother fell asleep on the couch, and I crept up to examine her still face. *So* this *is what she looks like*, I thought. Until that moment I felt I had never gotten a good look. It wasn't simply that she was always in motion. Moses had been instructed not to look upon God's face, and I imagined somehow that a similar injunction applied to my mother's face, for it seemed to radiate an otherworldly intensity. But now, on her deathbed, I could see that the face of my mother was the face of wisdom and understanding and goodness. I moved in close enough to study the patch of skin between her upper lip and her nose. Is there a word, I wondered, for that patch of skin? It had always looked velvety smooth. But up close, I saw a webby network of wrinkles and creases—the residue of a million kisses laid upon her children and grandchildren, upon my own forehead and temples and lips, dispensed with sincerity and, often, I would guess, a prayer.

Kisses that would never fall upon a child of mine. This is what I suddenly realized, staring at my mother's face. This is what death means. A state of no-more-ness. No more kisses, advice, questions. So many hours I had sat with her these past years, asking questions about her history and mine. As I beheld her placid, radiant face, questions began flooding my mind, obvious and unasked—*how could I never have thought of that?*— and now unanswerable.

When my brother Peter arrived, I got up so he could kneel at her head. After a time we all began taking turns, going at her with whispers, touches, ice chips for her lips. We nursed her for an hour or two the way she had nursed the eight of us for decades.

I took my place again at her head. I whispered in her ear. I told her she was doing beautifully. I told her we wanted to know if we could make her more comfortable. I told her that, if she could manage it, I would very much like to hear her speak one last time.

I dabbed her lips with the pouch of ice chips. I studied her kiss wrinkles. "I love you," I told her.

Her lips moved a bit. I leaned in to hear.

"Say it again," I said.

"I have never seen anyone . . ." she said, and stopped.

"I have never seen anyone," I repeated, coaxing.

"More relaxed . . ."

"More relaxed," I said.

"More relieved . . ."

"More relieved."

"More pain-free . . ."

"More pain-free."

These were the last words I heard. She spoke them as if watching herself from above. Then she fell into a deeper sleep, another place entirely, and her breathing stopped.

Her mouth slowly fell open, first a little bit, then into a wide "O." I couldn't help but think of her *FLAU-men* joke. Peter later admitted he'd been waiting for her to sit up and quote Groucho Marx: "Either I'm dead or my watch has stopped."

But she didn't. We went out and got the wives and husbands, the nieces and nephews, grandchildren and dogs. We poured the blackberry Manischewitz into tiny paper cups, and Peter offered a toast to my mother's life, a life lived in full accordance with the courage of her convictions, and I do not expect to ever drink to a toast that is more true.

THE NEXT MORNING, at a Comfort Inn, I woke up before dawn to write her obituary. Never before had words seemed so impotent: "A native of Brooklyn . . . a ballet dancer . . . baptized in the Roman Catholic Church . . . for many years active in the Right-to-Life movement, the Rosary Altar Society, the Charismatic Renewal . . . died with more than a dozen family members in attendance." All true but only a whisper of her life.

I was supposed to e-mail the obituary to the funeral director back in Duanesburg, but my laptop wouldn't cooperate. *Serves me right*, I thought, *for trying to cram a whole life into a strand of fiber-optic cable.* Finally, after a few frantic hours, it—she—passed on through.

At the wake, I met Father John Connelly, the current priest at Our Lady of Fátima. He was in his sixties, from Albany, the kind of Irish-Catholic priest they aren't making anymore.

"I read your book," he said, "so I know all about you and your mom. I thought you might like to say the Mourner's Kaddish during the Mass tomorrow. Maybe right before Communion?"

I thanked him. The Mourner's Kaddish, the Jewish prayer for the dead, is a nice prayer; it says nothing about death. It is an ode to God's glory, a poetic and in fact perfectly ecumenical prayer. Still, I told Father Connelly, in the interest of Catholic family and friends, it might be better to recite the Kaddish later, at the gravesite, rather than during Mass.

So the following day, after sighing and laughing and crying our way through Peter's eulogy, my big family and seemingly half of Duanesburg encircled my mother's new grave, careful not to step on my father's, where I'd stood alone so often in the past, and after Father Connelly recited the Catholic prayers, he passed around pumpkin-colored photocopies of the Mourner's Kaddish, and for the first time in my life I said the prayer not for my long-dead parent but for the long-lived one. *Today*, I thought, *I am an orphan.*

The following day was Thanksgiving. We told Thanksgiving stories, Mom stories. All of us were there, including brothers Dave and Joe from out west. On Friday, Peter was trying to keep everyone together for another day or two. I was ready to get back to New York, I told him. I was ready to go home and sit shiva for the remaining days.

Peter, who calls himself a lapsed agnostic, asked me what shiva was all about. I explained: a concentrated period of mourning, surrounded by family and friends, where you do your best to both celebrate and grieve. He nodded, said, "That makes sense."

Driving back to New York with Ellen, I fell silent. I was depleted. Every few minutes I thought of a new way in which I would miss my mother. I would never watch a Groucho Marx movie or drive past a Catholic church or think of *anyone's* mother—Ellen's mother, Franco Harris's mother—without thinking of my own. I felt like a piano player who suddenly breaks his middle C string: it is only one note but it figures in everything. It is a missing sound; it throws off every rhythm, dilutes every chord; it downgrades the entire enterprise. Had *she* been my hero all along? If a hero is someone who saves us, then perhaps she was. If a hero leads by example but ultimately challenges us to set our own course—well, she was that too. I felt a twinge of guilt: had I been so fixated on my father's absence all these years that I failed to appreciate my mother's power?

I also drove home feeling inadequate. A flock of my nieces and nephews, ranging from a few years old to their early thirties, had attended the funeral. At family gatherings, they tended to drape on me. I was the youngest uncle, theoretically the fun one. I was, a long time ago, the rock-and-roll uncle and then the New York City uncle and now the writer uncle. I was the rebel uncle—leaving the family religion, for God's sake (although, in my view, I reclaimed it). Over the years, a few of them had reached out to me, seriously, wanting help that went beyond the casual family camaradenrie. And I had never come through. I pretended to come through, but I didn't; I'd offer some advice and promise to follow up, but then I forgot about it. In too many ways I was still the wounded ten-year-old boy. I was nobody's hero. The sight of all my nieces and nephews at my mother's funeral made me think I never would be.

A few days later, Peter called from Connecticut. It was a Monday. He had gone back to work, he said, but he couldn't get anything done. All morning he sat in his office thinking about Mom. How would I feel, he asked, if he took the train into New York and sat shiva with me?

I would feel pretty good, I told him. He showed up within an hour or two, well before anyone else was expected. Ellen was out, at a doctor's appointment. Peter and I ate corned-beef sandwiches from a deli plate someone had sent over. Ellen came home. She said hello to Peter, smiled a strange smile, then asked to speak with me in the bedroom. That seemed odd. I also thought it odd that she didn't take the time to give Peter a hug.

In the bedroom, Ellen full-out grinned.

"I'm pregnant," she announced, this on the seventh and final day of sitting shiva for my seventy-eight-year-old mother.

So this is what people mean, I thought, *when they say that God opens a window every time He shuts a door.* An orphan and a father, all in one week. I grinned back and we hugged. And just as I'd realized in an instant the state of no-more-ness that my mother's death led me to, I realized this: now I will be someone's hero whether I like it or not.

11

GIVE EVERYONE A SMILE

——⟨∞⟩——

FRANCO NEVER DID CALL to reschedule my next visit.

That's all right, I told myself—he's busy bringing nutritious snacks to the schoolchildren of America, making sure the bones of our elderly don't snap in two.

It would be my responsibility to keep in touch. Franco had clearly seen that I was up to the task. He appreciated stamina. At Steelers practices, Franco took the handoff, ran through the line of scrimmage, and kept going, seventy yards at a sprint, all the way to the end zone. On every play. Come game time, he wanted to be the last man with fresh legs.

Winter had settled in. I left messages for Franco, maybe eight or ten. Jackie usually told me straight off that he wasn't in. A few times, though, she put me on hold. Was she checking with him? I couldn't get anything out of her. "I'll have him call you" was all she'd say.

One day, instead of cruel Jackie, a cheerful woman named Cindy answered the phone. Jackie was out sick, she said. And Franco, Cindy told me, was AWOL. "We actually haven't heard from him in a couple days," she said.

"Oh!" I said, and must have sounded concerned.

"No, I'm sure he's okay," she said. "That's just the way he is. He pretty much marches to his own drummer."

This news cheered me immeasurably. Franco wasn't dodging me; he was just scattered.

Finally, in January, I reached him.

"Happy New Year," I said. "Happy Millennium."

"Yeah, you too." He sounded preoccupied.

"How were your holidays?"

"Relaxing, just how I like them," he said. "How about yours?"

"Well, sadly, my mom died," I said, "so it's been a rough spell."

I flashed back to the fourth grade, a dress rehearsal for the school play, huddled in the darkened wings with a girl named Patty Horton, who refused to let me kiss her. So I said to her, "Jeez, I mean, my father just died and everything." Shameless! Shameless then and shameless now.

". . . sorry for your loss," Franco was saying. "I do accept death, that it happens to all of us." *What a strange thing to say*, I thought; *how could you not accept death?* ". . . just hope that there's not a lot of suffering involved."

"No," I said. "It was what you'd have to call a really good death. She was comfortable. Most of us kids were there."

"She sounds like some kind of lady, from what you told me," he said.

I asked about his business. He said things were fine, that he'd been traveling constantly. I asked when might be a good time for me to come to Pittsburgh.

"Well, maybe in the spring," he said, "since winter's so busy. Why don't you give me a call in early March."

"Maybe I could start interviewing some other folks in the meantime," I said. "Your mom maybe, some former teammates. Just to have some background."

"Well, let's wait on that until we get together," he said. Then, "Sorry again to hear about your mother," and that was that.

I started calling again, daily, on March 1. No luck.

"Are you *sure* he got the message?" I'd ask Jackie.

"I *gave* it to him," she'd say, huffy.

On March 7, Franco was turning fifty years old. I would have liked to wish him a happy birthday. I missed him.

It wouldn't hurt, I decided, to start making some background calls as long as I didn't call anyone too close to Franco. I didn't want word getting back to him.

I settled on Myron Cope, who had been broadcasting Steelers games since 1970. A native of Squirrel Hill, the old Jewish part of Pittsburgh, Cope (né Kopelman) had an adenoidal bullhorn of a voice and a style that could be called Overcaffeinated Cosell. On the air, Cope ranted, guffawed, and mewled; when the action got slow, he might sing "Goodnight Irene."

It was Cope who, back in 1972, publicly christened the Immaculate Reception. A few hours after the game, a Steelers fan called Cope from a tavern suggesting the name and, after pondering its heresy level for about fifteen seconds, he let it loose on the airwaves. Cope, in fact, had come to refer to himself as "the world's leading authority on the Immaculate Reception." On the play's twenty-fifth anniversary, he wrote an article for the *New York Times* explaining why this was so.

In the aftermath of the miracle play, Cope wrote, the Oakland Raiders disputed its legality. At the time, NFL rules prohibited an offensive player from catching his quarterback's pass if the ball was previously touched by another offensive player. So if Terry Bradshaw's pass, before caroming into Franco's hands, had struck John "Frenchy" Fuqua, the Steelers' intended receiver, and not Jack "the Assassin" Tatum, the Raiders defensive back who slammed into Fuqua, the touchdown shouldn't have counted. (The Raiders maintained that it hit Fuqua.) NBC's footage of the play, even in slow motion, did not make clear whether the ball hit Fuqua or Tatum. Cope, however, claimed to have taken the local television station's footage of the Immaculate Reception and cranked it, frame by frame, through an old-fashioned film viewer. His findings: "I'm the only guy on the planet who saw the film, and I can tell you that the Immaculate Reception was as kosher as a corned-beef sandwich in a Squirrel Hill delicatessen."

I didn't have a phone number for Cope, and he wasn't listed. I called the friend of a friend at the *Pittsburgh Post-Gazette* and was soon sucked into the happy, famous vortex of Pittsburgh hospitality.

"I don't know Cope's number," said the friend of the friend, "but I can give you the number of an insurance man I know who knows Cope."

The insurance man didn't have Cope's number either, but his nephew had just taken a job at the TV station where Cope used to work, so he gave me the nephew's home number.

The nephew's wife had supper on the stove and a baby crying, but she gladly gave me her husband's number at the TV station.

The husband-nephew couldn't find Cope's number, so he transferred me to a man he knew in the station's sports department.

"I'll call up Cope at home right now," said the man in the sports department, "and tell him to give you a scream."

My phone rang a few minutes later, and I heard what was indeed a scream. Cope had the voice of an old man imitating a little boy imitating Donald Duck.

"I'd recognize you anywhere," I told him, "from all the old Steelers highlight films."

"Yeah, some voice, huh?" he said. "I was a writer, you know. *Sports Illustrated*, a few books. When they first came to me about doing a radio show I said, 'Don't be ridiculous. Have you heard my voice?' They said, 'We see a trend toward obnoxious voices.'"

Cope asked what I was after, and I told him—Franco Harris stories of any vintage, any variety—and he said, "Well, you know about this thing tomorrow night at the Hilton, right?"

"What's that?"

"Franco's being roasted. It's his fiftieth birthday, you know. Every year Mel Blount has a fund-raiser for his youth home, and this year Franco's the roastee. A lot of the old Steelers will be there. You'll get all the stories you want."

Mel Blount, a longtime teammate of Franco's, was a Hall of Fame defensive back. I couldn't believe Franco hadn't told me about the roast.

"I can't believe Franco didn't tell me about the roast," I heard myself telling Cope.

"Well, Franco's Franco," he said, commiserating.

"I wonder if I should just show up. I don't want him to think I'm . . . I'm . . . *stalking* him."

"Yeah, it's possible he might think you were stalking him."

I got off the phone with Cope and dialed Franco's office. Jackie must have heard the determination in my voice, because she put me right through to Franco.

"Happy birthday," I said. "How's fifty feel?"

"You know what, not too bad."

"I hear you're getting roasted tomorrow night," I said. "I was thinking of coming down. But I didn't want you to think I was, you know, *stalking* you or anything."

I waited for him to say, "Of course not!" or, "Hey, come on down!" but he didn't say anything.

" 'Cause I'm not," I added.

He chuckled—at least I thought it was a chuckle—and then said, "If you do come, make sure to grab me and say hello."

I hung up and quickly called the Hilton, the airline, and Blount's charity to buy a ticket. Within fifteen minutes I spent one thousand and twenty-five dollars. I wondered: how many diapers would one thousand and twenty-five dollars buy?

But I was going back to Pittsburgh.

ON THE FLIGHT, I read Mel Blount's 1993 memoir, *The Cross Burns Brightly: A Hall-of-Famer Tackles Racism and Adversity to Help Troubled Boys*. Blount was hardly the only former Steeler to have written a book. Rocky Bleier, Andy Russell, Steve Courson, and Preston Pearson all did it; Terry Bradshaw has, at last count, published *four* memoirs. Another shelf of books have been written about various Steelers or the team as a whole. By now I had read just about all of them.

The white players' memoirs were, generally, upbeat stories of adversity overcome and victory seized. The black players told more bitter tales.

Blount's book was one long race rant. Not that he had to manufacture the racism: when he established his youth home in the hills south of Pittsburgh, the Ku Klux Klan burned a cross on his property. This news, sadly, failed to shock me. Rural Pennsylvania is a known redneck redoubt—the political operative James Carville has called the state "Pittsburgh and Philadelphia with Alabama in the middle." But Blount also targeted the Steelers, whom I had always considered a bastion of enlightenment. The Rooneys, though paternalistic, were said to be fair and certainly not racist; the Steelers were one of the first pro teams to actively scout black southern colleges.

Blount played at such a place, Southern University in Baton Rouge, having grown up in Vidalia, Georgia. Until he came to Pittsburgh, he wrote, he lived "in an all-black world." He was thoroughly unprepared for life in the NFL. After he let his man score during a playoff game against the Raiders, Blount heard a shout from the stands: "Bench that stupid nigger!" "Suddenly," he wrote, "I understood how the early Christians must have felt as they faced the lions. I could only trust that God's grace would deliver me from the white lions."

By 1976, Blount was an All-Pro but made less than $50,000. He thought he deserved a big raise. The Steelers offered him an extra $5,000. Blount thought they were kidding.

"Take it or starve," he was told.

Blount concluded that the Steelers had two pay scales, "one for the white player and another for the black player," he wrote. "Even when it came to promotion and publicity, the black player did not get much. If two players were needed to deliver a speech at two separate functions, the white player always came up with the better one. He would go to the plush hotel, give his speech, and dine on steak and lobster. The black player would end up in an inner-city school auditorium, eating hot dogs."

I argued with Blount as I read. For years, the Steelers' highest-paid player was Joe Greene, who is black. As for publicity, Greene got plenty (including the most moving Coca-Cola commercial in history), and Franco got far more than he ever wanted. I didn't doubt that Blount had experienced racism—one burning cross, I would think, is one too many—but he came off as an angry man who found it convenient to blame his every misstep on the white lions.

Franco didn't harbor such feelings, did he? He *had* told me how, when he first went into business, he was disappointed to discover so few powerful black men in that world. And the federal government's minority financing and set-aside programs, he said, "just make you laugh." But Franco didn't turn race into a weapon, offensive or defensive. A friend of Franco's once called him "an individual who transcends race, who transcends class," and that's how I saw him. Of course, I knew he had a black father and a white mother, that he thought of himself as black growing up, that his wife was white—but even when I was a boy, those facts were secondary. And in Pittsburgh, sitting across the table from him, race rarely entered my mind. Franco was Franco.

But was I being hopelessly naive? It's easy to say that race is secondary when your skin is white. Back in his rookie year, when Franco was fielding so many questions about his background, he told one reporter, "I guess the whole thing in this country goes by skin color. I mean, either you're white or you're not white. So that's what I've had to deal with."

Had he dealt with his race as coolly as it seemed? Or did he, like Blount, see a little bit of red every time he saw a white face like mine?

I ARRIVED at the Hilton ten minutes before the reception was to begin. Outside were a pair of television trucks, a cluster of hired sedans, a steady stream of tuxedoed men and begowned women. Fans in Steelers jackets and sweatshirts patrolled the perimeter with autograph books. It had been twenty years since Pittsburgh brought home a Super Bowl trophy, and the men coming tonight were the men who did it. Victory, even from a distance of twenty years, is a drug like no other.

I checked in, the lobby aswirl with handshaking and chatter, and wheeled my suitcase toward the elevator. I practically ran Franco over. There he stood, calm and courtly, at the center of a loose knot of tall people. His chin was raised for the affixing of a bow tie. The affixer was a young man, portly, with longish black hair and a wispy mustache.

Franco spotted me, and his face—I swear—brightened.

"Hey, Steve, you made it!" he said. "Steve, this is my son Dok." The portly young man said hello but didn't interrupt his bow tie duty to shake my hand.

Franco had remembered my face, my name.

"Hello," I said to Dok, and "Happy birthday" to Franco, and then, because he was about to be thronged, I said, "See you inside," and went upstairs to put on my tuxedo.

Riding back down, I shared the elevator with a large, heavily cologned black man, mid-fifties: Mean Joe Greene. He wore large eyeglasses and a sweet expression. When he caught me checking him out he gave me a yes-it's-me look, and I gave him a don't-worry-I-won't-harass-you smile, and when the door opened he said, "Have a great night."

On the mezzanine outside the ballroom, a thousand people drank and nibbled. Every face I saw was white. I wondered how Blount felt about taking their money: grateful? scornful? vindictive? A dozen people stood in line to pay twenty-five dollars to have their photo taken with the Steelers' four Super Bowl trophies.

I got to talking with a nervous, redheaded, fiftyish man, a lawyer, who wanted to hit up Franco for some kind of endorsement on behalf of minority construction workers. "When the U.S. Steel Building was built," he told me, seething, "there wasn't one black construction worker involved." He kept looking past me, trying to spot Franco. I found myself wishing, at least for tonight, that he wouldn't get to him.

Next I chatted up a friendly older couple, Dee and Tom Murrin, long-ago New Yorkers. Tom, a former Westinghouse executive, was now the dean of the business school at Duquesne University. Back in the day, he played football at Fordham under Vince Lombardi. "And Dee," Tom said, "knows more about football than most men." Dee smiled at that.

They had been supporting the Mel Blount Youth Home since the beginning, Dee said. And why, she wanted to know, had I come all the way from New York?

"To see Franco," I said.

"Are you a friend of his?" Dee asked.

I didn't know how to answer that. I said, "He was my childhood hero," and they nodded knowingly.

Dee and Tom couldn't say enough good things about Franco—his kind nature, his humility, his work with so many charities. "You really picked a good one," Dee said. "The Rooneys always recruited good, solid people. Not like some of the other teams, with players going to jail and that kind of thing."

"Well, you did have Ernie Holmes," I said. Ernie Holmes was notorious for, among other things, trying to shoot down a police helicopter.

"Oh, that thing with the helicopter was just for fun," said Tom.

I went to pick up my table assignment for dinner. On the phone, I had explained my mission and asked to sit up front, close to the action. Inside the ballroom, I found my seat—along the back wall. My tablemates were not football people, as I had hoped, but they were very pleasant. They included the man who made the ice sculptures for the event (since we were so far from the stage, he showed me the Polaroids in his pocket: a giant 32, Franco's jersey number, and a giant 50, for his birthday); an older couple who owned a jewelry store (in the family for four generations); a chipper man who worked at the Carnegie Museums and his commensurately chipper wife, a bridal consultant.

The old Steelers were introduced one by one, each man trailed by a camera. (The roast was being broadcast live in Pittsburgh.) Mel Blount and Joe Greene, Lynn Swann and John Stallworth, Andy Russell and Frenchy Fuqua, a dozen or so more. A few non-Steelers too: Lydell Mitchell, Franco's running mate at Penn State and now his partner in Parks Sausage; and Myron Cope, bald and tiny, dwarfed by the smallest football player. They all took their seats behind tiered banquet tables. And finally Franco, grinning like a kid picking up a Pee Wee Football trophy.

Mel Blount made some sober opening remarks about his youth home. He spoke graciously, deliberately. He has mellowed, I thought, since his book. There was one word that inevitably came up in any discussion about Blount, with either men or women, blacks or whites, a word that never failed to make me uncomfortable, and that word was *stud*. Now I saw why. At fifty-two, Blount still looked as if he could play football: six-foot-three, taut and muscular, perfectly erect, with a shaved head. He wore a cowboy hat with his tuxedo, and it somehow did not look foolish.

Lynn Swann, now an ABC sportscaster, was introduced as the evening's emcee. Swann was as slickly extroverted as Franco was low-key, and yet the two were said to be best friends. "Franco gets along with everybody," Swann once told a reporter, "but not everybody knows the real Franco." That, of course, was my challenge—to know the real Franco. Now, raising his eyebrows, Swann promised that when the roasting started, the real Franco would emerge, locker-room stories and all.

The dinner hour began with a viewing of the Immaculate Reception. The crowd turned as one to a pair of giant television screens up front. A chorus of gasps as Terry Bradshaw eluded his would-be sackers. A giant, pained grunt as Jack Tatum leveled Frenchy Fuqua. A breathy, expectant *ooooh*, the sound you let out approaching the top of a roller coaster, as the ball tumbled in slow motion to the turf. And a wild round of whooping as Franco snatched the ball and, with fulgurant speed, escorted it toward the end zone. As he crossed the goal line, the overdressed men and women banged their water glasses on the tables. They threw their arms heavenward to signal the touchdown. They turned to one another and grinned prideful grins, patrons then and still of a miracle.

The Immaculate Reception would be shown about forty-three times during the evening. Our reactions were always the same, and always perfectly timed. We knew every frame, every fateful twist of muscle and leather. It was the Zapruder film of sport, its outcome perfectly clear yet forever shrouded in mystery, its impact undiminished by one hundred viewings or even one million. It was a construction of beauty, thrill, and chance that no mortal artist could have created. Watching it there, with the iceman and the jewelry-store couple and, at the banquet tables up front, the old Steelers themselves, Franco craning his head like all the others toward the screen, I too felt a part of the miracle. A slight part, to be sure. A lowly apprentice to Michelangelo's frame-maker, perhaps, who many years hence discovers that his own face has been painted into the Sistine Chapel ceiling, the timid face of an angel of the Lord.

The Immaculate Reception was by now a divine touchstone. Although the Steelers didn't reach the Super Bowl that season, they began winning it repeatedly only two years later. In Pittsburgh, it was an article of faith that the Immaculate Reception had triggered all that victory.

And yet as I'd later learn from Father John Marcucci, the priest who used to wear a Steelers stole and deliver football sermons, many people confused the dogma for which the play was named.

"They hear 'Immaculate Conception' and they think of the Virgin Birth," he said. "But the Immaculate Conception doesn't have anything to do with Jesus—it's that when Mary was conceived in the womb of *her* mother, the stain of original sin did not touch *her.* That was God's big deal with the Immaculate Conception. And see, the big deal about the Immaculate *R*eception is that Frenchy Fuqua didn't touch the ball. So it's Mary not touched by sin, and this football not touched by Frenchy Fuqua."

And Franco, I asked Father Marcucci: what does that make Franco?

"Ah," he said. "Franco was God's winged messenger."

I had ridden around Pittsburgh with, had shared two meals with, had seen nearly naked God's winged messenger. And not once had I paused to consider: how does *he* feel to have been placed at the center of a miracle?

Watching him now watch himself on the vast television screen, I realized what a burden he must bear. For once you have been declared Immaculate, you cannot reverse field. Once the miracle occurs it grows only more holy, and it is your duty to safeguard it. God's winged messenger could not allow himself a single blemish.

And I: while I had come to Franco with the purest of intentions, he couldn't know that, could he? After all, who was I? Just another fan with just another story. But worse than that—a fan with a pen and a notepad. From where Franco stood, the story had already been written. And it was perfect. From where he stood, I could do nothing but damage. My pockets bulged with arrows, my mouth with lies. Was that why he had not yet taken me to his bosom? Did he expect me to harm him?

But I am innocent! I wanted to shout out. Like the shnook on some TV cop show who gets framed by his ex-wife: *Innocent, I tell you!*

After dinner the roasting began. Franco sat restlessly beside the podium. Despite Swann's promise of locker-room secrets, despite Myron Cope's prediction of stories by the bushel, it proved to be a tame affair.

Swann told the inevitable hungry-athlete story, how Franco used to order spareribs as an appetizer, then eat a thirty-two-ounce prime rib and a shrimp platter. Joe Greene recalled that Franco set aside Steelers tickets for needy schoolkids. Dan Rooney, who had run the Steelers since the Chief's death and was now an old man himself, said, "We hadn't won a lot before Franco came, and after he came we didn't lose a lot." (I was happy to see Rooney there, and surprised, since Franco's career ended so rancorously; even five years later, when Franco was inducted into the Hall of Fame, he thanked everyone down to his high-school English teacher—except for the Rooneys.)

Donnie Shell, a former defensive back known for his brutal tackles, took the podium and asked Franco, "Why's everybody being so nice to you?"

"I'm very intimidating," Franco said, so gently you could barely hear him.

After which Shell continued: "Franco had all the stardom, but he treated everybody with respect, whether you were a teammate or a fan. That rubbed off on me and made a great difference in my life."

The Friars Club it wasn't.

Frenchy Fuqua was in more of a roasting spirit: "The Immaculate Reception!—Franco runs away with the hundreds of thousands of dollars *I* would have made if *I* caught that ball!" Fuqua reminisced about a charity flag-football game in which Franco broke his nose. "And Dana gave him hell afterward. She says, 'How you going to make commercials now with your nose sitting over *there*?'"

Lydell Mitchell took his shot: "Franco doesn't know anything about time. Thirty-two years I've known him, he's never worn a watch. He says he'll pick you up at the airport at one-thirty, he gets there at three o'clock. He didn't tell me about this dinner until a couple weeks ago." (This made me feel a little better: even his closest friends were out of the loop.)

Rocky Bleier, on videotape, was the most direct: "Come on, Franco, you milked the Immaculate Reception for the last *twenty-eight* years. I mean, you got more publicity out of that than the shrine at Lourdes, let's be honest here. You just happened to be at the right place at the right time. *Nobody was around you.* Myron Cope could have scored. Now you got the Super Donut. What a great scam—I mean, a *nutritional doughnut*! The American public, they'll buy anything."

There was one truly treacherous moment. Lynn Swann, introducing a retrospective film of Franco's life, announced that a hidden camera had been trailing Franco for the past year.

Franco looked petrified.

"Just kidding, Franco," Swann said, and Franco hurriedly made light of his reaction—but I had seen it. Did he have something to hide?

After the film, after a giant birthday cake was wheeled out (topped by a hefty, lifelike replica of Franco's helmeted head), after a few more viewings of the Immaculate Reception, Franco took the podium. He seemed comfortable up there. He read a long list of thank-yous. He congratulated Dan Rooney on his upcoming induction into the Hall of Fame. He asked that we all remember the former Steelers and other footballers who had died during the past year. (He used the same strange line—"I do accept death, that it happens to all of us"—he used after I told him my mother died.) Then he began his speech, which wasn't really a speech at all, but a skein of inspirational verses:

> *Regardless of what you are or what you have been, you have the capacity to be what you want to be.*

Ah, yes. This was vintage Franco–cum–Norman Vincent Peale, the kind of saying that, as a kid, made me think him so wonderful. And then:

> *Risk more than others think is safe.*
> *Care more than others think is wise.*
> *Dream more than others think is practical.*
> *Expect more than others think is possible.*

And finally:

Be as enthusiastic about the success of others as you are about your own.
Forget the mistakes of the past and press on to the greater achievement of the
* future.*
Give everyone a smile.
Spend so much time improving yourself that you have no time left to criticize
* others.*
Be so strong that nothing can disturb your peace of mind.
Talk health, happiness, and prosperity to every person you meet.
Make all your friends feel there is something in them.
Look at the sunny side of everything.
Think only of the best, work only for the best, and expect only the best.
Be too big for worry and too noble for anger.

With each line I felt a bit smaller. These platitudes, Franco's recipe for human relations were . . . well, they were *nice*. Who could argue with them? But having been on the receiving end of his nicety, I was suddenly walloped by doubt: had Franco's warmth toward me been as *generic* as all that? Had we shared no special connection at all?

A businessman goes to his office every day because that is what he does. A young woman goes to Mass every Sunday because that is what she does. A little boy says the Pledge of Allegiance every morning because that is what he does. But do they *mean* it?

Give everyone a smile. Had Franco smiled at me, laughed with me, told me stories, because *that is what he does*?

The roast was over. Up front there was a free-for-all. Franco and some of the other Steelers were set upon by autograph seekers.

I said a quick hello to Myron Cope, and thanked him for letting me know about the roast. "Happy to help," he said.

Dana, Franco's wife, brushed past me, and I introduced myself. She certainly didn't recognize my name. She was self-assured, with a slender, pretty face and blond hair (though in the old photos it was brown).

"Maybe Franco's told you about the book I'm working on?" I said.

"No." She half-smiled. "It was good to have met you," she said, walking away.

A young woman stood with her father at the edge of the mob. He was bald, bone-thin, and looked to be about seventy. He was clutching a worn football, tightly, as if he were about to run off-tackle. I began talking to the daughter. She said her father was actually in his early fifties, suffering from cancer.

"He wants Franco to sign the ball," she said, "but I'm worried he won't get in there. He's not pushy enough."

The man got his football signed. Franco stayed and stayed, signing for every fan and busboy and security guard. After a half-hour, down to a dozen people, he spotted me.

"Hey!" he said. He looked surprised that I was still there, then seemed to make a mental calculation that he'd have to deal with me.

"Congratulations," I said.

An autograph seeker asked Franco how it felt to be fifty. Instead of answering, he turned to me: "How old are *you*, Steve?"

Talk health, happiness, and prosperity to every person you meet.

"Thirty-six," I said.

"Whoo," he said. "I don't know if I remember thirty-six."

Make all your friends feel there is something in them.

When he'd signed the last autograph, he asked me, "You ready to go?" Meaning, I realized, back out to the mezzanine for birthday cake.

We walked together. Someone had removed the replica of Franco's helmeted head from the cake and left it on a table. It was apparently inedible, a keepsake. Franco picked it up. He looked like a movie actor playing John the Baptist walking off the set with his own fake beheaded head.

On the mezzanine, the crowd had dwindled to a hundred people. Franco grabbed a piece of cake, handed it to me. He soon stood at the center of a cluster.

"Hey, Steve, this is Max Gomberg," Franco said, drawing me into the cluster, "my oldest friend in Pittsburgh."

Max and I shook hands. "Yeah, it's true," he said. Max was about Myron Cope's height and vintage. Back in Franco's rookie year, Max told me, Franco came to his son's bris; later, his kids' bar and bat mitzvahs and the Gomberg family's Passover Seders. "Franco's a brother to me," Max said. "We've traveled all over, taken our families together—his mother, Dana, her mother—to Europe, Austria, Italy, Mexico."

"Hey, Steve, this is Sammy Davis's wife," Franco said. He introduced me to a graceful, attractive black woman with an open face. Sam Davis was a former Steelers offensive lineman who not long ago, I had heard, either fell or was pushed down a staircase. He suffered brain damage and ballooned to four hundred pounds. Now he lived in an assisted-care home outside of Pittsburgh.

"It's good to meet you," I said, somberly.

"Where are you from?" she asked.

"New York," I said.

"New York!" she said, fondly, as if it had been too long. "And what do you do in New York?"

"I'm a writer."

"Oh! What do you write?"

"Actually I'm working on a book about—"

And as I turned toward Franco to say, "*him,*" I watched, mortified, as Franco reached over, gripped my forearm, and said, quietly but sternly, "Uh-uhn."

My face prickled. In that moment and in the hours and days afterward, I replayed that rush of mortification again and again. What had I done wrong? Why didn't Franco want Mrs. Davis to know? Was it because, with her husband incapacitated, Franco didn't want to play up his own appeal?

"Well," I managed to tell Mrs. Davis, "I wrote one book, and now I'm writing another."

"I see," she said, gently. She looked from me to Franco and back. I felt like a schoolboy who had just peed his pants while the teacher tried pretending to not notice.

A middle-aged white couple asked Franco if they could take a picture with him. "Sure," he said, "but let's leave your bottle of beer out of the picture, okay?"

I was about to ask Mrs. Davis how her husband was doing, but she excused herself. I watched Mel Blount stride toward me as, from his blind side, a pretty, fortyish, streaked-blond woman corralled him. She seemed half-drunk. She leaned into Blount, put her hand on his bicep.

"Mel, sign this," she said, shoving her program at him. "Say, 'To Pat, thanks for last night, Love, Mel Blount.'"

I sucked in my breath.

Blount didn't smile at the woman. He didn't even meet her eyes. He grabbed the program, scribbled his name, stormed off. I didn't blame him.

Franco came back. "There's a party up on twenty-two," he said. It sounded like an invitation so I followed him. I was afraid to say a word after he chided me in front of Mrs. Davis. When the elevator opened on the twenty-second floor, Myron Cope scooted past, clutching a cocktail glass and a cigarette.

Cope stopped. "Hey, Franco. How 'bout this guy, huh?" he said, meaning me. "Only last night I tell him about the roast, and just like that he hops on a plane from New York."

"Yeah, how 'bout that," Franco said.

Someone told Franco that Dana had just gone downstairs to fetch him. "Sheesh," he said. "Well, let me go find her."

"I'll go," I said. I was happy for the chance to help, to redeem whatever sin I'd committed with Mrs. Davis.

I found Dana on the mezzanine. She didn't look as if she remembered meeting me an hour earlier.

"I've been sent to retrieve you," I said.

She rolled her eyes. "Franco just had to stay down here, talking to every last person."

"He has a hard time saying no, huh?" I said.

"It's my favorite word, but Franco's never heard of it."

Back on twenty-two, the party had spilled from the Carnegie Suite into the hallway. Joe Greene and Frenchy Fuqua and Lydell Mitchell chatted in a cloud of cigar smoke. I overheard Tunch Ilkin and Jon Kolb, a pair of former offensive linemen, talking about the sorry state of the current Steelers. As parties go, especially football parties, it was pretty docile. The average height was about six-foot-two, the average age fifty.

I would have liked to talk with Greene and Fuqua and Mitchell. I would have liked to ask Fuqua if it was true that he used to wear platform shoes with live goldfish in the heels. I would have liked to ask Mean Joe Greene about the Minnesota Vikings game during which he lost his temper, grabbed some scissors from the first-aid kit, and charged the Vikings' bench. As for Lydell Mitchell, he was not only Franco's business partner but one of his oldest friends.

I didn't approach them, though. Their blackness held me back. A half-hour earlier it wouldn't have. But the encounter between Mel Blount and the streaked blonde shook me. When you're treated like a stud, literally, does every white face take on the shape of the devil?

Instead I introduced myself to Ilkin and Kolb. They were both white. Kolb, I remembered reading, was from Oklahoma. When he found out he was too small for high-school football, he took a job at a dairy so he could drink lots of milk.

"Wasn't much of a roast, was it?" Kolb said to me.

"I guess not," I said.

"If they'd let me talk," he said, "I would have done something good."

"Like what?"

"I'd have talked about his nickname, Sting Bee."

He and Ilkin laughed. "Where'd that come from?" I asked.

"The guy never blocked," Kolb said. "In practice, Franco's always saying, 'Hey, guys, this week I'm really gonna *sting* 'em.' And I'd say, 'Franco, you just stay out of the way and let the real men do the men's work.'"

I watched Franco moving from group to group. With other men he looked manly. With women he was gentle. With whites he seemed white, and with blacks he seemed black. He was a beaker of happy gas set free in a big room to ply his charm, to give everyone a smile.

"Yeah, Franco specialized in these very *convenient* blocking angles," Ilkin was saying, "designed so he wouldn't ever actually hit the guy."

Ilkin asked me what I did. I told him I was writing a book about he-

roes. He nodded earnestly. Then he quoted a New Testament passage—
Ilkin grew up Muslim but became a born-again Christian, he told me,
after "raising a few years' worth of hell"—saying that if the Lord has
given you a lot, you are obligated to give back. "Whether you like it or
not," he said, "the professional athlete is a role model, and he's got to act
like one."

Franco wandered toward us.

"Hey, guys," he said to Kolb and Ilkin. "Hey, Steve," he said, and shook
my hand. "Time to be heading out, I guess."

I didn't know if it was time for him to be heading out or me. But after
the Mrs. Davis incident, I wasn't taking any chances. I didn't ask Franco
about our next meeting. I didn't even say good-bye to Kolb and Ilkin. I
just scrammed. I rode the elevator down to my room, the beggar exiled
from the banquet, the clump of chaff shaken at last from the wheat.

I woke in the morning with a hangover even though I hadn't drunk a
drop. I felt as if I'd done something foolish and filthy the night before,
though I couldn't say what. Maybe I *was* stalking him.

My hotel room overlooked the Point, a jut of parkland beyond which
Pittsburgh's rivers join one another. Across the Allegheny, hulking in
the desolate rainy gray of a Saturday in March, was Three Rivers Stadium. I decided to go visit it.

A footbridge led over the river. As I reached it, the rain picked up. It
stung my face. I was lost not in some beery, bundled crowd but in a taut
silence of my own making. Suddenly, from downtown, the rataplan of
drums and the whine of bagpipes rose up, clattering off the skyscrapers.
A Saint Patrick's Day Parade.

The footbridge deposited me onto a concrete plaza. The stadium was
gigantic. And impregnable: not a single gap through which to see the
field.

Tremendous things had happened beyond those walls, of course. The
fact that I could not see inside didn't change anything. Things were happening inside Franco too. I was destined to see them. I had recently read
a novel whose narrator made this claim: "A talent is, at the start, nothing
more than a somewhat obsessive interest. But with careful guidance, it

can develop into that exceptional skill to which we generally refer when we speak of talent."

Franco may have begun as mere obsession. But now I was determined to make him my talent. Even if he turned himself impregnable. Even if I had just received my first inkling that he was trying to slip from my grasp. No: *especially* if he was trying to slip from my grasp.

12

FEELING VIDA BLUE

———•◦❀◦•———

BACK IN NEW YORK, I called Franco. I asked point-blank what I'd done wrong in telling Mrs. Davis that I was writing about him.

"I just didn't think it was the right time to talk about it," he said.

The right time? What was that supposed to mean? When would the right time be? His inscrutability was beginning to wear me down.

"That's some sad news about her husband," I said.

"Um, well, *yeah.*"

"Sounds like he's in pretty bad shape."

"Well, he's dead," Franco said.

"Dead?"

"Yeah, Sammy Davis Jr., he died like ten years ago."

Oops. So she was the wife of *that* Sammy Davis, not Franco's old teammate. I knew Franco had always kept a quiet coterie of show-biz friends. I didn't know it included Sammy Davis Jr. I was beginning to wonder what else I didn't know.

"Do you think we could schedule another Pittsburgh visit?" I asked.

He paused. "Why don't you give me a call in a couple weeks and maybe we can set something up for the spring."

I blurted out that Ellen and I were going to Italy in May. I was trying to keep him on the line. I was trying to let him know I had a life, that I wasn't just sitting around waiting to be summoned to Pittsburgh. (Although I was.) Italy would be our last trip for a while, I said, since we were expecting a baby in August.

"Wow, that's great news," he said.

"Does your mom still have family in Italy?" I asked.

"Yeah, outside of Florence. I'm going over in October."

"With your mom?"

"Oh, yeah, I always take her. I want to get a vineyard over there someday."

"Do you think about retiring there?"

"Well, it's a little early for that," he said. "But tell the country I said hello, no doubt about it, and tell them I'm coming soon."

NOT LONG AFTER, I dreamed that Ellen and I were spending the night at Franco's house. It was enormous. Dark, maze-like hallways fed into distant wings. Staircases abounded, up and down, half of them dead-ending before they reached another floor. Franco plainly didn't want us in his home but I had somehow cadged an invitation. My own house, I had told him, was unsafe—a problem with the chimney. "Maybe someone sabotaged it," Franco said, unsmiling, as if he could think of a dozen reasons why someone would sabotage my chimney. As if he wouldn't mind doing it himself. He told us how to get to our bedroom but the directions were so confusing that I asked him to escort us. He did, begrudgingly, then left. I went to lower the curtains, which were rigged with an extraordinarily complicated set of pullcords. I accidentally ripped one curtain right down the middle. Then Dana came in. She said she was checking to make sure we had everything we needed, but she wouldn't meet my eye. I gathered she was angry about the torn curtain.

After getting settled in, I went downstairs to find Franco.

"He went out," Dana told me.

"Will he be back soon?" I asked.

"I doubt it," she said.

IT IS GOOD to have good friends. They save us from ourselves in ways that even a spouse cannot.

I had decided by now to move to Pittsburgh. Just for a year. Although as a teenager I hadn't been able to persuade my mother to move there, I was pretty sure Ellen would go for it. She liked adventure. She was a photographer who had lived and worked all around the world. In Israel she dodged SCUDs; in Chechnya she was arrested by Russian soldiers and thought she was going to be executed. She could handle Pittsburgh. And I, given a year in Franco's town, could surely crack his shell. We'd bump into each other at restaurants. (Especially since I knew his favorites.) He would realize that my intentions were benign. Dana and Ellen would also bump into each other, maybe at the Andy Warhol Museum. They'd chat; they'd make plans. Pretty soon the four of us would be having dinners together.

"Isn't it amazing to think," Franco would say, patting his belly and swirling his brandy after a fine meal of Ellen's sesame chicken, "that we didn't even know each other until a year ago?"

I mentioned my Pittsburgh plan to a friend of mine, a former sportswriter who had covered Franco long ago.

"Jesus Christ!" he said. "Do you want to freak him out entirely? He'll get a restraining order."

I next considered hiring a private investigator. Not a sleazy one, of course. I only wanted to put some flesh on my skeletal understanding of Franco. He was spread out before me like a galaxy of dots I couldn't connect. Was his business devotion for real? Was he actually out of town all the time? Was he truly a family man?

I mentioned the PI scenario to my friend Jonathan, a novelist who is married to a rabbi. "Ooh, that's a fascinating idea," he said. "And a really, really bad one."

One night, Ellen and I were having dinner with our friend Barry, a writer and rare-book dealer. Ellen and Barry's conversation turned, somehow, to Napoleon's penis. Specifically, to the story of its having been surreptitiously cut off and preserved in formaldehyde by the abbé who conducted Napoleon's last rites. A few years back, Ellen recalled, the penis was offered for auction at Christie's but didn't meet its reserve price.

I had never heard this story, any of it, and said so. "And why," I asked, "did the abbé cut off Napoleon's penis in the first place?"

"He had a thing for him," Barry said casually, "the way you have a thing for Franco."

I DID NOT MOVE to Pittsburgh; I did not hire a private investigator; I did not even think about cutting off anyone's penis.

I had been persuaded that my Franco ardor had become a bit exaggerated. I needed to dial it down; I needed to take a step back and wait for an opening rather than rip my way through him.

In the meantime, I decided to embark on a different sort of hero-hunt. Other people had heroes too. How, I wondered, had their stories unspooled? Surely there were lessons to be gleaned from them.

I tracked down Richard LaPoint, my boyhood friend and devout Miami Dolphins fan. He was living in northern California; I found him on the Internet. Although we went through high school together, my memories of Richard stopped when we were about fourteen. That's when he became a serious athlete and I got serious about escaping Duanesburg.

"I don't know if you remember our rivalry—" I began.

"Hell, yeah!" Richard said. "We still do have that rivalry. You and Franco, me and Larry Csonka. I always have been and always will be a Dolphins fan. And Csonka, he really was my hero."

"How'd you get started on Csonka?" I asked.

"I always had an infatuation with winners," he said. "The Dolphins went undefeated in 1972, and I admired how they were the only team in history to do that. And Csonka—I really respected a warrior. As a kid, I didn't understand that the offensive line blocked for him. I got the impression he could take on any opponent all by himself. The way he ran through people—it inspired me to believe that any goal in life, you can achieve it if you really want to. And he seemed like a genuinely nice person. That was important. I needed to have a class act, needed him to treat people with respect."

"It sounds like you really fed off of him," I said.

"When my parents broke up, I looked inside myself and said, Richard, you're pretty much on your own for now. I was eleven. Nothing against my parents, but when you have two people who can't get their act together, you realize you're going to have to do it for yourself. Sports gave me a disciplinary direction to keep myself on the straight and narrow, because if you smoked or drank you got kicked off the team. So I always looked at Larry Csonka's work ethic. I channeled my energies through him. He'd get beat up every week but he wouldn't complain, and he'd come right back the next week. I made my whole life like that."

I remembered Richard's father, a little too well. He drove us home from Little League games in the back of his pickup, and he always "forgot" to stop at the foot of my road, even when I reminded him beforehand. That meant walking home from the LaPoints' house, a mile through brambly, snaky woods as night fell. I didn't know what Mr. LaPoint's angle was, but he certainly persuaded me that adults liked nothing more about children than keeping them powerless.

"What about your dad," I said to Richard. "Did you admire him?"

He gave a gruff laugh. "If you asked if I *feared* him, I'd say yes. I remember constantly throwing a baseball with him in the driveway. There weren't a lot of positives—more like, 'This is what you're doing wrong.' Later on we didn't spend a lot of time. He was always working and I was always pitching. I got up to ninety miles per hour in my prime, was throwing a pretty good curveball. The Toronto Blue Jays scouted me. I started having elbow problems, though. But I really believe that sports and religion, going to church with you guys, really was a blessing from God."

"Going to church with *us*?"

"Yeah. I didn't have a lot of inner family direction, but your mom—she was really my lifesaver."

I hadn't remembered that Richard used to come to church with us. We were always stuffing one more person in the car on Sunday morning. My mother's zeal had embarrassed me. I assumed that Richard felt the same way about church as I did, but apparently he hadn't.

"With church, I had a safe haven," he said. "It was like, Okay, if I don't have the two human influences of my parents in my life, at least I can talk to God, and He's going to push me in a good direction. I still go to church every Sunday."

We spoke a while longer. Richard told me about his construction company: he had twelve employees and built eight-thousand-square-foot homes in Silicon Valley. He had a serious girlfriend and was leaning toward marriage, but having grown up inside a brutal divorce, he wanted to make sure.

If Richard's life had turned out lousy, his messy childhood would have provided all sorts of handy excuses. But it didn't. Besides, Richard wasn't one to use excuses. Some of that strength seemed to have come from Larry Csonka. Also from God. And maybe—this was the thought that made my throat lump up as we said good-bye—the strength came from my mother too.

I SOON TOOK TO asking everyone—friends, acquaintances, seatmates on long flights—their hero-worship histories. A few people responded with a dull stare. Usually, however, the question brought on a dreamy look: of intimacy, of craving, of a distant salve.

My unscientific findings hewed to the scientific data I read. Males tend toward hero-worship slightly more than females. It generally peaks in the late teens and fades by the mid-twenties. (My Franco relapse was, like a May snowstorm, rare but not unheard-of.) A child who has lost a parent, whether to death or divorce or too-long office hours, is almost certain to have found a hero.

But as with love and religious devotion, no two tales of hero-worship were identical.

Queen Elizabeth I, Abraham Lincoln, Andres Segovia, Gertrude Stein, Ralph Nader, Vaclav Havel, Yitzhak Rabin, Joe Pepitone: these were a few of the names I heard. (Joe Pepitone!) Also, mothers and fathers, benevolent uncles and splenetic grandmothers, camp counselors and rabbis. And, again and again, Muhammad Ali, from men and women, old and young, black and white, boxing fans and boxing illiterates.

Some heroes were obscure. One friend of mine, a man in his late forties who played in high-school rock bands, used to idolize James Jamerson, the in-house bassist for Motown Records. "In my family, we had this Catholic working-class way," he explained, "this not-calling-attention-to-yourself way. That was my father's thinking. That anytime you call attention to yourself, things turn out lousy. That most of the people who want to be stars are making fools of themselves. The main thing was to avoid shame, not to achieve greatness. So I wanted to be in a band, but also I wanted to stand in the corner. James Jamerson's whole thing was that it was okay to be the backup guy—to do a secondary thing but do it extremely well." (It should be noted that my friend, an extraordinary editor, holds the number two job at a major magazine and has no designs on number one.)

Some heroes were imaginary. Another friend, an American Jew whose parents split up when he was thirteen, fantasized that his mother would start dating an Israeli archaeologist—"someone who'd accept hardship without fleeing," he told me, "preferably a combat veteran, someone brainy but brawny too, maybe with an eyepatch."

Some heroes were simultaneously imaginary, familiar, and bizarre. A man I worked with at the *Times* had a recurring childhood dream wherein his father turned into Superman and plucked him from a witch's cauldron. The witch, he realized upon waking, was his mother.

I came across one woman, the friend of a friend, whose hero story was very much like my own. So much so, in fact, and with such a disappointing ending, that it should have set off alarm bells.

Her name was Julie Irwin. In 1978, when she was twelve, she became infatuated with the baseball pitcher Vida Blue. She was an upper-middle-class white girl from Silicon Valley; he was a black man from a poor family in Mansfield, Louisiana. Blue had just been traded to the San Francisco Giants, and his star was beginning to fade. Early in his career he was a marvel. When he was twenty-one, he threw a no-hitter;

the following season he won the Cy Young Award. He made the cover of *Time* and helped the Oakland A's win three World Series.

But Julie Irwin didn't know any of that. Before 1978, she wasn't much of a baseball fan. When she began going to games, it was Blue who immediately caught her eye. She thought him perfect. His athleticism was still as dazzling as his name. She sat in the stands and sketched him. When she and her friends snuck down to the railing of the bullpen, Blue jogged over to sign their programs. He asked if they were having a good time. Whenever the Giants were mounting a rally, Blue stood up and exhorted the crowd to cheer, in sections, like a bandleader.

"That was a bad time for sports," Irwin said. "Athletes weren't all that friendly, but he took time to talk to a bunch of kids, repeatedly. He just struck me as pretty great."

Her enchantment lasted the four years that Blue pitched for the Giants. Then he went on to the Kansas City Royals, and Irwin went on to Northwestern University. She read about Blue in the sports pages as he entered a thicket of salary disputes, poor play, and cocaine abuse. When he was arrested for drug possession, Irwin was both heartbroken and ashamed of her heartbreak.

For her senior writing project, Irwin charted the decline of F. Scott Fitzgerald, who once described a character as "one of those men who reach such an acute limited excellence at twenty-one that everything afterward savors of anticlimax." Irwin realized that this description applied to Fitzgerald himself—and to Vida Blue. "I saw all these parallels between Blue and Fitzgerald," she told me. "Great promise that was never fulfilled. And *I* had always been the sort of student who teachers yelled at for not living up to my potential. I had this fear that the worst thing in the world would be to achieve something early and never live up to it."

Irwin became a writer. And, because Fitzgerald was long dead, she went looking for Vida Blue. She wanted to see what had become of him; she wanted to know, as I'd wanted to know with Franco, how her memory of Blue measured up against the reality.

She found him back in northern California, earning a few dollars at

Orlando Cepeda's All-Star Baseball Clinic. They went to a restaurant to talk. Blue was genial, polite, and happy to speak with Irwin. He didn't have a steady job or a family, but he seemed content.

"I freaked him out a little bit," Irwin said.

"How so?" I asked.

"Well, have you met Franco?"

I told her I had.

"The roles of fan and writer are not very compatible," she said. "You're not supposed to be fawning, but then you meet your childhood hero and start spitting out all these statistics from fifteen or twenty years ago. It's hard not to scare them a little bit."

"I guess so," I said, maybe a bit defensively.

"Anyway . . ."

"Anyway," I said. "So, how did you like him?"

"I was sort of indifferent," she said. "He seemed like a nice-enough guy, but no one I would come home and rave about. The fact that he'd been great and now wasn't great but still managed to be a decent guy made me happy. I think pity is the most unfair emotion in the world. But I do remember wishing he had a higher level of self-awareness. A lot had gone on in his life, and either he didn't want to think about it or he didn't want to share it with someone. It's a little disappointing when you're reading all these things into a person's life and—well, they're not there."

13

A BRIEF HISTORY
OF HERO WORSHIP

⸻◦◦⟨∞⟩◦◦⸻

THE CONVERSATION WITH Julie Irwin made me wonder: just how much had I read into Franco's life? It also led me to a broader question, which soon became all-consuming: how had it happened that Julie Irwin and I, and a few million others, in a country and a century that produced generals and astronauts and pop stars, would cast our hero-worshiping gaze onto . . . a ballplayer?

I decided to put myself through a crash course in the history of hero worship. I wanted to step outside my Franco obsession to see where it had come from and where it might be going.

I found no lack of reading material. Throughout time, man has spilled the majority of his ink in service of one hero or another. The Bible and every other religious text is built around heroes, divine and otherwise. So too are Greek and Norse and Roman myth, autocracy, Shakespeare (who used as source material the Greek essayist Plutarch's hero tales), art, industrialism, even communism (whose hero was meant to be the common man) and democracy (whose hero is the individual, acting in sacred union with a secular text, the Constitution).

In 1841, Thomas Carlyle established the modern church of the hero—and himself as its high priest—by publishing *On Heroes, Hero-*

Worship, and the Heroic in History. "Society is founded on hero-worship," wrote Carlyle. "Hero-worship *is* . . . as it was always and everywhere, and cannot cease till man himself ceases."

Carlyle considered himself a historian and man of letters but was in fact a moralist. His words still ring hot and moist. To read *On Heroes* today is to be trapped nose-to-nose, spittle and all, with a Jerry Falwell of the Victorian age: preening, condescending, self-contradicting, often preposterous—and nearly always compelling.

Carlyle was a pious Scottish Presbyterian living in London, born to a hardworking family. The heroes he celebrated in his book were, perhaps not surprisingly, rather like him: God-fearing, excitable, a bit fanatical. Among them were the prophet Muhammad; the poet Dante Alighieri; the Puritan revolutionary Oliver Cromwell; and Martin Luther, the Catholic monk so disgusted with, as Carlyle put it, the "scene of false priests" in Rome that he resolved to overthrow "the Popery."

Like most moralists—and hero-worshipers—Carlyle made no effort at ecumenism. He found Catholicism irreparably corrupt. Despite his praise for Muhammad, he called the Koran "insupportable stupidity." He detested Jews and their "deadly terrible earnestness." (Carlyle's admiration for the Book of Job led him to write: "One feels, indeed, as if it were not Hebrew.")

He especially hated democracy. Carlyle believed that history was shaped by a select few Great Men, each anointed by God and sharing at least one trait: "I should say *sincerity,* a deep, great, genuine sincerity, is the first characteristic of all men heroic." A nation, Carlyle believed, should be led not by quibbling parliamentarians but by a single Great Man, a Cromwell or a Napoleon or a Frederick the Great. But the Skeptics of the eighteenth century, he complained, had devalued the Great Man. "Heroes have gone-out; Quacks have come-in," he wrote. Europe had become "an effete world; wherein Wonder, Greatness, Godhood could not now dwell—in one word, a godless world!"

I had naively assumed that hero worship stretched in one unbroken chain from the dawn of the gods until the dawn of my own life. Yet here in the middle of the nineteenth century was Thomas Carlyle, bemoaning "this sad state Hero-worship now lies in."

I felt for him. Reverence came naturally to Carlyle, like it had to me. He was enraged by his belief that the Skeptics—and the Catholics and the Jews and the democrats—had killed off reverence. (One senses that Archie Bunker would have been a great fan of Carlyle's.) That rage was what drove him to write *On Heroes*. To bellow, even if into the wilderness, that only a Great Man could save the world from vanity and sloth.

For a time, I sided with Carlyle. Who could argue against sincerity? Franco was relentlessly sincere. That was his most appealing trait. He laughed when he thought something funny, objected if he found it distasteful, asked questions if he didn't understand.

But Franco hadn't one-tenth the zeal that Carlyle required of his heroes. As I read on, trying to ignore Carlyle's anti-Semitism and numberless other hatreds, I felt exhausted. His fundamentalism wore me out. Carlyle's heroes weren't father figures so much as God figures, summoned by Carlyle as a weak boy summons the schoolyard bully: to mete out punishment on his enemies.

Reading on, I learned that Carlyle's Great Man theory was often ridiculed, even during his lifetime. Henry James Sr. wrote that Carlyle was "ready to glorify every historic vagabond." More worrisome than the crowning of dead kings, however, was the possibility that Carlyle's theory would be applied to the living. He insisted that hero-worship "is always an inspiration to the good if its objects are good." But who was to decide if an object was good or bad? What if the wrong Great Man was anointed?

Carlyle died in 1881. A half-century later the Nazi leadership, so stirred by his lionization of the Great Man, his hatred of the Jews, and his contempt for democracy, adopted him as a sort of patron saint. German scholars, in articles entitled "Carlyle and the Führer Idea" and "Carlyle and the Jews," treated him as a biblical prophet. One such scholar insisted that if Carlyle were still alive, he would be "the most energetic and the most enthusiastic champion of National Socialist Germany and of its leader." Hitler's own language in *Mein Kampf* was a pitch-perfect echo of Carlyle's: "The front steps of the Pantheon of history are not for sneak-thieves, but for heroes!" And it was widely known that Joseph Goebbels, Hitler's chief propagandist, considered Carlyle's six-volume biography of Frederick the Great among the best books ever written.

In fact, while bunkered in Berlin during the hopeless final days of April 1945, Goebbels read aloud to his Führer long passages of Carlyle's heroic Frederick biography.

Is there a Hell? I personally doubt it. But if so, I would expect to find Adolf Hitler there, perhaps with Goebbels still reading into his ear. And I would hope that Thomas Carlyle, for all his Christian piety and love of sincerity, is made to visit them at least a few days each month.

A FINAL WORD from Carlyle: "Hero-worship," he wrote, "heartfelt, prostrate admiration, submission, burning, boundless, for a noblest god-like Form of Man—is not that the germ of Christianity itself?"

Yes, I do believe it is. Christianity may be the purest form of hero-worship the world has yet encountered. Which is why, I realized as I finished up with Carlyle, I had been so eager as a child to throw myself down, burning and boundlessly, before Franco Harris. I had been raised with a taste for a messiah; I simply substituted a football player for the Son of God. Christianity was in my mother's milk.

But so too was Judaism. And Judaism, as I discovered, thinks differently about hero worship.

"Who is a hero?" asks the Talmud. The answer: "One who overcomes temptation." Not, that is, the Great Man who defeats armies, but the plain man who defeats his own flaws. As a plain man well acquainted with his own flaws, I found this concept inspiring; as a Jew, I wanted to learn more.

The historian and rabbi Arthur Hertzberg has described Judaism as "a call to the breaking of idols." Hertzberg, an iconoclast himself, was referring to a midrash, or rabbinic commentary, about Abraham. The midrash holds that Abraham, the first Jew, was the son of an idol-maker. Left behind one day to watch his father's shop, he grabbed an ax and smashed the idols. This was a revolutionary act on three fronts: Abraham was declaring war on polytheism; he was breaking with his father's beliefs; and he was proclaiming that no earthly object, human or otherwise, should be deified.

So much for idols and false gods. But what about heroes? "In Judaism, idolatry is the idea that anyone, or anything, is perfect," Hertzberg told me when I called him for further comment. "Now, that doesn't mean we Jews don't hero-worship. In *Pirkei Avot*, we are commanded to get dirty with the dust picked up by the feet of the great scholars. But we are also supposed to remember they are not perfect. If a Talmud Jew wrote the biography of Babe Ruth, he'd certainly include the drinking and the womanizing."

The heroes of the Torah are, like Babe Ruth, openly flawed. Abraham, afraid of Pharaoh's troops, passes off his wife Sarah as his sister and allows Pharaoh to take her into his bed. David exploits his office as king to sleep with Bathsheba and then send her husband to death in battle. Moses, the great leader and prophet, kills a man in anger; he routinely quarrels with God and occasionally disobeys Him; to his own people, Moses is a persistent scold.

Even God is hardly perfect. Beneath all that love and mercy, He is moody, quick to anger, vengeful, impatient, and vain. He becomes so frustrated with the Israelites that Moses must persuade *Him*, God, to not strike them down.

The removal of such blemishes seems to be a Christian impulse. In the New Testament, God has mellowed; the Jesus of the Gospels is, morally at least, flawless. In the official histories of Catholic saints, rare mention is made of madness or vice. (The satirist Ambrose Bierce once called a saint "a dead sinner, reviewed and edited.")

When I was a child, nearly all my Bible reading was New Testament. We occasionally dipped into the Torah (which we knew as the Old Testament), but we didn't treat it as a Bible on its own. The Old Testament was essentially a foundation to shore up the New Testament.

The great shock of reading Torah as an adult was seeing the humanity of its heroes. Not only were their flaws not buffed away; the flaws were central to their character—and, I now saw, central to the Jewish understanding of heroism.

Toward the end of the Torah, Moses so angers God—instead of ordering water to spurt forth from a rock, as God commanded, Moses strikes the rock with his rod—that he is forbidden to enter the Promised Land. Sadder yet, Moses dies alone, within sight of Israel. He is buried in Moab, an enemy kingdom. "And no one," says the Torah, "knows his burial place to this day."

But why? Why is Moses, the most beloved hero of Judaism, treated so shabbily, his very bones unmarked?

"So that his grave would never be turned into a shrine," Hertzberg told me. "So that Moses would never be deified." Moses may have been a hero, but the message was clear: a hero is not perfect, and a hero is not God.

When Ellen and I visited Italy, we toured a sixteenth-century synagogue in Venice. It was crammed into the top floors of a poor little building. Up near the ceiling, barely noticeable, hung a series of woodcuts depicting scenes from the Exodus. They were extremely humble; from where we stood they looked like children's drawings. Up close, they became even humbler. Because of the Jewish ban on idolatry, the pictures were entirely absent of one main ingredient: people. Plenty of sea and sky and manna but no Moses, no Israelites, not even any Egyptians. The next day, not half a mile away, we visited the Church of Madonna Dell'Orte, home parish of the sixteenth-century painter Jacopo Robusti Tintoretto. Above the altar, Tintoretto had painted his vision of Moses receiving the Ten Commandments. And what a Moses! He was strapping and bold, his bare chest rippling with muscles, arms thrust skyward in exultation. This was a Moses that a Jew would never have painted.

Even in the Haggadah, the Exodus text read aloud during the Passover Seder, Moses is barely mentioned. "The rabbis who compiled the Haggadah, in the third and fourth centuries, wanted to emphasize that God and God alone was the hero of the Exodus story," Hertzberg told me. "But there's one other thing. These rabbis were ever more aware of the competition and the pressure of the early Church, and they were very nervous about being seen as turning Moses into another Jesus."

It isn't that Judaism doesn't believe in a messiah. It does. But to most Jews, the messiah is less a person than an idea, a hope, a yearning—as I once heard a Jewish scholar put it—for the world to have a happy ending. The messiah isn't a hero from the past; it is the future itself.

Yes, that was what Franco represented to me as a child: the future itself.

And yet Thomas Carlyle seems to have been right in at least one regard. Even among Jews, hero worship is a human condition that "cannot cease till man himself ceases." Despite the prohibitions against idolatry, despite the Torah's insistence that God is God and man is man, Jewish history is pocked with false messiahs. Some of these self-proclaimed messiahs were madmen. Others were charlatans, leading their followers to death but arranging an escape for themselves. Almost always they appeared in the wake of a tragedy—which, given Jewish history, was not infrequently.

It stands to reason that the Holocaust, the greatest Jewish tragedy yet, would again provoke a hunger for a messiah. Among the Jews not killed by Adolf Hitler was a rabbi named Menachem Mendel Schneerson. Born in Russia in 1902, he was studying in Paris during the Nazi occupation. He barely escaped, arriving in New York in 1941. A wise, generous, and charismatic teacher known simply as the Rebbe, he became leader of the Lubavitcher sect of Hasidic Jews.

The Rebbe did not dwell on the horror of the Holocaust. From the Crown Heights neighborhood of Brooklyn—the same streets where my mother grew up—he instead masterminded a gleaming future. He built schools, synagogues, charities; he sent emissaries around the globe to revive dormant Jewish communities. The Lubavitchers flourished, eventually numbering two hundred thousand worldwide. They treated the Rebbe like a king. Politicians and movie stars sought out his blessing. And a small but noisy minority of his followers turned a whisper into a roar: the Rebbe, they hinted, was *Moshiach*, the Messiah.

Several years ago, on assignment in Russia, I visited a Lubavitcher summer camp outside of Moscow. Until the fall of the Soviet Union, most of these children had not known they were Jewish, their parents having hidden this potentially dangerous fact. Now the parents clamored to send them to a Jewish camp: free food, plenty of sunshine, a few prayers. Maybe even a ticket to America. I watched a flock of boys finish a game of football and march into the cafeteria for lunch. They were no older than ten.

"One-two-three-four, we want Color War!" They chanted in unison, in English, sunburned and knickered, banging plastic cups on the table.

And then, also in English, "We want *Moshiach* now! Bring us *Moshiach* now!"

"Who is *Moshiach*?" I asked one boy.

He had blond hair, dazzling green eyes. He looked at me as if I were the dumbest person on earth.

"The Rebbe," he said.

The Rebbe died in 1994. It is impossible to say how many of his followers believed he was *Moshiach*. Today some of them do not even believe he is dead. *"Der Rebbe firt der velt"* is a common saying in Crown Heights—"the Rebbe runs the world." Unlike Moses, his burial site is well known: Old Montefiore Cemetery in Queens. Thousands visit his grave; hundreds send fax or e-mail prayers every day. Shortly after his death, a billboard was erected outside the cemetery. Beside a huge picture of the Rebbe, the message read, "Let's Welcome Moshiach with Acts of Goodness and Kindness!"

Thomas Carlyle, for all his malice toward the Jews, would have been impressed with such zealous adulation. And I, for all my devotion to Judaism, knew that this wasn't the kind of hero-worship that I was interested in. Not anymore.

I decided to go looking for other quintessentially Jewish heroes. I was charmed to discover that the boldest Jewish hero of modern times wasn't a religious figure at all. He wasn't even flesh and blood. He was the comic-book superhero.

Superman, Batman, the Green Lantern, Spider-Man, Captain America—all of them, it turns out, were Jewish creations. As Alan Oirich, a scholar of the field, told me, "The list of early comic-book pioneers reads like a synagogue mailing list." Binder and Blum, Fine and Klein,

Gillman and Meskin, Schuster and Siegel. Many took Anglicized by-lines, the same sort of country-club names they gave their superhero characters (Clark Kent, Bruce Wayne, Alan Scott). But if you knew where to look, Oirich explained, their Hebrew-school roots showed. The Guardian of the Universe, for instance, a wizened sage in the Green Lantern books, was drawn on the likeness of David Ben-Gurion.

Superman, the first and greatest of the superheroes, was also the most Jewish. He was born into the House of El ("House of God" in Hebrew) on the planet Krypton, which was run by a male council of elders much like the Sanhedrin of ancient Israel. When Krypton was destroyed, Superman mourned its loss much like the Jews mourned the loss of Jerusalem, vowing to keep alive its rituals and language. In time, he learned that a small remnant of Krypton had survived, called Kandor ("here is the generation" in Hebrew). Superman was famous for his red boots, but they were a last-minute change; originally he wore lace-up sandals modeled after Samson's.

Superman was invented by Jerry Siegel and Joe Schuster, a pair of high-school students in Cleveland. The only night they couldn't work on him was Thursday—the breadboard they used for drawing belonged to Joe's mother, and she needed it to bake her Sabbath challah.

The original Superman, like most comic-book characters of the time, was a villain. But as the Depression deepened and Hitler rose, trumpeting himself as the incarnation of the Nietzschean superman, Siegel and Schuster changed their plan. They came up with a new, heroic Superman, the Man of Steel, devoted to fighting evil. He was introduced in June 1938 with a tale familiar to any reader of Exodus: like baby Moses set astream by his mother to escape Pharaoh's infanticide, baby Superman was placed in a rocket ship by his father as Krypton was about to explode.

During World War II, Superman and his peers regularly tangled with Hitler, Mussolini, and Hirohito. They always won. (At American PXs, comic books outsold by a ten-to-one margin *Reader's Digest, Saturday Evening Post,* and *Life* combined, suggesting that the superheroes may have inspired the real-life defenders of liberty.) But they were hardly flawless. Superman was desperately lonely (and imperiled by

Kryptonite). Spider-Man had no luck whatsoever with girls. Batman seemed clinically depressed, and with good reason. As an eight-year-old, he had witnessed the murder of his own parents—a murder that Alan Oirich likens to the Nazis' early attacks on German Jews. The superheroes especially chafed under the burden of carrying a secret identity. Poor Clark Kent: he lusted after Lois Lane, who lusted after Superman, who *was* Clark Kent but couldn't tell Lois.

Their creators also chafed under a dual identity. In reality they were pale, scrawny immigrants' kids whose cousins back in Europe were on the run from Hitler. On the page, they became muscular do-gooders who had Hitler on the run. It was both a military and an assimilationist fantasy. But it was also a magical, audacious act of hero-worship: on the page, these immigrants' kids became their own heroes. It is worth remembering that Superman pretended to be Clark Kent, not vice versa. The Man of Steel was real; the nebbish was the disguise. Siegel and Schuster were telling the world that inside every bespectacled, ninety-eight-pound Jewish kid lay a Samson. All you had to do was find a cape.

I never read comic books as a kid. But, I now saw, I shared the impulse that drove their creators. My cape was a Franco Harris jersey. I can still feel it on my skin. Scratchy rayon, too tight around the shoulders, riding up on the wrists. After the Steelers won their first Super Bowl, I wore it to school every day for a month. The jersey was my way of telling the world that beneath this fragile and fatherless boy lay a man, a winner, strong and true. My mother would have preferred that I wear a crucifix. But a child, more than anyone, knows what he truly believes. When you are a child, belief is your sole freedom. You are not free to choose your family, your religion, your school. A timetable is dictated to you. On schedule, you wake up, eat breakfast, run for the bus, avoid the bullies, pay attention, read aloud, eat lunch, play kickball, drink milk, pay more attention, on and on. At home it's more of the same but also you pray and pray and pray, and then you are sent to bed. Your imagination is the only corner of your world that adults do not control. And so you summon into it the one person you most need, the person you must become, the person you know you truly are—even if your mother cannot see it.

WHILE THE SUPERHERO was a Jewish creation, he was, most significantly, an American creation. Just as Franco and I, the offspring of immigrants and slaves, were also American creations. And America, if I was to believe the historian Dixon Wecter, writing in *The Hero in America*, was "the premier nation of hero-worshipers."

American hero worship, however, would not be what Thomas Carlyle had in mind. This was a country born of democracy, shorn of kings. A democracy might cherish greatness but it would never, as E. M. Forster wrote in *Two Cheers for Democracy*, "produce that unmanageable type of citizen known as the Great Man."

In its infancy, the United States quite naturally worshiped its father figures: George Washington, Thomas Jefferson, Benjamin Franklin. This was the Silver Age of our patriotism, as Wecter called it, when one "could hardly see the hero for the incense."

By the Civil War, such thick sentiment had already been replaced by grim reality. The assassination of Abraham Lincoln was the sort of apocalyptic event that sent people scurrying for a messiah. Lincoln himself became the prime candidate. To those who recalled the Old Testament's claim that a messiah would usher peace into the world—a feat that even Jesus did not accomplish—Lincoln seemed positively messianic. He was shot just five days after Lee's surrender at Appomattox, and on Good Friday no less. He sacrificed his life for peace. His recent urging toward reconciliation—"with malice toward none, with charity for all"—sounded as if it might have come from the mouth of Jesus himself.

In death, Lincoln became even greater than in life. His biography, especially the log-cabin birth and dying mother, leant itself to mythmaking. How could America, a motherless nation, fail to idolize a man who said, "All that I am, or hope to be, I owe to my angel mother"?

At least Lincoln may have said that. The construction of his myth, I learned, was never hindered by the truth. The story about young shopkeeper Lincoln walking several miles to return the pennies he overcharged a customer? Sheer invention. His deep religiosity and his legendary charm over the opposite sex? Also fictional. "A small book might be made," wrote Dixon Wecter, "of Lincoln sayings that the man himself never uttered." Long after Lincoln's death, a University of Wisconsin freshman wrote this memorable line: "Abraham Lincoln was born in a log cabin which he built with his own hands."

This mythic man, Honest Abe, appealed to a particularly American belief: that it was possible to rise from humble beginnings to greatness. In *The Hero in America*, Dixon Wecter argued that, by the turn of the twentieth century, the truest American hero was Success. Get-rich-quick pamphlets had become best-sellers. It was the millionaire playboy and the bootlegger who caught the eye—not in the old-fashioned, inspirational sense of a hero but in a new, aspirational sense. People didn't want so much to be like their heroes as to have what they had. Wecter called this time "the Age of the Great Debunking." Old truths had lost their power; heroes had lost their sheen. Even World War I hardly intruded. It was the first war after which America did not send a general to the White House. Patriotism seemed a limp and long-ago sentiment. A newly sophisticated and cynical America considered itself, as Robert Penn Warren wrote, "Just Another Sucker for having been conned into a crusade to Make the World Safe for Democracy."

And then came Charles Augustus Lindbergh. When he flew an airplane nonstop across the Atlantic Ocean in the spring of 1927, Lindbergh swept away the miasma that had settled over America. In truth, *he* was the first superhero. Lindbergh's flight met every heroic criterion and then some. It was a life-risking feat of strength and stamina, patriotic but also universalist, performed in solitude, an imaginative foray into uncharted territory by a man who, afterward, professed he couldn't see what all the fuss was about.

According to A. Scott Berg's biography, some thirty million people—one-quarter of the population—came out to salute Lindbergh on his victory tour of America. In print he was called "the new Christ." Another journalist wrote: "Five centuries have been required to make a saint of Joan of Arc but in two years Colonel Charles A. Lindbergh has become a demigod."

But those claims turned out to have been wrong. Lindbergh was indeed the start of something new, but it wasn't a religion. It was bigger than that.

Hero worship—as I, the former Franco Dubner, can freely attest—certainly has a religious component. But Charles Lindbergh's fame ripened into a far noisier and more secular version of hero worship: celebrity.

Lindbergh's flight coincided with an explosion of new technologies. By 1927, a mass media had come into being. Between the radio, telephone, radiograph, and most recently the sync-sound motion picture, Charles Lindbergh could be seen and heard, instantly, around the world. This was an intoxicating development. Lindbergh's flight was not simply a fantastic event to be recorded, duly and dully, for posterity. It was instead the popping of a cork, the mere beginning of a party that would last for years. Lindbergh would become, in Berg's words, "the most celebrated living person ever to walk the earth." That would seem to include even Jesus, who had the bad fortune of arriving twenty centuries early.

Lindbergh's celebrity ushered in an Age of Artifice. He would see his image shaped, reshaped, distorted, and ultimately tarnished. He learned, as would every celebrity to follow, that his public image was not necessarily a product of reality. This was the miracle that mass media made possible: the image *became* the reality.

A great many people began using this miracle to their advantage, especially advertisers, entertainers, preachers, and politicians. In 1939, *The Wizard of Oz* seemed to suggest that even Great Men, like the ones currently plotting to carve up Europe, were nothing but small men with very large microphones. The enduring American image of World War II? The flag-raising atop Iwo Jima—which, while not a staged photo, was a photo opportunity, the reprise of a flag-raising that had taken place earlier in the day.

It did not take a cynic to believe that World War II had been fought not in honor of Great Men but *because* of them. Hitler and Mussolini and Stalin were, after all, heroes in at least their own minds. In the war's wake, many Americans decided that heroes were for suckers. Celebrities—movie stars and pop singers, television cowboys and even ballplayers—were much safer. Joe DiMaggio and Marilyn Monroe couldn't start a war, quite, even when married to each other.

As hero worship yielded to celebrity, the hero-worshiper was shoved aside by the fan. Fans followed the celebrities' doings as if they mattered while taking comfort in the knowledge that they didn't. It was fantasy hero worship. Better to follow celebrities than to put faith in someone who could truly make trouble. Politicians were the worst: they were fakes who pretended to be real. Movie stars at least didn't pretend they weren't fake, and ballplayers were obviously real.

Weren't they?

When I was a child, I believed every baseball story I heard. Unlike the history of Christianity, the history of baseball had been ruthlessly recorded in newspapers. As the son of a newspaperman, I could not have asked for more reliable sourcing.

But I had been duped. My crash-course reading had now brought me to a book called *The Sports Immortals: Deifying the American Athlete*, by Peter Williams. It made clear that the official history of baseball is shot through with lies. Abner Doubleday, "the father of baseball," probably never even played the game and certainly didn't invent it. (He was a Civil War hero who, years after his death, was declared baseball's founder by a blue-ribbon panel eager to give the sport a classy pedigree.) When the Chicago White Sox, led by Shoeless Joe Jackson, were said to have conspired with gamblers to throw the 1919 World Series, a little boy stood on the courthouse steps and cried out, "Say it ain't so, Joe!" It's just what I would have done. But the boy, I now learned, was a sportswriter's fabrication. Sportswriters apparently fabricated at will. Babe Ruth was credited with more bogus witticisms than anyone since Abraham Lincoln. Joe DiMaggio's famous bedside promise to a sick boy was marred by just one fact: the boy was already dead by the time DiMaggio reportedly made the promise. Even Red Smith, the best and most levelheaded sportswriter of his time, was warned by his editor to "stop Godding up those ball players."

It set me to wondering about all those Franco articles I read as a boy. They weren't fabrications, were they? He really did let neighborhood kids follow him home on their bikes and then fix them hamburgers . . . didn't he?

But even if he hadn't, I knew that what I saw on the field was real. That was the difference between a ballplayer and everyone else. My mother, waging her war against abortion, was always telling me how politicians said one thing behind closed doors and another in public. Movie stars and pop singers too: even I could tell they were pure artifice.

How was a boy to counter such artifice?

My antidote arrived a few hours later, in our living room at home. Kneeling before the television, my body humped over my father's hassock, the fake-leather brown hassock I had to beg my mother not to throw away when he died, I would watch Franco and know that every play was 100 percent real. The game was fierce and fast and live. There was no closed door or Wizard's microphone to hide behind. The winner won and the loser lost. In order to try to win, you had to be willing to lose, in public; that risk was what made it most real. Best of all, the game had no script. It happened the way my own small life was happening—in bursts and lulls, things seen and unseen, often a parade of unremarkable transactions but then, out of nowhere, *release:* Franco catches a three-yard swing pass and, after a head-fake toward the sideline, cuts back inside, hits full gait, and then freezes, up on his toes, leading a pair of defenders to comically maul each other instead of him, then continues, stiff-arming the last pursuer, and suddenly he is in the end zone, teammates leaping onto his shoulders. I leap about with them. I pound the hassock as if I too am pounding Franco's shoulder pads. It sends up little clouds of dust. And he just trots back to the sideline, a glimmer of a grin behind the face mask. Nothing but a little swing pass. Franco wasn't even the intended receiver. It was never meant to be a grand gesture. But he turned it into one, and I was his witness.

If a three-yard swing pass, an afterthought, thrown in desperation, could bloom into a sixty-yard touchdown play, why couldn't a fatherless boy in Duanesburg, New York, turn himself into a clever bird and fly out of the grasp of everything that bound him—his church and his mother and even his father's hassock, which leaked stuffing through its dung-brown vinyl covering but which he clung to as if it were a life raft?

MY CRASH COURSE in hero worship had by now delivered me into the time of my own childhood. Robert Penn Warren, writing in 1972, pointed out that "without the context of the communal soul, there can be no true hero."

So that is what happened. By the time I was born, our communal soul had been shattered. I could not have articulated this as a boy, but anyone alive during that time certainly felt it. I thought back to Julie Irwin and her Vida Blue obsession.

We were about the same age, Julie Irwin and I. We were born into the shadow of John F. Kennedy's assassination. We were young children during the late 1960s, the Great Falling-Apart, those sudden few years during which every institution was hauled under a bright light and pronounced suspect. Government: good or bad? Religion: good or bad? Parents: good or bad? Our tender brains struggled to compute; we were not equipped to untangle such mysteries. Even within my family's rural Catholic cocoon, the outside world pressed in. The Russians were scary; Watergate was confusing; Vietnam was both. No one could glue together those 1960s and 1970s. Martin Luther King Jr. and Bobby Kennedy tried, but even their martyr's deaths couldn't close the deal. We were each of us left to seize our own hero—or, just as likely, to choose none at all.

We grew up with a mordant chant droning through the air: *There are no heroes anymore! There are no heroes anymore!* It was both lamentation and statement of fact. The customary heroes, it seemed, had expired. We knew dimly of a past that was different. We knew that our parents spoke of FDR as no one spoke now of Nixon. We knew that mothers, on their knees, had thanked God nightly for Jonas Salk. We knew that Lindbergh was a prince of invention and daring and not, like the astronauts, a pawn in a desperate space race. We knew that there was such a thing as a Good War, in which plain men performed extraordinary feats, and that Vietnam was not such a war.

But just because you are told not to hero-worship does not mean that you won't. You may as well be told to not fall in love. If you are prone to it, hero worship is a rite of passage, as right as rain. And so Julie Irwin and I latched on to the last hero standing: the ballplayer. He had not yet been sullied; he too was a prince of daring, a plain man performing extraordinary feats. We projected onto him all the traits that, a few generations earlier, we might have projected onto a president or an inventor or a revolutionary.

In hindsight it seems obvious: a ballplayer was the only hero a boy in my position could have conjured. Television had made it so. He came to me each week, late on the Sabbath, a seductive flicker of speed and power and *alchemy*, turning nothingness into something. He was real but, unlike my mother, distant (and that distance was a virtue). Unlike my teachers and priests and other adults, he was not interested in deceiving me or holding me powerless. Unlike God, he could not steal any more members of my family. He did good, honest deeds, in public, and refused to gloat about them. He was not afraid to show how badly he wanted to win.

That will to win was the thing that always captivated me.

People who watch sports are often criticized by those who don't. "You shouldn't be watching!" my mother hollered out on Sunday afternoons. "You should be outside, playing!"

This strikes me as unfair. Museum-goers are rarely criticized for not painting portraits, nor philharmonic audiences for not playing the cello. There *was* something to be learned from watching a football game. The will to win—to escape, to beat back the powerlessness of childhood— was the will to survive, and I learned that not by going to church or by studying history but, for better or worse, by watching Franco Harris play football.

14

I AM NOT A STALKER

———•··◦∞◦··•———

JUST BEFORE Ellen and I left for Italy, I called Franco.
I did not tell him that I intended to visit Pietrasanta, his
mother's birthplace. (It would turn out to be a drowsy, inhospitable
town, best known as the source of Michelangelo's marble; still, as a pil-
grim strolling meaningful streets, I was satisfied.) Or the chapel behind
the Tower of Pisa where his parents were married. (I grew misty there,
thinking of his GI father and nineteen-year-old mother, as if visiting the
site of my own parents' wedding.)

What I did say was that I'd be gone for a few weeks and that I sure
would like to visit him when I returned.

"Okay," he said. Just like that. And we set the date, June 6.

Finally, I thought, *I have won him over.* Or worn him down.

We almost never made it back from Italy. By the end of our stay, Ellen
was seven months pregnant and rather protrusive; the Alitalia agents in
Rome didn't want to let her board the plane. She essentially had to
promise to not give birth in flight. We touched down in New York, still
infanticipating, on the last Friday in May 2000.

A few days later, I made the seven-hour drive to Pittsburgh. It had
been just over a year since my first visit. I approached from the east,
newly seeded fields giving way to steep budding hills. The sun was full,

the sky pristine. Pittsburgh is no longer a dirty city—the failed blue-collar industries have been replaced by successful white- and pink-collar ones, especially medical technologies—but that news has traveled slowly. A group of Russian pollution experts recently visited Pittsburgh expecting to find its skies as inky as their own. "You are known internationally for pollution," one of them told the *Post-Gazette*. "But we are pleasantly disappointed."

I chose to drive rather than fly because impending fatherhood had frightened me into thrift. I also wanted my own car in Pittsburgh, for I planned on exploring. Just as Italy had given me a taste of Franco's mother's life, and as an earlier trip to Poland had given me a taste of my long-dead grandparents' life, I believed that Pittsburgh might yield some wisdom about Franco. To that end, I was arriving several days before our appointment. And if things went well—if he warmed to me the way I knew he would—I hoped to stay on an extra week or two.

I checked into a Wyndham Garden hotel in Oakland, one of the oldest parts of town, its avenues packed with newsstands and shoe stores and delis. Oakland was a neighborhood thick with ghosts. Franco had lived nearby when he was a rookie. (I hoped to have him show me his old apartment, to help describe that glorious first year.) Andy Warhol grew up poor and sickly in Oakland, clipping Marilyn Monroe pictures. Jonas Salk discovered the polio vaccine here, at the University of Pittsburgh. By now the university had sprawled its way across the neighborhood. The law school stood on the former site of Forbes Field, which the old, bad, pre-Franco Steelers had shared with the Pirates. When Forbes Field was torn down, a remnant of its outfield wall was left standing to commemorate Bill Mazeroski's bottom-of-the-ninth home run that won the 1960 World Series. Prior to the Immaculate Reception, the Home Run was Pittsburgh's supreme mythical moment. Even now hundreds of fans gather at the site every October 13 to listen to a tape of the broadcast, which always ends the same perfect way.

On my first night in Oakland, I summoned a few ghosts of my own. Over room-service pasta, I watched a videotape I'd brought from home, the 1975 Super Bowl. It too ended the same perfect way, with Franco

leading the Steelers to victory and receiving the Most Valuable Player
Award.

I spent my first few days just kicking around town. Pittsburgh, I discovered, was a mecca of hero worship. You couldn't walk a block without
seeing the Steelers' logo—on coffee mugs, on spare-tire covers, on babies' bonnets. In the waiting room of a storefront dental clinic, I
counted seven of the eleven patrons wearing a Steelers garment.

But the hero-worshiping urge went well beyond sports. I visited
Saint Anthony's Chapel, a nineteenth-century hilltop church that
houses more than 4,200 relics. The bone chips of a great many saints lie
there in jeweled reliquaries, including Saint John the Baptist and Saint
Stephen, my namesake martyr. The collection, said to be the largest
outside of the Vatican, was assembled by a wealthy, saint-struck German priest. His own father, I noted, died when he was ten years old.

I toured the Carnegie Museums, where one great hall contains nothing but plaster copies of Greek and Roman sculptures, from gods to
discus-throwers. Andrew Carnegie, like his countryman Thomas Carlyle, was an unabashed hero-worshiper. "The false heroes of barbarous
man," he once wrote, "are those who can only boast of the destruction of
their fellows. The true heroes of civilization are those alone who save or
greatly serve them." In 1904, he established the Carnegie Hero Fund
Commission, which still exists, giving cash awards to civilians who risk
their lives to save others.

I learned that Pittsburgh even had its own mythic folk hero, a Paul
Bunyan of the steel mills named Joe Magarac. As the story goes, Joe was
eight feet tall, made of steel himself, and he could shape a hot beam with
his bare hands. He went on to make more steel than any hundred men
who ever lived. Like many a Pittsburgh steeler, Joe was an immigrant
eager to prove his American patriotism. His mill got a huge order for
steel beams, which needed to be flawless, for they would be used in an
important new government building in Washington, D.C. That's when
Joe Magarac, man of steel, flung himself into a cauldron of molten ore. It
was a sacrifice as selfless as Christ's: in death, Joe's flesh was turned into
the most perfect steel beam ever.

I visited a tiny museum devoted to Stephen Foster, composer of "Oh,

Susannah!" and "Camptown Races." A woman of uncertain age, a bliz-
zard of kerchiefs and cardigan, was straightening some brochures.

"From otta tahn?" she asked.

"Pardon me?"

"You from otta tahn?"

"One more time?"

"ARE . . . YOU . . . FROM . . . OTTA . . . TAHN?" she said, as if to a
deaf child.

"Yes." I am from out of town. In the Pittsburgh dialect, vowels perform amazing tricks of self-expansion, and consonants bend down before them. "I didn't know Stephen Foster was from Pittsburgh," I said.

"Ya know Gene Kelly's from here too, yah?"

"No, I didn't."

"And William Powell."

"Really? The Thin Man?"

"That's right, the Thin Man! That's right! There was a lotta great
people come from Pittsburgh."

She turned back to her brochures. Her happy Pittsburgh chauvinism
reminded me of my mother's feelings for Brooklyn. Although she made
exactly one appearance in Brooklyn after moving upstate—and that
upon her mother's death—she never stopped claiming it. "The whole
world's from Brooklyn," my mother liked to say, "not just me." Then
she'd name names she thought would interest me: Jackie Gleason,
George Gershwin . . . Vince Lombardi!

Leaving the museum, I stopped at a library to hunt for famous Pitts-
burghers. The museum lady was right: there was a lotta great people
come from Pittsburgh and its environs. I already knew about the football players. It's been said that western Pennsylvania has sent more men
to the NFL than any other part of the country. The quarterback output
alone is remarkable: George Blanda, Johnny Unitas, Joe Namath, Joe
Montana, Dan Marino, Jim Kelly. The list of musicians (beyond Stephen
Foster and Earl "Fatha" Hines, of course) was just as impressive: Billy
Eckstine, Lena Horne, Billy Strayhorn, Errol Garner, Oscar Levant,
Stanley Turrentine, Ray Brown, Art Blakey, Henry Mancini, Bobby
Vinton, Perry Como, Byron Janis, and, most recently, Christina Agui-

lera. Dancers too: Gene Kelly, Martha Graham, and Paul Taylor. There was the famous battery of barons: Carnegie, Frick, and Mellon. Also, George Romero and George Benson and George Westinghouse and George S. Kaufman and General George C. Marshall. And Jimmy Stewart, a favorite of my mother's. ("Why can't everyone behave like him?" she once said.) David O. Selznick was born in Pittsburgh but didn't stay long. Ditto Mary Cassatt and Gertrude Stein, both of whom fled for France. There were plenty of writers: Rachel Carson, Willa Cather, August Wilson, David McCullough, Annie Dillard, John Edgar Wideman. And anchoring the neighborhood for as long as anyone could recall, Mr. (Fred) Rogers.

For a time, Franco Harris was as big as any of them. I was reminded of this the following day over lunch with Myron Cope. Aside from naming the Immaculate Reception, Cope had, according to legend, midwifed a meeting between Franco and a certain American icon. I wanted to know if the legend were true. Cope agreed to meet me at a restaurant near Three Rivers Stadium and tell the story.

As we headed for a table, a pretty blond woman, late forties, cut us off. "Mr. Cope," she said, "I just want to say that you *made* Pittsburgh."

"Thank you, dear," he said, and blushed. Cope was in his early seventies and barely five feet tall. But having broadcast Steelers football for thirty years, he was a star, an impish totem of the city's most beloved institution.

We ordered lunch. Cope lit a cigarette and, over a cocktail, a fish sandwich, and several more cigarettes, proceeded to tell a story that even I had the good sense to not interrupt:

"Franco very rapidly became a folk hero, you see?" he began. "In his rookie year, even before the Immaculate Reception, everybody wanted a piece of him. He was the final ingredient that made the Steelers start winning, and with all the steel jobs going down the toilet, the winning was *huge*. Plus he was so damn good-looking and everything. He had all kinds of national publicity, and when Franco's Italian Army, his fan club, took off, it was all over the wire services.

"Now, the Steelers were going out to play their final regular-season game against San Diego, and if they won, they'd clinch the first division title in their forty-year history. Chuck Noll decided to take them to Palm Springs for a week of practice to get them acclimated to the warm weather.

"So the Italian Army—that is, Tony Stagno, the five-star general, and Al Vento, the four-star general—they came to me and said, 'Cope, we got a mission for you.' I said, 'What's that?' They said, 'Well, Frank Sinatra'—who at that time had been in retirement for a year or two, in total seclusion—they said, 'Well, Frank Sinatra, as you may know, lives in Palm Springs, and we'd like you to find Sinatra, bring him out to practice, and induct him into the Army.' I was a one-star general myself, see.

"Well, on Wednesday night out in Palm Springs, we're sitting in a nice restaurant, out on Frank Sinatra Drive if I'm not mistaken, called Lord Fletcher's. There's about twelve guys at our table—reporters, broadcasters, Steelers front-office people. Buff Boston, the Steelers' traveling secretary, he says to me, 'How's your Sinatra search going?' I said, 'It's going nowhere, I'm quitting it, because I came out here expecting to have a good time, and all I'm doing is hunting around for leads on Sinatra.'

"So Buff was facing the front door and he says, 'Well, don't give up now because here comes your man.' There's Sinatra. He's in the company of Leo Durocher, the baseball manager, Ken Venturi, the great golfer, and a tall, good-looking brunette. They're ushered to a table clear on the other side of the restaurant. Everybody at my table's yelling at me, 'Here's your chance, Cope, here's your chance!' I said, 'Settle down!' I got a cocktail napkin, wrote a note on it: 'Dear Mr. Sinatra, we're a bunch of newspaper, broadcast, and Steeler guys. You've probably heard of Franco's Italian Army. I would like to invite you to the Steelers' practice tomorrow to be inducted.' I signed my name, then I wrote, 'P.S.: Franco's also from Hoboken.' Which was a damn lie—he's from Mount Holly, New Jersey. But I figured, What the hell, it's a shot.

"So I gave the curly finger to Lord Fletcher, who comes to the table, and I said, 'Would you mind delivering this note to Mr. Sinatra? If you think it's an intrusion, never mind.' He said, 'Nah, he'll get a kick out of it.'

"So he takes it over, and the guys at my table are saying, 'He's getting the note! He's reading the note! He's coming over!'

"So here comes Sinatra, trailed by his two flunkies, Durocher and Venturi. He picks up a chair from an empty table and puts it down right beside me. It was always rumored, you see, that Sinatra was a huge football bettor, ten grand a day. And that week the big story from the Steelers' practice site was that Terry Bradshaw's baby finger had been dislocated. But earlier in the week I'd gone to Chuck Noll and said, 'Listen, level with me, how's the quarterback's finger? I won't use it on the air, but I want to know.' So Noll says, 'He's throwing the football better than he ever has in his career.'

"So Sinatra, the first words out of his mouth were, 'How's the quarterback's finger?' I said to myself, It's true, he *does* bet. I told him, 'The quarterback's finger is fine, Mr. Sinatra, don't worry about it at all. Now, how about coming to practice tomorrow to join Franco's Army?' And he said, 'Sure, I'll do it.'

"So I called Tony Stagno back in Pittsburgh so he and Al Vento can hop on a plane and do the induction ceremony. It's after midnight there. Tony's asleep—he's a baker, gets up early. I tell him what's going on with Sinatra. He says he can't come. I say, 'Why not?' This was shortly before Christmas. He says, 'I'm behind on my Christmas cookies. I've got to tend to business.'

"Now, unbeknownst to me, after we hang up, Tony's wife tells him, '*Sinatra!* You're going to California!' See, the Christmas story was a phony. The fact was, Tony had never flown on an airplane in his life and he was scared stiff.

"Anyway, after dinner we all celebrated. Hell, *Frank Sinatra was going to be at practice!* The next morning, outside the hotel, Noll comes up to me and says, 'What's this I hear about you planning a distraction at my practice today?' I say, 'Listen, you're only two years younger than me, which means you're just as big a Sinatra fan as I am, and don't tell me different. Besides which,' I say, 'I've got the worst hangover in my life, so don't hassle me.'

"So practice gets under way. No sign of Sinatra. An hour goes by, still no sign. All the newspaper guys are walking by me saying, 'Cope's a loser again.' It sure looked that way. Meanwhile, about two hundred photographers had showed up. See, nobody had a new picture of this guy in two years.

"Now, Buff Boston is on a pay phone talking with Joe Gordon, the Steelers' publicity guy, who's up in San Diego advancing the game. Gordon asks Buff, 'Did Sinatra show?' And Buff says, 'Sinatra's a no-show and Cope's a loser again.'

"And with that, Buff feels a hand on his shoulder. He turns around and it's Sinatra. He says, 'When Sinatra says he'll show, he shows.'

"So Buff yells, 'He's here!' It turned out he'd been there the whole time, wearing an orange sweater and a white porkpie hat, sitting up in the bleachers by himself just watching practice.

"So all hell breaks loose. Sinatra comes out to the sideline. The photographers are racing to set up. And guess what—here comes Tony Stagno and Al Vento trotting across the field! They got on the plane after all. The timing was perfect. They arrive just as Sinatra reveals himself. See, that rookie year of Franco's, everything surrounding him was just magical. They're carrying baskets of prosciutto and cheese and bottles of dago red. Because, see, the ceremony involves all that, and much kissing of both cheeks.

"So I said, 'Hold everything, boys! Franco's got to be a part of this.' Without thinking, I raced out into the middle of practice. I stopped and said, 'Jesus Christ, what the hell am I doing, racing out into the middle of Chuck Noll's practice?' Anyway, I say 'Franco, get over here, the *man's* here.'

"Now, Franco was a very humble rookie. He said, 'Myron, I can't do that, I'm practicing.' I say, 'Hell, get over here, the *man's* here. *Sinatra!*' He says, 'I can't do that, Myron, I'm in practice.' He didn't want to be looked on as having special privileges. He didn't want to look like he's a star. Whereupon, from twenty yards away, Noll yells, 'Franco, get over there!'—revealing himself, as I knew he was, as a Sinatra fan.

"So now we do the ceremony. They put the battle helmet on Sinatra and induct him into the Army. It must have lasted fifteen minutes.

There's a lot of toasts with the wine and the kissing of cheeks. The first thing Tony does afterward is call his wife to tell her about it. He said, 'It was like kissing God.'

"So the Steelers go on to win the game and the title, and I guess Sinatra won however much he bet. And the next week was the Immaculate Reception game. It's about an hour after the game and Franco's the only player left in the locker room, sitting on a stool, cornered by about six reporters. So I go over and stand on the fringe, and here comes Joe Gordon, who reaches in and hands Franco a telegram. I'm looking over Franco's shoulder. It simply said, 'Go Steelers Go,' signed 'Colonel Francis Sinatra.'"

So how, I asked Cope, did Franco react to meeting Sinatra?

He blinked. "Well, you know," he said. "Franco's Franco. He was very polite. He says, 'Gee, Mr. Sinatra, it's a pleasure to meet you,' something like that. Franco's never one to get very excited, especially when he's the center of attention."

Franco's subdued reaction didn't surprise me. Nor did his reluctance to participate in the induction ceremony. He had a job to do—just like I now had a job to do—and even Frank Sinatra was nothing more than an interruption.

Cope asked me how my book was coming. I told him that I was seeing Franco in a few days but that he'd been hard to pin down. He's been on the road a lot, I explained, for Super Bakery. Cope asked if maybe Franco, in the time-honored tradition of athletes everywhere, wanted to be paid for his time.

"No!" I said. "He's not like that!" I was flabbergasted. How could Cope even suggest a motive so impure?

The vigor of my comeback seemed to chill Cope. We gathered the check and left. I felt sheepish—but not wrong. For, although Myron Cope had known Franco Harris more than thirty years, it was I who knew his heart.

THAT NIGHT I had a dream. Franco and I were eating lunch at Gibby's Diner. When I was a kid, the greatest treat in the world was to go to Gibby's with my father, just the two of us, for a bowl of vanilla ice cream. That probably only happened once or twice—there were so many of us and he was so diminished—but in my memory it was a landmark of ritualistic import. We sat at the counter. My legs dangled. My father poured some of his hot coffee onto his ice cream. "Wanna try it?" he asked. I nodded hard. He poured. My ice cream melted to a brown puddle. It tasted terrible. But I spooned up every drop. More recently, Gibby's was where we had all gathered after burying our mother. We ate turkey and potato salad and dinner rolls and bread pudding; it tasted exactly as it had twenty years earlier. Now, in the dream, as Franco and I ate, I was pressing him to critique the food. For some reason, I badly needed to know that he approved of my hometown diner. But he wouldn't commit to anything. He ate and he smiled but he wouldn't judge. Then we got in my car. I wanted to show him my old house, the yard where the Dream took place, where he handed me the football and said, "Kid, you're going to have to take it from here yourself." But I couldn't find my own house. I turned left even though I knew I was supposed to turn right. The meadows I knew had become forests, and the hills were ravines. And then, just as I found my way, I looked over and Franco had vanished.

IN THE MORNING, I called his office. It was Friday. Jackie answered, coolly. She said that Franco wasn't in. I asked her to let him know I was looking forward to our get-together on Tuesday, and that I had come to town early. I left my cell-phone number. She took the message with a complete lack of gusto.

I was fantasizing that Franco, upon learning I was in Pittsburgh, might call before Tuesday.

"Hey, you're here already?" he'd say. "Why don't we go to the Pirates game on Sunday?"

Or: "Hey, we're having a barbecue out at the house on Saturday, Lynn Swann and Rocky Bleier and some of the guys—why don't you drop by?"

Or: "Hey, me and Dana are cleaning out the basement and going through some old scrapbooks—you want to come over and take a look?"

But I was also calling to let Franco know that if he was having any eleventh-hour doubts about our meeting, the eleventh hour had passed. I was already here.

On Friday afternoon, I had an appointment with Joe Gordon, the Steelers' longtime public-relations man and business manager. He had retired three years earlier. If a poll were taken among football writers, asking them to name the best PR man in recent memory, Joe Gordon would win 95 percent of the vote. (The rest would be Raiders partisans.) In the den of paranoia and deceit that is modern professional sports, he was known as a pillar of truth and decency.

I parked on the street outside Joe's apartment building, a lone tall tower sunk into the face of Mount Washington. His wife, Babe, answered the door and led me out to the balcony. Joe, feet propped up, wore retirement clothes: shorts, a T-shirt, deck shoes. His was the face of a man whose little-boy features—crinkly eyes and easy grin—had never receded.

Joe and Babe's balcony looked down on the best parts of Pittsburgh: the jagged skyline, the curling rivers, the solemn stadium, the cramped hillside neighborhoods. For the next few hours, Joe told me Steelers stories. He would gesture into the distance as he spoke, like a history professor gesturing toward a wall map, using the city beneath him to indicate the settings of his tales. Saint Peter's Church, where the Chief attended daily Mass and, eventually, drew an overflow crowd at his funeral. The apartment building where a thin-skinned Terry Bradshaw sequestered himself during his years in Pittsburgh. The park where Franco played tennis and then—yes, Joe said, the story was true— played Pied Piper, a pack of kids trailing him home on his bike.

I didn't doubt a word. Joe was a loyalist but also a realist; he didn't sugarcoat or dress up the facts. There was little he didn't know, but when he didn't he said so. For what I was after, talking to Joe Gordon was like talking to someone who'd been around when the Bible was written. He knew what was real and what was later added for flavor. He knew the heroes, the villains, and the thin line that often separated them.

My phone rang as Joe talked, five long rings, but I ignored it. The Franco stories were flowing fast, and I didn't dare interrupt. How

Franco never turned down a charity request. How he hosted all-night poker games on the Steelers' day off. How he was the only Steeler to live on the hardscrabble North Side except for the Chief himself, who loved Franco, and whom Franco always visited on Christmas Day. How Franco stubbornly negotiated every deal—every Steelers contract or personal endorsement or Wendy's franchise agreement—to within a comma of its life.

That stubbornness, Joe explained, was what ended Franco's football career. I had heard the outlines of this story, but Joe knew it from deep inside.

In 1984, Franco was set to begin his thirteenth season with the Steelers. He was thirty-four years old but healthy, and poised to break a major NFL record, Jim Brown's mark for career rushing yards. The Steelers planned a ticker-tape celebration; they put Franco on the cover of their media guide, the first time any one player was so featured.

Then Franco didn't show up at training camp. He had held out before, even in his rookie year, looking for a bigger signing bonus. This time, he and the Steelers had already agreed to a contract in principle. But now, Joe told me, Franco began making new, arcane demands. Eventually he asked for a new contract entirely.

"Franco was just the victim of bad advice," Joe said. "He had a young agent who didn't have a clue. The Steelers were going to pay him I think nine hundred thousand dollars that year, which was a lot of money in those days. Dan Rooney said to me, 'You call Franco and tell him he can have the money any way he wants it: normal payment period, every two weeks, or he can have it all deferred or all up front. If he wants we'll give him a check for the nine hundred thousand when he gets to camp.'"

Steelers coach Chuck Noll, meanwhile, had a camp full of young, eager running backs. As each day passed an aging, pricey Franco became more expendable. When the Steelers beat Dallas in a preseason game, Noll was asked about Franco's contract status.

"Franco who?" he replied.

In football-mad Pittsburgh, all this was front-page news. One columnist pleaded: "Come home now, Franco, while the doors are still open and a light still burns in the window." Another blamed Franco's agent: "Why has he taken pro football's No. 1 gentleman and turned him into pro football's No. 1 holdout?"

Franco and the Steelers finally agreed to terms. But Noll by then no longer wanted him. And the Steelers, unlike most teams, gave their coach the final word in personnel matters.

"So I called Franco," Joe said, "and told him, 'Listen, you're going to have to go to Chuck's house and convince him that you still want to play for the Pittsburgh Steelers.' I told him to call me when he got back. I waited a couple hours, but I never heard from him. Finally I called him. I said, 'What happened?'

"He said, 'Nothing.'

" 'Did you go out there?'

" 'Yeah.'

" 'Nothing happened?'

" 'No.'

" 'How long were you there?'

" 'About five minutes.'

"At that point," Joe told me, "I knew it was over."

Instead of ticker tape and nearly a million dollars, Franco Harris was cut from the Steelers. The Pittsburgh newspapers reacted as if a president had died. "All of us—Franco Harris, the Steelers, the fans—feel cheated," mourned the *Press*. Fans were split: some called Franco greedy, some called the Steelers disloyal. No one was not disappointed. "When Franco left the Steelers," Joe said, "under those circumstances and conditions, that was the low point of my career. And the low point of Dan Rooney's career too, I guarantee it."

A few weeks later, Franco was signed by the Seattle Seahawks. After all those years in black and gold he looked silly, like a big children's puppet, in the Seahawks' indigo, green, and silver. He played just as poorly. He failed to break Jim Brown's record and was cut by Seattle. His football life was suddenly, anticlimactically over.

"It should have never happened like that," Joe said, shaking his head. "Because this guy was an icon. And what he did for this franchise—you never saw a city electrified the way Pittsburgh was, beginning in 1972."

By now a lightning storm had chased us inside. Joe invited me out to dinner with him and Babe. He went to shower and left me in the den. There was a Rolodex on his desk. I turned away from it. Instead I sat down and leafed through some old Steelers books, June rain pelting the windows. The storm and the contract story put me in a melancholy mood. How could Franco have screwed up so tragically? What did it say about him that he'd so badly misread the situation? *Was* it greed? Had Cope been right—was Franco all about the payday? No, I told myself. Not possible. He gave away so much money—to Penn State, to a long list of charities. My eyes fell again on Joe's Rolodex. Surely it bristled with Steelers secrets. Franco's home number, at the very least. But I made no move toward it. *I am not a stalker.* Though I may have exhibited some *slight* stalking tendencies, I had come to Pittsburgh with honorable intentions. Rules were rules.

I rode with Babe and Joe to dinner, contentedly, in the backseat of their clean Chrysler. I felt like a kid home from college. We went to a mall restaurant. After dinner, Babe went off to shop while Joe and I watched the Knicks' playoff game on the bar TV. During halftime we chatted about this and that: the upcoming Steelers season, New York City versus Pittsburgh, Gore versus Bush. Joe told me that Franco had been campaigning in Pittsburgh for the Gore-Lieberman ticket.

I said I was surprised that Franco, out of football for so long, remained a big draw.

"Are you kidding me?" Joe said. "He's more popular than ever. And the Immaculate Reception, because it's constantly replayed on television, is far more famous than it was twenty-five years ago."

Pittsburgh had obviously forgiven him for the contract debacle. Franco, I realized, had become a brand name, cultivated in his youth and, presumably, well-guarded in his middle age.

I asked if Franco had ever involved himself directly in politics.

Joe made a noise, half-chuckle and half-groan. "Not exactly," he said, and then told me one more Franco story.

"A few years ago, the Ku Klux Klan was holding a march downtown, in front of the County Building," he said. "Before it started, I get a call from a friend in the mayor's office, who says that Franco is camped out on the steps. Not hidden but not too conspicuous, just sitting there with a book, some food, a canteen of water, like he's prepared to stay for a while."

Franco had heard that some neo-Nazis would be marching with the Klan. As it turned out, it was the neo-Nazis—not, as one might have assumed, the Klan—that got Franco agitated, for his mother had lived and nearly died under the Nazi occupation of Italy. So he had made a poster condemning the march.

"I tried calling Lynn Swann," Joe continued, "who's Franco's best friend and who has an office downtown, but he was traveling. Then I called Dan Rooney. He decided we should get over there immediately. We called the mayor's office and asked them to clear the way so we could get through without attracting any notice."

They reached Franco within fifteen minutes.

Dan Rooney said: "Franco, you're playing right into their hands. It may cause a riot, and with all the television cameras, that's exactly what they're hoping for."

Franco responded: "Listen, we have to stand up for our rights. I know what my mother went through under the Nazis, and it was terrible. Somebody has to express that."

"I'm 100 percent behind what you're saying," Rooney told him, "but where you are right now is causing a problem. They're going to single you out."

For some time, Joe recalled, they went back and forth. And then Franco decided that Rooney was right, and he packed up his things and left.

Such a strange, admirable, naive, stubborn, autonomous creature was my Franco Harris.

It was past eleven o'clock by the time we got back to Joe and Babe's. Joe steered the car into his underground garage. We made plans to go to the Pirates' game on Sunday. "Unless," I told him, "Franco calls and wants to get together."

"Of course," Joe said.

I took the elevator up to the street. The sky was still, a murky midnight blue. I walked to my car. Something looked wrong with its tail end. The license plate—it was missing. I remembered bolting it on my-self; it hadn't just fallen off. Someone had helped himself to my license plate under the murky midnight blue. I checked to see if the front plate was still there; it was.

Oh, well. If the price of a new friend was a stolen license plate, so be it. Joe Gordon was willing to talk and, far more rare, worth listening to. I felt as if I'd finally slipped behind the partition that Franco had erected around himself. But even if Joe had never known Franco, I would have been glad to have met him. He was, as promised, a pillar of truth and de-cency. It was a good day.

I climbed into my car and just sat, my mind pancaking under the weight of so much Franco lore. I took the cell phone out of my pocket. The message light blinked red in the dark. I pressed the button. I heard the robotic voice-mail lady recite the time of the message—3:38 P.M., the call I ignored on Joe's balcony—and then I heard *his* voice: "Hi, Steve, this is Franco Harris calling."

For an instant, I thought my mind was conjuring his voice from the night. But he continued.

"So you're in Pittsburgh. Wondering if you're just passing through, and also, I'd like to hear about your trip to Italy."

Sure, I'll tell you about Italy, but . . . *you're wondering if I'm just passing through?*

"Listen, unfortunately, Steve, I'm not going to be able to meet on Tuesday."

Well, Monday then, or Wednesday. It doesn't really matter.

"I got a nice paying gig down in Florida."

A paying gig? Meaning . . . a lecture? I know—I made some calls: your asking price is twenty grand. For that price, I hope you have some-thing better than your Give-everyone-a-smile talk from the roast. That one, I found out, was lifted verbatim from something called the Opti-mist Creed.

"I'll be down there Monday, Tuesday, and Wednesday."

Well, how about later in the week?

"And then on Thursday, I'm going to Nashville to my ex-teammate Joe Gilliam's football camp."

Wait a minute! We had an *appointment*. We had a *date*! I *drove to Pittsburgh to see you!*

"So, sorry about that—"

Sorry about that?

"—but I really can't pass this gig up."

You can too!

"Okay, Steve, have a good weekend, and I'll talk to you soon."

The son of a bitch! Before I knew what was happening, I began to cry—shoulders shaking, face melting into a teary, snotty mess.

That was the moment I snapped. That was the moment that all my Franco expectations and curiosities and confusion boiled over and turned to scalding steam.

If he'd left his home number, I would have called and said something regrettable. Instead I drove back to the hotel through dark and empty streets. The parking attendant stared when I got out of the car. He asked if I was all right, if I needed a doctor. I'm fine, I told him.

"Hey," he said, "you're missing a license plate."

I couldn't call Ellen. I was too ashamed to admit that I'd been stood up. Her consolation would feel like pity, and pity was the thing I had always feared the most. I was ashamed when my father died too. Because he died at the start of Christmas break, we were out of school for two weeks afterward. On the first day back, a friend came to me at recess and he said, with a sweetness I could not appreciate at the time, "I'm sorry that your dad died." And I said, "No, he didn't!"

I did phone the Pittsburgh police and report my license plate stolen. The clerk asked if I suspected anyone in particular.

"Franco Harris," I said, and she laughed, but I didn't.

I AWOKE Saturday morning with a stirring thought: *I know where he lives.*

I had recently paid $39.95 for an Internet search ("Franco Harris, male, 50 years old, Pittsburgh, Pa.") that combed tax rolls, lien filings, court documents, and the like. I took out the report now and looked it over.

It had some interesting information about Franco—which I cannot divulge here, for in order to receive the report I had to sign the following statement: "I intend to use the information ONLY for a use which will clearly cause no emotional or physical harm to a reasonable person who is a subject of the inquiry."

It could be argued, of course, that a man who so brutally stood up another was not "a reasonable person." It could be argued that *he* was the one inflicting the emotional harm. But rules are rules.

The report listed his various addresses: home, office, and the old brick house on the North Side that he still owned. Studying them, I made a discovery. If you added up the street numbers of his home and office addresses, the sum equaled his old North Side address. I somehow felt this might be significant. Was a coded message being sent to me? Inspired, I began to search his street names for anagrams. The first one I tried said it all: West North Avenue = *Steve Want Hero, Nu?*

So I had been reduced to this. Sitting in a Pittsburgh hotel playing word games and voodoo math.

The situation called for action. *Risk more than others think is safe*—was that not Franco's own advice? On a map of Pittsburgh, I located the street where he now lived. In red pen, I traced the route from my hotel to his house. It looked to be a forty-minute drive, out to the horsey end of town. What would I do once I got there? An image came to me: I rush his porch and smack the bricks with my fists, the way a child climbs into Daddy's lap when he's reading the newspaper and smacks his chest so he will pay attention.

I was searching for my keys when another scenario came into my mind's eye. I am driving past his house—once, twice, three times, checking for activity. Dana watches this from an upstairs window. She calls the police. She gives them the license-plate number (from the front of the car) and they check their database. *A stolen plate.* A pair of policemen, sunburnt and thick-necked, tear through those horsey, cul-de-sacky streets and yank me out of the car. They sneer at my protests—*Just let me talk to Franco! He'll clear up everything!*—and throw me in jail, where I spend the next ninety days among winos and pickpockets, missing the birth of my first child.

I put away the map.

Instead I drove up to Grove City, an hour north of Pittsburgh. I had heard that some of the current Steelers would be signing autographs there, at an outlet mall.

The drive through the countryside was calming. I felt my hysteria easing up. The hardwood forests were thick and uncomplicated. The sun shone happily. Polka played on the radio.

I was expecting a quaint scene—a few dozen kids, football cards in hand, milling around their favorite Steelers. After all, this team hadn't even been to the playoffs in three years. The Steelers of Franco's era, I'd been told, still drew much larger crowds.

But there were hundreds of fans, maybe a thousand, snaking through roped-off lines outside a Steelers merchandise shop. Most of them wore Steelers gear, and nearly all of them were white. All of the players, meanwhile, were black, and none wore Steelers gear.

The main draw was Plaxico Burress, the team's No. 1 draft pick, a wide receiver built like a basketball player. "Dang, he's tall!" one woman said, eyeing him from the line. The fans handed him objects to sign—a Steelers lunchbox, a miniature Michigan State helmet (Burress's alma mater), a size-fifteen Nike cleat—and Burress wordlessly complied. A pudgy man, his bicep tattooed with a Confederate flag, approached, suppliant. "How you enjoying training camp so far, Mr. Burress?" he said. And I could not help but think that if Burress were not a Steeler, this same man might call him something rather different than Mister.

In the long, sunny line of seekers, a familiar sight caught my eye: a Franco Harris jersey, No. 32. The woman who wore it was built like a small fullback and had a friendly look about her.

"I like your shirt," I told her.

She beamed. We introduced ourselves. She was Bee Huss, a customer-service representative at a bank in Bowling Green, Ohio. She had awoken at four-thirty that morning to drive to Grove City with her teenage son and a girlfriend. "My husband," Bee said dismissively, "is a *Bengals* fan."

Bee, who was two years younger than me, had liked Franco ever since Penn State. I asked her why. "It was his demeanor on the field—and off too," she said. "He wasn't a jerk, like so many of these guys. He didn't dance in the end zone, he didn't fight."

I noticed that her earrings bore the Steelers logo, and she noticed me noticing. "Oh, yeah, and this and this and this and this," she said, pointing to her wristwatch, her necklace, her shorts, even her socks. They were all official Steelers issue. She opened her purse. It was a logjam of Steelers paraphernalia: key ring, wallet, pens. Then she flipped open a little photo album containing pictures of herself and Franco Harris. He wore the same earnest, toothy smile he'd shown me a few times.

"It was two years ago," Bee said as if in reverie. "He's a wonderful man. I came with my family to Pittsburgh for a Steelers game. We were staying at the Best Western, and we went to Vincent's"—a known Franco hangout—"for calzone. I was wearing this jersey. We were walking in, and the lady said, 'You are dressed so *appropriate*. You won't believe who's inside.'

"I had told everybody I knew," Bee continued, "that before I died or he died, I would somehow meet him. He's the only person I ever wanted to meet. I tapped him on the shoulder, I said, 'Mr. Harris, I've wanted to meet you my whole life.' I started crying."

Bee cried again, even now, telling the story. Her girlfriend giggled, and then Bee did too.

"He said, 'Thank you very much.' He was with Dok and a friend of Dok's. They just finished playing tennis at the gym. He was drinking a beer. He starting signing my jersey on the front and back. He signed everything I had. He looked at me, I'm still crying, and he said, 'You need to sit down.' I did, and he invited my husband and dad to sit too. He told the waitress to give him their check—but when Franco wasn't looking my dad paid the check. I couldn't eat. We stayed for two and a half hours."

Despite myself, I was cheered by Bee's encounter. It portrayed Good Franco, the one who brought me to Pittsburgh, not Bad Franco, the one who abandoned me. It also made me a bit jealous.

"What'd you talk about?" I asked.

"About Penn State, about the Steeler Pounder poster for Nike—you know, with the sledgehammer and the steel beams. We had a great time.

Then we took these pictures. I wanted to get them signed, so he gave me his Super Bakery address. That's the only address I asked for. I said, 'I'm not one of those kind of fans who's going to harass you.' He sent the pictures back, wrote a little note on each one. He wrote, 'To Bee, truly my No. 1 fan.'"

It struck me suddenly that I had no photographic evidence of my own bond with Franco. Nor did I own a single piece of his handwriting—even though I had eaten two meals with him *in one day*. I mailed him a thank-you note after that first visit, but he didn't write back. I later sent him a few of my current articles, to prove that I was not entirely fixated on him. No reply. I'd recently sent him a gift, a book called *Radical Marketing*, which my brother Peter thought might appeal to a small-company CEO like Franco. Again, no response.

Bee, meanwhile, was still smiling broadly over her signed photographs. "And I haven't contacted him since!" she said, with what sounded like pride—the pride of, say, an investment banker who has executed a large and complicated transaction so perfectly that the need to review or revisit it, ever, was inconceivable. Whereas I, in my every transaction with Franco, seemed to create further complication.

"Well, you don't want him to think you're some kind of freaky idiot," her friend was saying.

"No!" I agreed.

"Like a *stalker*!" Bee said, laughing.

"A *stalker*!" her friend shrieked.

"A *stalker*!" I said.

"It was the happiest day of my life—better than getting married," Bee said. "I will be buried in this jersey. He's a wonderful man."

By the time I left Grove City, I was massively conflicted. In Bee Huss's experience, Franco was purely Good; perhaps, therefore, I was the Bad one. Had I become just the sort of "freaky idiot" that Bee had had the wherewithal to not become? Franco had been kind to me once too. On that magical first visit. And yet that wasn't enough for me, not nearly enough. To the untutored eye, Bee was the fanatic. She owned so much Steelers clothing, she told me, that she could wear a different outfit every day for a month. But I was the one who had bought Franco's home address. I was the one forcing myself on him. I had told myself this was appropriate because Franco and I had so much in common—because I was, in some small way, a part of him. But what if Bee Huss was also a part of him? And how many Bee Husses were out there? We couldn't all be special, could we?

ON SATURDAY AFTERNOON, I left a message for Franco at his office, knowing he wouldn't get it until Monday at the earliest. I first put the message in writing. I wanted to control the tone, to convey disappointment without churlishness. I wrote one version after another, stopping at eight. Each version was less angry than the previous one. I finally settled on No. 5. "Yeah, here I am in Pittsburgh," I read into his voice mail. "I'm glad you've got a good gig in Florida, but I'm definitely disappointed we can't get together Tuesday. I could stick around till next Friday or Saturday, if you'd have time to see me when you get back. Please call me as soon as possible so I can plan accordingly."

I spent the rest of the weekend scrounging for crumbs.

On Saturday night, I wrangled an invitation to an opening at the new Andy Warhol Museum. I thought that Franco and Dana, reputed to be civic boosters and cultural progressives, might attend. They didn't. The crowd, dotted with drag queens, was large and raucous. A young Warhol fan I met, however, complained that the crowds only came for parties, that the museum stood empty during regular hours. "If Andy Warhol had played just one down with the Steelers," he said, "this place would be packed every day."

On Sunday, Joe Gordon took me to the Pirates' game at Three Rivers Stadium. Afterward he walked me through the Steelers' empty locker room. I had vowed to be unmoved, but when we came to Franco's old locker I grew jittery inside. Then Joe showed me the equipment room, a messy, tool-strewn cave full of exploded shoulder pads and smashed face masks. A dozen retired helmets were suspended from a ceiling rack, Franco's among them. They dangled lifelessly, upside down, like shot-gunned deer strung up to bleed out. Franco's helmet hung well beyond my reach. Too bad. I would have liked to finger its nicks and dings, to feel its heft, to examine its lining for sweat and blood. Instead I gazed up at it until my neck spasmed. It propelled me into a far deeper state of awe than had the bone-chip relics of Saint Stephen.

When Joe went home, I took a walk around the North Side neighborhood. Without meaning to, I found myself outside Franco's sturdy old brick house on West North Avenue. *(Steve Want Hero, Nu?)* It stood motionless but appeared to be occupied—rented out, I imagined. The nearby houses were smaller, in worse shape, and the slate sidewalks were buckling. I began to circle the block and, feeling forlorn, chatted up a few of Franco's old neighbors. I didn't learn much. He was known to give out the best Halloween candy in the neighborhood (full-size Baby Ruth bars). I was told that Dana's mother used to live with them—she walked Dana's dog, answered Franco's mail, and helped look after Dok. One man, a retired carpenter who introduced himself as Rock, remembered Franco playing touch football with neighborhood kids. Rock played once too, he said, and his team beat Franco's team.

"And Dana—she was pissed *off*!" Rock said with a nasal laugh.

Because, I asked, Franco might have gotten hurt?

"No. Dana says to him, 'You're a *professional*—you shouldn't get beat by these guys.'"

Another old neighbor, an accountant, told me that his daughter had gone to school with Dok. "Nice kid," he said. "A little weird, but nice." Then he asked, "Is Franco still with Dana?"

I was caught off-guard by the question, which seemed impolite. And as a harvester of Franco information, I was unaccustomed to providing it.

But I also felt empowered. Yes, I told the accountant—as a matter of fact, I saw them together just a few months ago, at a fiftieth-birthday celebration for Franco.

"That marriage was always trouble," he said.

Maybe, I concluded in a blaze of clarity, *that's* why Franco had been keeping me away. He and Dana were breaking up. That made sense! He certainly was on the road a lot. (But why couldn't Franco have told me? Didn't he know I would lend him a sympathetic ear?) I recalled my brief exchange with Dana at the birthday roast. When I escorted her to the after-hours party, she complained to me—a total stranger—that Franco was always late because he couldn't say no to anyone or anything. (Except, apparently, me.)

A few months back I'd phoned Roy Blount Jr., a former *Sports Illustrated* reporter who wrote a masterful book about the Steelers of Franco's era. Not surprisingly, the book didn't have much Franco in it. Blount told me he'd found Franco "reticent, although not threateningly so," and "extremely unneedy." Dana, he said, was "very friendly, smart, and unmysterious—not like Franco, more direct and more accessible." When I asked about the dynamic between them, Blount chuckled. "I think," he said, "Dana was a little vexed with Franco's etherealness."

So maybe now, with Dok gone to college, Dana had finally had enough of Franco's "etherealness"—his inability to say no, his marching to his own drummer, his Steelers-contract stubbornness and neo-Nazi distress—and booted him out of the house. The "paying gig" in Florida was, surely, a cover-up. Maybe he had an old girlfriend down there. And he couldn't tell me the truth because he was ashamed of having been abandoned. (Just like me!) Rather than invite my pity by baring his shame, he tried to pass himself off as callously mercenary—a *"paying gig"* indeed!—which he should have known that I knew he was not.

Or maybe the marriage was fine, but Franco had contracted a terrible disease, some new brain cataclysm, and had gone to Florida, *with* Dana, in search of a miracle cure.

Or maybe *Dana* was the one with a brain cataclysm.

Or maybe one of Franco's employees in Florida had sold company secrets to Krispy Kreme.

Or maybe—and by now my mind was acting on its own, adhering to neither the constraints of logic nor the physics of conscious thought—Franco's company was capsizing. Perhaps a mouse living inside the boiler-room wall of a factory in Utica, New York, one of the three factories used by Super Bakery (the others were in California and Indiana), ate a rind of moldy cheese and, poisoned, crawled inside a batter-mixing drum to die, contaminating a batch of Super Donuts and thereby sickening the entire third and fourth grades of an elementary school in Orlando.

Anything could be true. Or not. The truth was, I had no idea. What did *I* know? What did I really, truly, convincingly know about Franco Harris?

Not much.

This startling, rancid truth struck me just as I circled back around to Franco's old house and stood, desolate, in the shadow of its unwelcoming red brick.

The house may as well have been Franco himself. Its walls were handsome and mute. Its windows, reflecting the dying light of a summer day, were impenetrably useless; they had the cruel look of eyeholes in a Crusader's armor mask. The wrought-iron gate, with its "FH" inlay, seemed to sneer at me: *even I, a creaky gate, have more of an affinity with him than you.*

I sat down on a low wall across the street. Sirens and shouts cracked the falling dusk; the neighborhood felt unsafe and I didn't care. I tried to recall the bond we had forged on my first trip to Pittsburgh—it *was* a bond, wasn't it? Like a prisoner trying to recall freedom, like a sick man trying to recall health, I struggled now to taste again the joy of a year ago. The easy, lazy driving tour through town. Our lunch at Piccolo Mondo, talking family and politics. More of the same at dinner—and at the tennis club, his willingness to stand before me naked. But had he actually revealed himself to me? I surely thought so at the time. I thought he saw me as a kindred spirit, a new friend worth confiding in—but now, raking through the "revelations" he shared with me, I saw them as innocuous stories, mere incidentals. He probably told me nothing he wouldn't have told Bee Huss. I had been blinded by excitement.

The excitement of that first visit was twofold. To simply be with him after such a feverish, long-dormant infatuation was a sensory thrill, like the first fifteen minutes in front-row theater seats: *I can see the actors' spittle, for God's sake! I can hear the prop man rattling the teacups!* Such thrills, however, fade. The second excitement was more lasting and even more thrilling: the promise of future visits. On that day, I envisioned myself deeply intertwined with Franco over the coming weeks, months, years. I would insinuate myself into his life so completely that it would be impossible to say where he ended and I began. He had *promised.*

"I guess I have no problem with that" is what he said when I described the book I wanted to write.

"We'll work it out" is what he said when I pressed him for a quick follow-up visit.

Don't those sound like promises? I banked on his words, knowing they would come true.

And now they weren't coming true.

What struck me was not just how poorly I knew him but how resolutely he insisted on not being known. Did that make him heroic or paranoid? He certainly was, as Roy Blount Jr. said, extremely unneedy. He had no need to relive his glory days or brag about his business success. He had no need to dredge up his family's past, as I had mine, searching for clues to his own identity. He had no need, it seemed, to consider his identity at all. No need to talk talk talk about himself or think think think or write write write—that constant, slapdash effort by which certain people attempt to wring from the mysteries of life *an answer.*

But I did. Even now, so long removed from boyhood, I was a needy person, starving for revelation. Hunting for answers, solutions, verities. "What kind of father are you?" I'd asked him on that first visit. His reply—"How do you even answer that question?"—should have told me what I needed to know: there wouldn't *be* any answers. None that would satisfy me at least.

Perhaps I was naive for expecting otherwise. But I had been certain that, once introduced to each other, Franco and I would, like a pair of otherwise ordinary chemicals, perform a magical alchemy. He, dulled by needlessness, and I, quivering with need, would produce a radically splendid partnership.

Instead of alchemy, we created an allergy. His resistance only made me more needy; my neediness made him more resistant.

Was it all because I am a writer? Would he have let me in if I were still an innocent child? But in my heart, I told myself, *I still am.* In pursuit of Franco, I had regressed. This was apparently the price of seeking out a childhood hero. I couldn't see the regression in the moment, but later it was obvious—my keening voice on our interview tapes; my ragged shame when he shushed me in front of Sammy Davis Jr.'s wife; my teary meltdown in the car outside Joe Gordon's apartment. In the presence of Franco, I became a little boy full of admiration and need. But that's not who he saw. He saw a grown man with a notebook and a tape recorder. The same kind of man who, long ago, constructed his myth. And could now tear it down. He had never trusted writers. I remembered what he said back in his Steelers prime: "I don't want anybody really nosing around, snooping into what I'm doing." Now here I was, in his hometown, somewhere between snooping and stalking—but whose fault was that? Who had stood up whom?

He was the deficient one, not me. He was the one with intimacy issues, unable to embrace my affection. He was the one who wrecked my trip, who had the bad manners to leave his bad news on my voice mail. "Sorry about that," he said—like a teenager! He couldn't even muster a real apology?

Night had fallen on West North Avenue. Police sirens still rang out; the air smelled of peanuts, menthol cigarettes, deep-fry exhaust. Sitting on a stone wall opposite his former residence, I had convinced myself that, in sum, I had acted more honorably than Franco Harris. The satisfaction this brought, however, was a joyless one, for I knew that he would call in a day or two to apologize, and, like a child, I would forgive him everything.

HE DIDN'T CALL on Monday. Or Tuesday or Wednesday. I passed those days in a windowless, concrete-block media room inside the Steelers' offices at Three Rivers Stadium. Although it was fully three months before the first game of the season, two dozen local reporters toiled all around me. They were covering the Steelers' pre-training-camp workouts. "There's a saying here," Joe Gordon had told me, "which is largely true. They say baseball season ends when the Steelers' workouts begin, and hockey doesn't start until the Steelers have cleaned out their lockers." The reporters, just back from their locker-room interviews, cradled tape recorders between shoulder and ear, transcribing onto their laptops, madly rewinding and fast-forwarding, the players' voices blanketing the room like a chorus of squirrels. I, meanwhile, read through a three-foot stack of faded newspaper clips about Franco. I felt like the hapless newspaper reporter in *Citizen Kane*, sent to unbury the secret of a dead man's life. After a while, I couldn't even tell what I was looking for—proof of Franco's goodness or signs of his deficiencies?

On Wednesday afternoon, I called his office. Jackie, my longtime tormentor, answered.

"I gave Franco your message from over the weekend," she said. "He's got your number."

"I know," I said. "But he hasn't called back."

"Well . . ."

"Can I ask you for some candid advice?"

She didn't say no, so I asked.

"I know Franco's busy," I said, "but I've gotten stood up here pretty good. We had an appointment, and he left town. I can't get him to call me back. So what I want to know is, should I be reading something into this?"

"Oh, *no*," Jackie said, laughing, friendly for the first time ever. "I don't know what you two are working on—he doesn't tell me anything—but that's typical Franco. I'll get a call from two different people at two different restaurants, waiting for him to show up for lunch, and he's actually someplace else entirely."

So maybe I wasn't the problem after all. But it's a funny way to treat people, I thought, and a funny way to run a business. I had already inflated his goodness; had I inflated his competence as well? It would hardly be the first time a man with a pen had turned an athlete into a symbol of something he wasn't.

On Thursday, I packed up my car and checked out of the hotel. Just as I pulled onto the highway, my phone rang. It was Franco. He was still in Nashville, he said. He'd be back in Pittsburgh tomorrow night but he was busy through the weekend. He'd be in New York early next week, he said, and he'd call me then. Maybe, he said, we could grab lunch. He was perfectly cordial but he didn't apologize for standing me up. And I, who turned twelve years old again every time I spoke with him, didn't object at all. I made the long drive home from Pittsburgh and, instead of taking my very pregnant and patient wife to the mountains to escape the summer's first heat wave, I stayed in New York awaiting Franco's call, which I doubted would come, and which didn't. Later, he'd tell me he lost his phone book. By then I no longer believed him.

15

YANKED FROM THE PEDESTAL

———··⟨∞⟩··———

M Y ALLEGIANCE TO Franco had expired. I was still determined to solve him as I'd once tried solving my father, to
unravel him like the human genome. But no longer would I ask his permission to do so. His broken promises *were* my permission.

I took to the phone like a losing candidate on Election Day. Only his
family and closest friends, I decided, were off-limits. (For now at least; I
wasn't ready to slam the door on future meetings with Franco, and ha-
rassing his loved ones would surely do that.) I did call former teammates and coaches from Pittsburgh, Penn State, and Rancocas Valley
Regional High School. I did track down old neighbors and family
friends, business associates, even his former lawyer.

They all sounded like a bunch of Jewish mothers, or a gaggle of Vatican
saint-makers. "It's almost as if Franco was sent here on a mission to better the human race," said one Steelers executive, and he wasn't kidding.

Even as a child, I was told, he played the peacemaker. He kept the bullies away from the weaklings; when choosing up sides for stickball, he
made sure the worst player was on his own team. The Harrises, all
eleven of them, lived in a three-bedroom apartment in Mount Holly
Gardens, a small housing project on a dead-end street some ten miles

from Fort Dix. That was the street where families like theirs lived—
black soldiers with wives from Italy or France or even Germany.

In Mount Holly Gardens, Franco was a ringleader. He organized the
ballgames and the bike races. When a neighbor's car battery died,
Franco rounded up a wagon and led an expedition to the service station.
He was kind and he was canny. He shoveled driveways after every
snowfall and, although he didn't ask for money, his first stop was always
the lady he knew would give him fifty cents. In high school, he was offered the student-council presidency because of his football stardom but
turned it down in favor of someone who had worked for it.

"He had a smile for everyone, and he was always looking to help out,"
one family friend told me. "You couldn't help but like him." He was—if
this were possible for a teenager with a black father in a largely segre-
gated town in the 1960s—a golden boy.

He grew homesick during his first semester at Penn State and hitch-
hiked back to Mount Holly. He had to be talked into returning. He was,
one assistant football coach told me, a patriot and an innocent: after his
first game, when Penn State whipped Navy in Annapolis, Franco stood
alongside the midshipmen with his helmet over his heart as the Navy
band played "Blue and Gold," his jersey the only white one in a mass of
blue, even though Joe Paterno was hollering to get off the field.

He was given a summer restaurant job by a Penn State booster
named Walter Conti, but proved so undependable that Conti nearly
fired him.

So his undependability, I saw, had a long history.

And yet—and here is where the summer-job story, like so many
about Franco, took on the weight of parable—instead of resenting
Conti's scolding, he humbly began to apply himself, accepting Conti's
fatherly advice. Twenty-five years later, on the night Conti shut down
his restaurant for good, Franco flew in from Pittsburgh to thank him
one last time.

That was the kind of touch Franco became known for, his friends told
me—showing up at restaurant closings, graduations, bar mitzvahs, funerals. He was, they said, the most loyal man ever born. Even after stardom found him in Pittsburgh, he loved for his old friends from Mount

Holly to visit. At the end of every football season, he anonymously sent every teammate a keg of fancy beer. When his backfield partner Rocky Bleier retired, Franco gave him a bronze sculpture of a running back with an engraved message: "Rock, you made it happen."

Franco played sports with handicapped kids, bought bicycles for poor kids, paid visits to sick kids. He used to miss flights all the time, his former lawyer, Lee Goldberg, told me, "because he'd stop at Children's Hospital on the way out of town. He truly recognized what it meant to be a role model."

He seemed constitutionally incapable of cockiness. One friend recalled a party where Franco was introduced to Chuck "Concrete Charlie" Bednarik, a legendary NFL strongman. When Bednarik got in Franco's face and said, "You wouldn't be running like that if *I* was still playing," Franco smiled and said, "You know, Mr. Bednarik, you really are one of the greatest football players of all time, and it's a pleasure to meet you." He was tactful, selfless, almost pathologically attuned to the underdog. "He'll give the whore on Liberty Avenue as much time as the Queen of England," his mother-in-law was once heard to say, though not necessarily as a compliment.

If anything, he was too soft a touch. He lent money to friends or, if their prospects were no good, he just gave it to them. When his father died, in 1980, Franco became his family's anchor and, too often, its checkbook.

No one was surprised when he went into the food business after football. As one friend put it, he had "some sort of a calling" when it came to food. He'd get genuinely excited by discussions of riboflavin content or the cancer-fighting properties of soy. He could be fanatical about what he would or wouldn't put into his own body. No aspirin, ever—bad for the stomach.

His earliest business ventures were not successful: some Wendy's outlets that he let his brothers manage, a botched bottled-water deal, an "Aussie meat pie" that never took off. But his enthusiasm never waned. He studied his failures in order to not repeat mistakes; he constantly sought out mentors; he read business books by the dozen.

With Super Bakery, everything came together. He gradually built it into a national company—the only doughnut available in all fifty states, he liked to say. Franco personally made hundreds of sales calls. It was not lost on him that his customers, particularly the buyers for large urban school districts, were of the generation that watched him play football and, often, were black—including Shirley Watkins, who was Undersecretary of Agriculture for Food, Nutrition, and Consumer Services in Washington when I interviewed her. She first met Franco when she was with the Memphis city schools. "I cannot begin to tell you how excited I was, that here was a black man starting his own business and starting something that could be pretty successful," she said. "I wanted to do as much as I could to help him. We gave Franco the names of contacts in all the large school districts—L.A. and Chicago, Dallas, Newark, New Orleans, Fort Lauderdale—so that he'd have lots of friends in those places."

He was a champion networker. He memorized clients' names, their spouses' names, and where their kids were going to college. Every year he invited prospective customers to the Super Bowl. He didn't even have to talk shop to make a sale. "He's a very astute businessman, but he's also the greatest magnet I've ever seen," one longtime business mentor told me. "He's one of the most recognized athletes of all time, and when he goes to meet people they just fall all over him."

Like the best politicians, Franco had the ability to make everyone he met feel special. "He's always looking for the goodness in a person," one friend, an entrepreneur named Art Baldwin, told me.

Baldwin and his wife Cynthia, a lawyer, were so taken with Franco's people skills that they asked him to be the honorary campaign chairman of Cynthia's election campaign. She was trying to become the first black woman elected judge in Allegheny County.

"He said, 'If I do this, I'm not going to be the honorary chair, I'm going to be the *real* chair,'" Cynthia recalled. "I said, 'You don't know what you're getting into.'" But Franco liked the idea of helping get a black woman elected, so he signed on.

When she lost the election, Cynthia immediately decided to run again in two years. "Franco literally stayed involved those whole two years," Art Baldwin told me. "He'd go to the VFWs and the Masonic

halls and the bingos. Not only that—he'd reach into his pocket to provide money, and not just a little bit of money. He'd even alter his business schedule if there was something of import in the election. He was
able to pull people together, very subtly, without even making any refer-
ence to race. He's a remarkable human being."

Elections in Democrat-heavy Pittsburgh are virtually decided on Endorsement Day, when a thousand Democratic Committee members
gather to choose the slate that will go to the voting public. It is a day of
double-talk and horse-trading. Candidates give away whatever they
think might win them votes: hot chocolate or meatball heroes, cork-
screws or shoehorns emblazoned with their names. But on this Endorsement Day, in 1989, only Cynthia Baldwin was giving away Franco
Harris. He arrived at 6:00 A.M. and stayed well past the voting deadline,
dispensing Super Donuts and his famous smile. All day long he was
swarmed. He eventually shook the hand of—in Art Baldwin's estima-
tion—"just about everyone."

And Cynthia Baldwin became a judge.

ONE DAY, I found myself no longer interested in these fairy tales,
these too-good-to-be-true Franco stories. In the past, I would have
sucked them down like pure oxygen. Now they seemed stale. Now they
seemed fraudulent. The Baldwins' experience with Franco ran so
counter to my own that it hurt.

The difference was that Franco obviously deemed Cynthia Baldwin's
cause to be worthier than mine. The same for the handicapped kids, the
down-on-their-luck friends, even the whore on Liberty Avenue. As
much as I professed to need Franco, he wasn't buying. He didn't want
me around. He especially didn't want to be written about.

Maybe I was just jealous of the unadulterated good vibes he sent in
every direction but mine. Or maybe . . . maybe he *did* have something to
hide. I kept thinking of that fleeting tense moment during his fiftieth-
birthday roast: Lynn Swann announcing that Franco had been trailed
by hidden cameras, and Franco cringing until he realized Swann was
joking.

I took to the phone again, casting a wider net. By now I ached to know all the things about Franco that he would never tell me.

This turned out to be a sleazy, titillating endeavor. It brought to mind the boyhood summer afternoon that I stole a glimpse of my friend's sister in the outdoor shower, a mystifying blur of pubic hair and soapy elbow.

I learned, for instance, that during college Franco was caught driving down to the Jersey shore in a van full of girls and empty beer cans. But the cops recognized him—he was by now the starting fullback on an undefeated Penn State team—and let him go.

I learned that one of Franco's closest friends in Pittsburgh went to jail for insurance fraud.

I learned from some former law-enforcement men that Franco himself once flirted with jail. During his early Pittsburgh years, he was friendly with a man named Robert Hawkins, who turned a federal jobs program into a no-show racket. He was offering free money, and at least two other Steelers accepted. Franco "never took a nickel himself," one source told me, but he did reportedly steer seven friends and relatives to Hawkins's phony payroll. Hawkins was eventually sent to prison; Franco was investigated but never charged.

I learned that he badly miscalculated his leverage during the 1984 contract holdout that ended his career. "I remember him saying, 'I never thought I'd ever get paid this much money to play football,'" an old friend told me. "So I said, 'What the hell are you waiting for, then? Just go back!' But by then he had this feeling of invincibility."

I learned from a Super Bakery employee that Franco was an enthusiastic but sloppy boss, making big messes for others to clean up. A number of people told me that Franco had woefully underthought his purchase of Parks Sausages, that he didn't have nearly enough experience to run the company, and that, until he sold off its factory in desperation, Parks threatened to sink Super Bakery.

Following one lead and then another and another, I found a woman who had known Franco very well for a very long time. In a single ninety-minute conversation, I got more dirt on him than I'd ever wanted.

"I like Franco a lot, and he is a genuinely good-hearted human being," she began, "a truly gentle soul. But he's got his personal quirks and flaws like anyone."

She proceeded to enumerate them. "He's not stupid by any stretch, but he's not terribly bright either. I remember one time sitting in his living room when he was hatching this business scheme, and it was basically a pyramid scam. But he wasn't being duplicitous—he's just gullible."

She told me that his relationship with Dana was, as I had by now gathered, highly imperfect. And although he came around to fatherhood, he hadn't taken much interest in Dok until a few years ago.

What about Franco's brothers and sisters, I asked this woman: is he close with them?

She laughed. "I don't think he's ever gotten close to *anybody,*" she said. "You can't really be giving out a whole lot of pieces of yourself when everyone's asking for them. So you become more careful and more distant."

From what I had seen, even he and Dana were distant. Why, I wondered aloud, had they stayed together?

"A combination of things," she said. "Being inert is one of them. Leaving her would require action—and confrontation. Franco really backs away from conflict."

I half-hoped that this woman was lying, or at least exaggerating, but I later checked her stories and found them to be reliable. Worse yet, nothing she told me rang false; her information jibed perfectly with my own Franco encounters. He *was* distant and he *was* inert and he *was* afraid of conflict, all to the point of being maddeningly disengaged. In the past I had seen his disengagement as charming somehow, as if the world were too coarse for his sensitive nature. But now it just made me sad.

I suppose it was natural that I would want to tear Franco down at some point. A Freudian might say that, because I never had the chance to turn against my own father, Franco became my stand-in. Especially after he had the nerve to abandon me, just like my father did. (I didn't stop to acknowledge that, since Franco *wasn't* my father, he didn't really owe me anything; and that, in truth, what he did to me fell well short of abandonment.)

After a few weeks of phone calls, I had accomplished what I set out to do: yank my hero off his pedestal. I had imagined that pulling him down would somehow lift me up. But it didn't. He fell right on top of me, crushing the both of us.

A MONTH AFTER Franco stood me up in Pittsburgh, my phone rang and it was him. He asked how I was doing and how Ellen's pregnancy was coming along. (Does he keep an index card, I wondered, so that he has my personal information handy?) Fine, I told him. And how are you, I asked. Busy, he said, with a heavy sigh, as if to preempt me from even suggesting that we meet anytime soon.

He didn't sound like himself. Even by his standards, he seemed distracted. *Or maybe*, I thought, *guilty*. For having stood me up. Franco was known to respond to guilt. I had recently spoken to a friend of mine who interviewed Franco and his mother long ago for an Italian-American magazine. "Never underestimate the guilt that an Italian mother can inflict on her son," said my friend, who knew firsthand whereof he spoke.

If this *was* guilt, it might pass—so I pounced. I told Franco that, since he and I hadn't been able to get together, maybe I could finally start interviewing his family. I asked for his mother's phone number. He hesitated for only a moment, then gave it to me.

"Let me know what happens with the baby," he said, and we hung up.

I dialed his mother immediately, before Franco could change his mind and warn her off. She had a tiny voice, mired in Italian accent, and she sounded so downcast that I asked if something was wrong.

"No," she said, "just a-lonely."

"Well, would you mind if I came to see you?" I asked.

"Whenever you want," she said. I told her that, because my wife was expecting our first child in a few weeks—"Oh, my *good*ness!" she said—I'd like to come right away. She still lived in Mount Holly, New Jersey, less than a two-hour drive from New York. "Right away is good," she said.

I was elated. So many times Franco had put me off when I asked to speak with his family. Now I was in! His mother would surely tell me everything I needed to know.

That evening, I mentioned (bragged, really) to a cousin of mine (a psychologist) that Franco had finally given me permission to interview his mother.

"Duh!" she said, and laughed hard. "You think a mother's going to have anything bad to say about her son?"

It was such a good and simple question that I hadn't considered it.

"You think *your* mother would have breathed one word against you?" she went on. "What would you do if some guy was chasing *you* around, writing a book? Your mother is the first place you'd send him!"

She was right. Even if an inquisitor had strapped down my mother and threatened to flay her skin with steel combs, she would not have spoken ill of her children. (Except, perhaps, to say that we didn't visit her enough in Florida. I wondered suddenly if Franco was actually *grateful* for my interest in his mother—as if my visit might count toward his quota.)

My cousin's words also led me to consider my hero-hunt from a new perspective: the hero's. I had been pursuing Franco with such abandon—blithely at first, intoxicated by the sheer fact of our union, and punitively of late, stoked by rejection—that I hadn't contemplated the effect of such pursuit. I thought now of Odysseus, such a wise and crafty hero—and in the end, so put upon. According to one of Plato's myths, all that Odysseus wanted in the next life was to come back an anonymous man in a quiet corner of the world. The hero grows weary; the hero doesn't have it easy. What *would* I do if some guy were chasing me around, writing a book? The idea literally made me shudder. It was a horror-movie moment, the hunter becoming the hunted. How positively awful.

Book Three

A HERO AND HIS BOY

16

A MOTHER IS A MOTHER IS A MOTHER

———⟨∞⟩———

A H! I'M SO GLAD you came!" said Franco's mother. "I'm so glad you're going to have your baby! I love-a the babies. I came here *quando* I was nineteen. Then I was thirty-five, I had nine children. The only thing that I wish is to enjoy the baby. I never had a baby-sitter, never wanted nobody *touching* my babies. Oh, the babies, I love-a the babies! I like to kiss them so *much*!"

She was suddenly cradling an imaginary baby. She assailed it with kisses, one cheek and then the other, again and again. In the murmur of skin above her lips I saw an intricate web of creases just like my mother's, the byproduct of a lifetime kissing their children.

My mother: I missed her.

The sun hung high in the midsummer sky. The New Jersey Turnpike had let me off a few miles from Mount Holly, a Revolutionary-era town of prim colonials and haphazard mini-malls. I found the high school and then, just past it, the house the Harris family moved into when they finally left the Mount Holly Gardens housing project. Franco was a teenager by then. It was a modest two-story brick house with pink shutters and trim. The tiny, fenced-in front yard didn't have a scrap of grass; it was done in gravel and stone, a taste of Italy.

She had answered the bell wearing a flower-print dress with white stockings and white shoes. Her hair was still black. She was, at most, half the size of Franco. How had she borne him—and eight more? I reached for her hand, but she pulled me in and grazed each of my cheeks with a kiss. I knew that her youngest son—a financial planner who worked in Manhattan—was just about my age. Maybe I reminded her of him?

Inside, the house was cool, spotless, silent. The walls were white and pink, hung with Italian tchochkes and enormous paintings of flowers. "I love-a the flowers," she said happily. What kind in particular, I asked. "Oh, all kinds," she said. "Roses. Hi-biscuits."

She led me through the kitchen and into a glassed-in patio as large as a small restaurant. Beyond it lay a sloping backyard. Like the front yard, it was done in the Italian style, though far more so. Tiled paths were woven through elaborately terraced gravel, all of it abounding with potted flowers. And statues too, a flock of them, pietàs and nymphs and Davids and Venuses. On the patio, several tables were set with plastic placemats at perfect right angles. (I recalled how Franco, at our first meal, had squared the menus with the corner of the table; the right-angle gene, it seemed, came from his mother.) The overall effect was a hopeful blend of greenhouse, quarry, and sidewalk café that no customer had yet discovered. It was a very grand but very empty nest.

"Wow," I said.

"Ah!" she said.

We sat down.

"Do you miss children in the house?" I asked.

"Well, I live alone now, so I miss company, but I have grandchildren. I don't drive. I never go hardly anywhere. But what I need really is to take a vacation. I want to go back to Italy."

"Isn't Franco taking you in the fall?"

"I hope so," she said. "He promised me. I make my suitcase in ten minutes. But I don't want to bother him. He's supposed to ask *me*."

"How often do you talk to Franco?"

"I never call him, he call me. He called me yesterday, he need to know how you spell *paisano*. Sure I know how to spell. No, I don't call him unless maybe it's been one month. I don't call nobody in fact, even my daughter, she lives nearby. That is just the way I am."

Her claim to self-sufficiency reminded me, again, of my mother. I was swept through with filial feeling. I would have liked to at least mow her lawn (but there was no grass) or drive her to the grocery store (although, when I offered, she said her daughter took her whenever she needed). With my own mother this feeling came to me so hard and so briefly, only at the tail end. Rubbing the small of her back with Tiger Balm, laying cold cloths on her swollen ankles: I had felt as shy, as ill-equipped, as unsure as a virgin. I was able to give so little to someone who had given me her everything.

"I've always wanted to know," I said. "Is it true that you played 'Ave Maria' just before the Immaculate Reception?"

"Oh, yeah, and I still got that record. Beniamino Gigli. I was putting up the manger in the front of the house. Giuseppe and Michele were watching Franco on television, and they weren't saying nothing. I knew they were nervous, so I knew the Steeler were in trouble. I say, Oh, my God, they gonna lose. So I put on 'Ave Maria,' and *quando* the record was playing, they started screaming—that's when I know that he catch-a the ball."

Suddenly she leaped out of her chair. "Oh, my God! 'Scuse me! Oh, my God!" She ran to the patio door. "Michiko, come on! Come on! That's-a my girlfriend, Michiko!"

Michiko and her husband, Vance, were old neighbors from Mount Holly Gardens, long since relocated to California. They apologized for not calling ahead, but Mrs. Harris was thrilled for the visit. Vance was a retired Air Force mechanic, and black; Michiko was Japanese. Mrs. Harris kissed them roundly and announced that we were all going out for lunch, Italian, her treat.

She and I rode in the backseat of Vance's rental car. As we entered the restaurant, the waiters all called out to Mrs. Harris in Italian. When the wine came she made a toast—to old friends and new—but she wouldn't let Vance clink his glass since he was drinking water. "Bad luck," she said.

While she and Michiko got caught up, Vance told me Franco stories.

He was such a good, loyal kid, Vance said, that he called Michiko and Vance whenever the Steelers were playing in California. Once, they all went out to a restaurant after the game. A little girl at the next table was staring at Franco. It was unclear, Vance said, whether she recognized him or was simply enchanted. When the waiter came, Franco smiled toward the girl and said, "I'll have what *she's* having." The girl, misunderstanding, immediately scraped half of her meal onto a bread plate and gave it to Franco.

"That's the kind of effect he has on people," Vance said, shaking his head in wonder.

Hearing this, Michiko admitted that, of all Mrs. Harris's children, Franco was always her favorite.

"He knew how to con Michiko," Vance explained. "In the summer evenings, Mr. Softee would come by, and as soon as he heard the bell he'd run over and sit with Michiko. She'd ask him if he wanted one, and naturally he'd take it. He was always a politician."

I asked Mrs. Harris why she'd named him Franco.

After a friend in Italy, she said, smiling.

"A boyfriend?" I asked.

She paused.

"Well, yes!" she said, in a strange tone—sheepishness? surprise at the candor of the question? She seemed to drift away for a moment. Then her face crinkled dramatically and her mouth turned down. Her hands flew up to cover her face.

And then her hands fell back into her lap, her smile reappeared, and she ordered some penne carbonara. It had been a tearburst, the shortest crying jag I ever witnessed. She would pass through a half-dozen more that day.

After lunch we went on a drive through town. Mrs. Harris pointed out the hospital where her husband died. He collapsed over the steering wheel, she said, as he drove to the bank. We pulled into Mount Holly Gardens. It was a sunbaked suburban clot of low-slung brick apartments.

Michiko gasped at how run-down it looked. "Used to be a dream here," she said.

I expected them all to get out and walk around but we just sat at the curb, in silence, in the air-conditioned car. They could see from there what they needed to see. A black man, his Japanese wife, an Italian widow. I watched them replaying memories in their minds—kids, bikes, bills, jobs. Mount Holly Gardens was America as they knew it. And it had worked. Everyone came from somewhere else, and when they left they were somewhat larger. I had thought that Pittsburgh would tell me about Franco, what kind of person he was, but I should have come to Mount Holly Gardens first.

After a while, Mrs. Harris asked Vance if he wouldn't mind driving up to the cemetery. " 'Course not," he said.

Climbing out of the car, we were smothered by the heat. Mrs. Harris grabbed my hand, and we walked to her husband's grave. The rough skin of my knuckles caught the fabric of her dress, like a burr.

The grave was topped by a gorgeous, massive slab of marble, whitish with gray streaks. I asked if it came from Pietrasanta, her hometown. "Ah!" she said. "No, from Alabama." It bore the same military cross as my father's gravestone. That stone read S. PAUL DUBNER, the name his father gave him reduced to an initial in favor of its Christian successor. This stone read: CADILLAC HARRIS, HUSBAND OF GINA, FATHER OF DANIELA, MARIO, FRANCO, MARISA, ALVARA, LUANA, PIERO, GIUSEPPE, AND MICHELE.

A statue of the Virgin Mary stood at the head of the grave. It looked to be the very same statue my mother had erected at my father's grave. Mrs. Harris bent from the waist and vigorously plucked some weeds. She even pulled weeds like my mother! If I had taken a picture of Mrs. Harris at that moment and shown it to my brothers and sisters, I am sure that every one of them would have thought it was our mother.

One Memorial Day, she was telling us, she came here and found no flag on her husband's grave. "So I took from another one and put on his," she said. Then she broke into and out of another tearburst.

Vance and Michiko dropped us off at Mrs. Harris's house and said their good-byes. It was too hot for the patio, so we settled around the kitchen table. I pulled out my notebook; I was armed with several pages of questions about Franco. But I found myself more interested in the mother than the son. So I asked.

"When I was a little girl," she said, "I was living with my parents along with my brother. But we moved and something must have happened with my parents because my father didn't move with us."

By the third grade, she hired herself out every night to wash dishes. That year, her mother fell ill and went into the hospital. She was alone with her mother when she died.

She was sent to live with her father, who sold hardware from town to town. She quit school to work as a maid. Her father, she told me, would go out to play billiards at night, locking her and her brother inside. When he came home, he beat them with a belt.

"And then the war came," she said. "We had to go up in the mountains. We moved about twelve times. There was nothing to eat and my father was scared to go anywhere and told me to go to Pietrasanta to see if any store was open. We stayed in the churches. The Germans hanged the priest outside the church for hiding people."

Her brother was taken prisoner by the Germans. "The Germans kept the prisoners until the Americani came," she said. "Then they tortured them and cut them into pieces." After a time, a large box arrived in Pietrasanta with the remains of the dead, including her brother. His funeral was held in the same church where she had been baptized.

Cadillac Harris of Baldwin, Mississippi, was among the American soldiers stationed in Italy after the Germans were defeated. She was seventeen when she met him in a dance club. "I used to be scared of black men," she said. "I mean, I never *saw* one before."

"So what did you think when you first met him?" I asked.

"He was a nice man," she said flatly. "He had a girlfriend. He came to me and I said, 'Well, if you want me you got to come to me and leave her.'"

And he did. She wrote to the Pope for permission to marry Cad, since he was a Baptist. Afterward, they took a troop ship to New York and then a bus to Chicago, where he had family. He left her with them, pregnant, when he shipped out to Kentucky.

"What was that like," I asked, "for you to come to this country, not speaking English, your husband leaving you in Chicago with his family—"

"Tell me about it! I wanted to go home! Yah! I mean, I was too young. I was lost! I never was in the elevator before. Everybody's working, I was alone, they told me to not open the door for nobody."

"Were you scared?"

"No, because I didn't open the door!"

She began having children in the Midwest and continued, from Franco onward, in New Jersey. "The only time I went outside was on the first and fifteenth of the month, to buy groceries at the PX," she said. "And I go outside to hang the laundry too. I used to wash every day until late at night. But I was happy. I was happy! I tell you, I love-a the babies so much—so beautiful, oh, my *God!*" Their apartment in Mount Holly Gardens cost one hundred fifteen dollars a month; Cad brought home just three hundred dollars a month from his two jobs. "Nobody ever knocked on my door and asked me to pay the bills," she said, "because I was good with the money."

It was she who managed to save seven hundred dollars for the piece of land near the high school, and it was she who walked across town to buy it—alone, since she knew her black husband would be turned away. It took another seven years to save enough money to build the house. Her children never had fancy things, she told me, but their clothes were always clean and no one ever missed a meal.

Now she leaned close, as if to impart the cruel secret of the universe. She spoke in an insistent whisper, drawing out each word like a dagger: "Never forget who feeds you. Your mother and father—never forget, they feed you *quando* you were small. *Never* forget that."

I thought of a parable I had read not long before:

A bird set out to cross a stormy sea with her three fledglings. The wind was so strong that she could carry only one fledgling at a time. Halfway across the sea with the first one, she said, "My child, look how I struggle and risk my life for you. When I am old, will you do the same for me?"

"If you only bring me to safety, I will do everything you ask of me," said the fledgling, whereupon the mother bird dropped it into the sea, saying, "This is what becomes a liar!"

The mother bird returned to shore and set forth with the second fledgling. She asked the same question, received the same answer, and dropped that child into the sea as well. "You too are a liar!" she cried.

She asked the same question of the third fledgling. Its answer: "My dear mother, it is true that you struggle mightily on my behalf, and risk your own life. And it would be wrong of me to not repay you when you are old. But I cannot bind myself. All I can promise is that when I am grown and have my own children, I will do as much for them as you have done for me."

"Well spoken, my child, and wisely," said the mother bird. "I will spare your life and carry you safely to shore."

Would I be able to do for my children what Mrs. Harris did for hers? What my mother did for me?

This is what a mother endures: we laugh at her, rage at her, ignore and disrespect her, carp and plead and lie to her. And in spite of all that—or maybe *because* of all that, for if we weren't so miserable we wouldn't need a mother to save us—she grabs us up and carries us safely to distant shores, hoping we will one day return the effort but knowing we won't.

Now that is heroic.

WE PARTED AFTER another hour or two with the heat still lying heavy in the air. The hi-biscuits were drooping. We parted with kisses to the cheeks and a promise, happily extracted and happily made, to let her know when the baby arrived.

A FEW DAYS LATER, I dreamed yet again of Franco. As usual, I was pursuing him. I had somehow barged into his house, which was small and cheaply built, right on a busy road. His son was home from college. The son was petulant, arrogant, and directionless. He immediately began using me against Franco, trying to make me a co-conspirator in his slacker life. Franco, meanwhile, wanted to straighten him out. Franco counseled him, firmly, to take control, ease up on the drinking, get serious about life. Franco had a big rip in the seat of his jeans but didn't seem to care. Dana was there too, warm and friendly. I wanted to get Franco alone but couldn't. After a while we all went out to eat. At the restaurant, I tried to interview Franco, but he kept counseling his son. The son poured ketchup into my tape recorder. Franco grew more and more agitated but wouldn't let himself lose his cool; he kept giving advice even while his son ignored him.

I didn't need to call my psychologist cousin to interpret this dream. Franco had no use for my attention (even though I, competing for the role of son, was the "good" son while his own son was a jerk). Nor was he concerned with appearances (the cheap house, the ripped pants). He was focused on just one thing: being a father to his son.

I had by now dreamed about Franco many times. But this one was different. Upon waking up, the character with whom I most strongly identified wasn't "me" and it wasn't "the son." It was Franco. The drive I felt upon waking was not the drive to be a son (especially to a father figure who never asked to be my father figure); it was the drive to be a father.

I had been sleepwalking lately. Most mornings, Ellen and I would wake up to find our bedside table bare. Apparently I was getting out of bed during the night and moving the lamp and stacks of books to the floor.

One night, Ellen caught me in mid-act. "What are you doing?" she asked.

"Making room for the baby," I said.

"Get back in bed," she told me, and I did.

When I was a child, I dreamed a child's dream—of a man coming to rescue me. Now, at last, I was dreaming the dreams of a man. My subconscious was sending a message: long ago I froze myself in place at the time of my father's death and summoned a stranger—a younger, mightier, less mortal man—to watch over me; now it was time to let myself thaw. I had a more pressing duty than chasing my childhood hero. In that long-ago Dream, Franco spoke only one line. I couldn't grasp then what it meant (or maybe I just didn't want to). But as I now—finally—understood, his line wasn't a promise of rescue at all. It was an exhortation, a prophecy: "Kid, you're going to have to take it from here yourself." Franco didn't have any solutions for me, then or now. He wasn't the answer; the answer was me.

It has often been said that a son lives his life to make his father whole. I suppose this may be true. All along, I had imagined my life as an offering to my dead father. That was why I became a writer: to finish the books he never had the chance to start. That was the way I would make him whole.

But I had been wrong. No book could ever accomplish such a thing. No book, as hard and bloody as it might be, was suitable sacrifice. It would take a riskier, more painful project to fulfill my offering: fatherhood.

17

SOMETHING LIKE LOVE

＊━◦◦◦◦━＊

H E WAS BORN in a hurry, an unfrozen slice of time.
Ellen was doing her hard work, and I—where was I? day-
dreaming? numbed by expectation?—saw him abruptly hoisted out of
her belly, out of my imagination, and whisked to a metal table. The doctor began tossing him about, the way a butcher tosses a chicken. The
baby sputtered loudly.

"Go to him," Ellen said.

The doctor poked, measured, prodded. His metal table was crowded
with metal instruments, medieval but for their gleam. A heat lamp dangled above, flooding my son's eyes. I held up my hand to throw shadow
onto his face.

"He *needs* the heat," the doctor said tersely.

"Is he all right?" I asked.

"So far, so good."

"All this is standard?"

"All standard."

"Can I touch him?"

"Be my guest."

I shyly lowered my index fingers as if he were a bird in need of a
perch, not knowing which fragile piece of him to stroke.

The doctor picked up a long, slender, evil-looking hose.

"What's *that* for?" I asked.

"Gets the mucus out of his nasal passages," he said, and rammed it up the baby's nostril.

His miniature hands, gummy and cool, suddenly gripped my index fingers—what strength! I had no idea, on the first day of his life, he could do such a thing!—while his face, all cheeks and chins, exploded into a wail. His thin scarlet tongue quivered like a bell's clapper gone mad. His eyes pleaded with me through tender slits. His fingers dug into mine, turning his red and mine white. How he needed me! My heart surged with hurt for his hurt, and it surged with joy at the hugeness of my responsibility. I knew instantly and forever that I would gladly fly him across a stormy sea. I would throw myself in front of a truck, a bullet, a bully. He needed me! *I love you love you love you,* I told him. *I will not let you down,* I told him. *I will not die or disappear, leaving you to adopt some distant, helmeted hero whose job is not to steer you through life.*

The first days were a blend of wonder and frenzy. Ellen and I stared at him and each other. We knew we should sleep while he slept, but we couldn't tear ourselves away. As they had done nine months earlier during my mother's shiva, friends brought food and spoke in low tones. But gone was that state of no-more-ness. This was new life, the diametric opposite of fresh death. I had entered a state of extreme here-and-now-ness. And, even better, I felt a thirst for the future I hadn't known since I was a child. I could not look at the boy without my thoughts tumbling forward to how we would teach him, raise him, love him. If someone had asked me just then about Franco, I might have responded as Chuck Noll once did: "Franco who?"

On the eighth day, we took him to synagogue for his *brit milah*, the ritual circumcision marking the covenant established by Abraham, the original idol-smasher. It was also the day that we would make public his name.

I was so deliriously, tearfully excited that I did not trust myself to speak from memory during the service. I wrote down what I wanted to say, and I type it here straight from the note I held that day in my damp hands: "My father, who was also named Solomon Dubner, died when I was ten years old. Ever since, the world somehow seemed incomplete. It was like a jigsaw puzzle that always had one piece missing. Eight days ago, the last piece turned up. It would have been ridiculous to name this boy anything but Solomon. We hope his life is as eventful as King Solomon's, that he will be wise and inventive and bold (though not so bold as to have seven hundred wives). And we hope that, like my father, his children will love him until the end of time."

My only sadness was that my mother did not live to hold him. Every hard edge she presented to the world disappeared when she was with her grandchildren. She offered them unadulterated love and they returned it in force. Even at the end, when she was lassoed by oxygen tubing, the youngest grandkids had to be restrained from leaping into her lap. Solomon was her thirteenth grandchild (plus four great-grands), the first one she missed. I thought of her every time I picked him up. He looked just like her. And how the two of them would have gotten along! He was, like her, curious and buoyant and headstrong (quite literally in his case: on the day he was born, while slung over my shoulder, he raised up his head—he looked like those fuzzy photographs of the Loch Ness monster—to take a look around). Sometimes, when his stubbornness got the better of us, Ellen and I would tease him with a one-word scold: "*Veronica . . .*"

I remembered to send Franco's mother a birth announcement. Two days later she called, so riled up by vicarious baby-thrill that I could hardly understand her. (Over the phone, her accent made her sound like Chico Marx—yet another link, however tenuous, to my own mother, who was so fond of Groucho.) What I could make out was that she wanted me to send a picture of the baby, so I did.

The next week's mail brought a card from her: "Dear Ellen, Stephen and Solomon, I received your beautiful baby picture. He is so perfect, and so loveable, please receive my deep congratulation. With affect, Gina."

Into the card she had folded a terry-cloth bib. It read: "Thank Heaven for Little Boys." A few days later came a second card, this one with a $100 U.S. savings bond tucked inside. And she asked for more pictures.

We began writing back and forth, two or three times a month. "One day, hoping to come to New York and see all of you great family," she wrote. "With affect, Gina." And: "I must say, Franco and I, we will be going to Italy the November 5. Please kiss the beautiful baby and your lovely wife. Ciao, Gina." With a Roman postmark came a package of goodies—a change purse for Ellen, a keychain for me, a picture frame for baby photos—and a snapshot of Gina and Franco. They waved at the camera from beneath a twenty-foot sculpture of an angel: "To all you Family, from all our Family, love, Gina and Franco, Italy Roma."

I sent her updates and, always, pictures. Solomon proudly naked in the bathtub. His first smiles—crooked, knowing little smirks. Oatmeal spread clear across his face, proof of his graduation to solid food.

One day, Ellen was holding Solomon up to look at the photographs on our walls. He ignored them. He fidgeted, cooed with boredom. But when they arrived at my parents' wedding portrait, I watched him fixate on it. After a full minute or so (a lifetime, by a baby's standards) he reached for their faces. When his fingers bumped the picture—cold and glassy, not real at all!—he turned to me. Was that disappointment in his eyes? I quickly thrust forward my warm, real face. He reached for me, even squeezed out a smile. But still he looked melancholy.

"He recognizes your mother," Ellen said.

"You think?"

"I do. I think he innately gets what it means to be related to another person, even in a photograph."

I wanted to believe that too. Might he even have recognized himself in my mother's photograph? The shape of their mouths was identical—the upper lips especially, each with two sharp peaks, just like the Brooklyn Bridge.

But if he did recognize my mother, wasn't it all the worse to discover that her picture was not really *her*? It was the further loss of something he had already lost and didn't even know it.

I was grateful, therefore, whenever I packed an envelope with photographs for Gina Harris. It cheered me immeasurably to know that there *was* a set of hands, grandmother's hands, to receive them. To know that she would admire his round face in the sunlight streaming through her south Jersey *piazza*. To know that she considered this child of mine—as she put it in one of her letters—"a treasure."

I was a man who had journeyed home looking for the site of his boyhood dream but found instead a sex farm. And I was a man who went looking for a hero but found instead . . . *a mother.*

It made me wonder if I had mislabeled the enterprise I'd been engaged in here. I had always called it hero worship. A hero is many things: savior, champion, inspiration, role model. Above all, for me at least, I had come to think of a hero as a guide. But when my father died, it wasn't so much his guidance that I lost; it was his warmth. His stubbled chin against my smooth cheek. His goofy wordplay, his love of baseball, his laughing Brooklyn accent. His *happiness*—which, on those rare days it broke through, having been sent into exile by his depression, was as contagious as poison ivy.

Years later, when I chased down Franco Harris, it wasn't really his guidance I sought, was it? (Even in the Dream he wasn't much of a guide; he had no answers, no advice.)

What I truly wanted from him, then and now, was his warmth. When I first traveled to Pittsburgh my fantasy was that Franco, so charmed by my long-ago infatuation and so impressed by my moxie, would invite me into his life. He would shine on me the light that he saved for special friends.

He, however, was having none of that.

But his mother—she had warmth to spare! And when she began spreading it in my direction, the true purpose of my mission became evident.

It wasn't the guidance of a hero I'd been after all along. It was something both smaller and larger than that; it was something like love.

18

FINISHED BUSINESS

———··◄◦∞◦►··———

O N THE THIRD SATURDAY of December 2000, the Pittsburgh Steelers would play their final game at Three Rivers
Stadium. Only thirty years old, it was to be demolished and replaced by
two new stadiums, one for football and one for baseball. This extrava-
gance had been the subject of much local debate. In the mill towns dot-
ting the three rivers that flow through Pittsburgh, schools and churches
and entire neighborhoods had been going broke. But where the rivers
come together, the new stadiums were already rising at the cost of half a
billion dollars.

I was writing an article about the demise of Three Rivers for the *New
York Times Magazine.* The Steelers planned an elaborate ceremony after
the final game, to include speechifying, video highlights, fireworks, and
an ingathering of the old heroes who brought home four Super Bowl
trophies. I had seen by now that Pittsburgh is a town where the hand-
shake between religion (particularly Catholicism) and sport (particularly football) is so firm that it can be hard to tell where one hand stops
and the other begins. Indeed, the shuttering of Three Rivers was being
treated like the deconsecration of a cathedral. The lockers of the most
beloved Steelers, for instance, would be dismantled and reassembled,
like a church fresco, in the new stadium. The farewell ceremony would

conclude with a real-life re-creation of the Immaculate Reception. It promised to be an interesting show, with Franco its star.

I called him to say I was coming back to town.

"That's fan*tas*tic," he said. (I knew he meant the *Times* article, not my visit.) "Let me know when you get in, and I'll pick you up at the airport."

No thanks, I told him. Because I'd be spending nearly two weeks reporting in Pittsburgh, Ellen and Solomon were coming with me; we'd rented a car and an apartment. The baby was four months old.

I passed my days doing interviews (former Steelers, the mayor of Pittsburgh, city planners and sports pundits, a great slew of Rooneys) and my evenings singing made-up songs to Solomon. Some were vaguely educational ("These are your feet / These are your feet / Left-right / One-two / Left-right / One-two . . ."); others, practical ("Calm down / Calm down / Nothing's wrong in / Solomon Town . . ."). He diligently watched videotapes of old Steelers games with me. (Ellen was not so diligent.) One night we all went out for dinner with Babe and Joe Gordon, a nice Italian place, but Solomon was a bad sport and slept right through it.

Franco, after a few false starts, agreed to one last interview. He pushed for neutral territory (a restaurant), but I lobbied, long and hard, for his house. It seemed silly to have so maniacally peered and leered inside his life without at least seeing where he lived. But even more than that, I wanted to win this standoff for the sake of winning. It was Franco who long ago gave me the will to win; our recent history made me want to use it, just this once, against him.

Finally he relented. I would visit him at noon on Sunday, a week before the last Three Rivers game.

On the drive over, my cell phone rang. As soon as I heard his voice, I was sure he was canceling. I was more relieved than disappointed: did I honestly still need to be shadowing this guy? But he wasn't canceling. He said he wanted some cheese and was running out to the store, so I might beat him to his house.

The day was raw and sleety, the highways empty. I drove toward downtown, crossed what felt like twenty bridges, headed toward the airport and, beyond that, the posh and hilly hinterland where Franco lived.

Here the streets were wide and quiet and old, with quaint signage and gleaming SUVs. I stopped at a supermarket to pick up some clementines for Franco. In the checkout line my phone rang again. Him again.

"Hey," he said, "are you there yet?"

"I'm at the Giant Eagle," I said.

"No way. Me too. I'm at the checkout."

"Me too," I said. I turned around and saw him, a few aisles down, and he waved. We laughed, hung up our phones. On his way out, two boys, born long after Franco retired, stopped him for an autograph. He signed and they ran off, giggling.

"What do you have there?" he asked, pointing at my bag.

"A box of clementines. You like them?"

"You didn't have to do that," he said, at which point the plastic bag broke, the box hit the floor, the flimsy rubbery netting failed to contain the clementines, and they skittered off in a dozen directions. Franco helped me gather them up.

I followed his car, up steep hills and around blind curves. His house was a typically gigantic exurban affair, a brownish brick contemporary built on a reclaimed golf course.

Inside, I sat in the living room while he fixed himself a plate of cheese and grapes in the kitchen. He offered me some, but I'd eaten. It was a lived-in house, happily cluttered but desperately quiet. His knife on the cutting board rang out like an ax in the forest. A corner of the living room was given over to football trophies; a LeRoy Neiman print of a New York bar scene dominated one wall. Big windows looked out on a midwinter-brown ravine speckled with fresh snow.

Dana came downstairs, said hello. She was going out for a drive with Salty, her bichon frise. She told Franco not to bother cleaning up his kitchen mess, that she'd take care of it. She sounded like a mother talking to her teenage son. She was polite to me, friendly, bordering on chatty. I found myself wishing she would stick around.

Franco led me down to a finished basement: a bar with leather-cushioned stools, more football trophies, a pool table, a rack of silky patterned shirts (very 1970s, apparently bound for Goodwill), one wall of windows. We settled into a pair of corduroy easy chairs facing the televi-

sion. Franco turned on CNN to get caught up with the Bush-Gore election recount in Florida. He had campaigned for Gore, who narrowly
won Pennsylvania, but on this day it seemed ever more likely that the
courts would, like a rich uncle, slip the presidency into George W.
Bush's pocket.

On another channel, the Steelers were playing the Giants. Franco
began flipping back and forth, the volume low. He put his feet up. He
wore a red flannel shirt, tan khakis, patterned socks, and brown loafers.
As he ate he deposited the grape seeds neatly on a paper towel spread
across the arm of his chair.

I began asking questions and he began answering them, but both of
us stared straight ahead at the television. An hour, then two, then three
of Wolf Blitzer–Kerry Collins–John Sununu–Kordell Stewart–Mario
Cuomo–Michael Strahan punctuated by our halfhearted conversation.
Sometimes I thought Franco had fallen asleep, so long were his pauses
and so low his voice.

As before, he preferred business talk. He admitted that buying Parks
Sausage had been a mistake. (I immediately realized the irony of this ad-
mission: if he hadn't bought Parks he would have avoided the cover of
Black Enterprise magazine and, therefore, *me.*) He was unhappy that his
ownership of Super Bakery had become such public knowledge ("I just
don't think it's anybody's business," he said). When I asked how his
growth plans for Super Bakery were playing out, he produced a finely
wrought koan, a veritable Yogi Berra–ism: "I guess I do eventually catch
up to what I've been thinking for a long time."

When it came to personal matters, his answers were brief and color-
less. He told stories that others had told me with a thousand percent
more enthusiasm.

His grape seeds by now lay desiccated on the puckered paper towel.
Behind us the thin winter daylight had faded. He massaged his stiff
right shoulder; he sank deeper into his chair. He looked exactly like a
tired fifty-year-old businessman at the end of one long week and about to
begin another.

"This is what I do now, a lot of times," he said. "Watch football games,
fall asleep. Nothing like a Sunday afternoon, you're zonked—'Okay,

what happened, what'd I miss? Man, how'd that score change all of a sudden?' You realize you slept a lot longer than you thought."

A long pause. "So," he said, "are we done?"

I had neither desire nor reason to prolong the interview. I had finally gotten what I wanted: Franco alone, in his house, uninterrupted, with the liberty to ask him anything. And yet . . .

I felt as if I'd spent a lifetime tracking the habits and habitats of some exotic creature, and now that he was in my capture I had no idea what to do with him.

I followed him upstairs. The kitchen was dark, quiet, empty. He asked if I wanted to go have an early dinner. Sure, I said. "Italian okay?" he asked. Sure, I said. He went off to change his clothes. I found a bathroom. I didn't go through his medicine cabinet or steal his toothbrush. He had lost his power over me. Downstairs, in his corduroy easy chair, he finally *had* revealed himself. He was a man who got tired, whose shoulder ached, who liked to fall asleep on Sunday afternoons. That's what men do when they work hard. That's what I would have seen my father do had he lived. That's what I'll be doing not so many years from now, if I'm lucky.

A WEEK LATER, I was at Franco's side again. We stood in the very back of the end zone at Three Rivers Stadium. The Steelers had won their final game, against the limp Washington Redskins. The farewell celebration was reaching its climax. Franco, wearing a crisp new version of his old jersey, was positioned just out of public view, eyes aimed at the overhead JumboTron screen along with fifty-eight thousand Steelers devotees.

"How about one more look at the greatest play in NFL history!" the PA announcer said, and the crowd made happy, prayerful noise.

The Immaculate Reception played across the JumboTron in super-slow motion: the desperate throw, the brutal collision, the balletic catch, and Franco's furious gallop into the very end zone where we now stood. The crowd's happy roar built to a jubilant peal, and when the tape was over and Franco himself trotted onto the turf—"Here we go," he said, perhaps to me, perhaps to himself—they screamed as if a god had just climbed down off his mountaintop.

From midfield, he waved to the crowd. He wore black trousers with his football jersey and, since he'd known the turf would be wet, rubber-soled shoes. A football was tossed to him and he set out, at perhaps one-third the original speed, to reenact the play that changed his life—and mine?—forever.

Although my infatuation was by now in deep recession, I could not fail to note, as Franco jogged sixty yards down the soggy field, that I had just crossed two more items off my Franco Wish List: No. 1 (Walk through Three Rivers Stadium with Franco) and No. 4 (Watch tape of Immaculate Reception with him). I had already taken care of No. 6 (Spend time at his house) and No. 5 (Meet Dana and Dok)—No. 5 in generous measure before today's game, when I spoke with them for an hour outside the stadium while Franco signed autographs. I bet I could have even conquered No. 10 (See Franco naked) had I really needed to.

Then came the fireworks, the black-and-gold confetti, and "Auld Lang Syne." The fans cheered and wept and eventually went home. I made my way to a post-postgame reception for the old Steelers. I saw Franco there. He seemed both bashful and excited over the attention he'd been receiving all day. He asked me if I'd had a good time. Yes, I said, which was true—although my good time had come more as a jour-nalist than a hero-worshiper. Franco shook my hand and drifted away; Dana drifted over. She told me where they and some other folks were having dinner after the party. It was a half-invitation, maybe three-quarters. But I didn't go. I was eager to get back to my own family.

FOR WEEKS AFTERWARD I didn't contact him, and then the weeks became months. I was dazzled by fatherhood. Even on deadline, I would rush home to give Solomon his bath and help put him to bed, then return to my studio to write. I loved to stare into his deep brown eyes, so brazenly curious, and wonder what they would one day see. Love made me forgetful, it made me humble, it made me cocky. Love sometimes made my jaw ache: I found myself unconsciously clenching my teeth when I was near Solomon, as if to keep from gobbling him up. Together we read books, we counted taxis from the window, we belly-laughed, we burped and slurped, and, lo and behold, we took to our feet. The key to not being needy, I discovered, was simple: being needed.

Franco was a world I had entered and, finally, departed. I played the hero game to its end; I may not have won but at least I finished in one piece. It would be a lie to call it a happy experience. I had been stung by his rejection and baffled by his obfuscations. But I was a more desperate person then.

Now, from a growing distance, I see things more clearly. I see that Franco was as kind to me as any sane person in his position might have been expected to be. He was, I have to admit, wise for refusing my most aggressive advances. Though he was defiantly unknowable and even unquantifiable, he was just as defiantly decent (for the most part). Whether or not he had the capacity to offer something like love to a total stranger should not be the mark by which his goodness is mea-sured. He *is* a good man, as far as I can tell. Full of quirks and faults, to be sure, but who among us is not? In the end I came to see him as more human than hero—more Moses than Jesus—and as humans go, I think he is a very fine one. I am not remotely ashamed that he was the man I reached out for when I was a brittle young boy. I was fortunate to find him when I needed him; I am grateful that he let me know him, at least a little bit, when I thought I still did.

ONE DAY SHORTLY AFTER Solomon turned a year old, he didn't awake at his usual early hour. By nine o'clock, when I was ready to leave for the day, he was still asleep. I stalled; I wanted to say good-bye. In the kitchen, I pulled out my laptop and went online. Reading the words "Two airplanes crash at World Trade Center," I pictured a pair of tiny two-seaters, Piper Cubs, tangled amid a skyscraper's roof antennae. We lived in the West Fifties of Manhattan, a good four miles north of the Trade Center. The plane-crash headline was barely enough to make me turn on the television, but I did. Then I marched into the bedroom and pulled Ellen by the arm into the kitchen. For a long, long time we stood wordlessly and stared at the images. Finally we heard Solomon stirring and we both ran for him. He had slept till nearly noon. It was as if his small and pure soul were somehow attuned to the morning's horror and couldn't bear to acknowledge it. We scooped him out of the crib with a greed that frightened him.

Our reactions to the September 11 killing spree were disparate. I, most typically, veered from one emotion to the next: shock to fear to anger to grievous confusion. Ellen, who had photographed war in Chechnya and Afghanistan and Israel, was able to do so only by quarantining its dangers to a far corner of her mind. She now reflexively did the same. For five or six days she was pure stone, hardly seeming to register what had happened. When at last she did, she broke down entirely. Solomon, meanwhile—babbling, toddling, laughing, and provoking laughter at will—was blessedly oblivious. In time, his oblivion became our blessing. He didn't need us to watch CNN eighteen hours a day; he needed us to be his parents, so that's what we did. During those benumbed early days, he became our sole link with normalcy.

One night I had a dream and then it repeated itself four or five times. It was the first recurring dream I'd had since childhood, since *the* Dream. But Franco wasn't in this one. I hadn't dreamed of him at all, in fact, since that sleepy visit to his home the previous winter.

In this dream, the first Trade Center tower had just collapsed. I was seeing things from the perspective of a TV camera pointing at the chaos—the result, surely, of watching too much news footage. People were running from the collapse, choking on debris, shouting and screaming. A secretary in one high heel, a fat man with blood on his eyeglasses, a bug-eyed bike messenger without a bike. And then I saw myself in the dream. I was running awkwardly, shoulders tucked in. I had something in my arms. I had Solomon in my arms. I had his face buried in my chest to keep the smoke out of his lungs. We made it to safety.

In the dream I wasn't a fireman; I wasn't a football player. I was me. This is what it took—nineteen hijackers committing mass murder—but at long last, I was the hero of my own dream.

Three hundred and forty-three firemen died at the World Trade Center. In the mind's eye, as a numeral, 343 was not so striking. But one day the *Times* ran a double-page spread with thumbnail portraits of all the firemen. Now each numeral had a face, a name. Three hundred and forty-three people! Three hundred and forty-three people *who did not have to be there*, who ran into the burning buildings to make sure that other people, regular people could get out. It was understood that such bravery was as unnatural as the atrocity that necessitated it.

The country seemed to regain, albeit involuntarily and perhaps fleetingly, a communal soul. In New York, every firehouse was soon awash with flowers and candles and casseroles. And that antique word, *hero*, was dusted off. It was chanted, everywhere and loudly, as if it were the only prayer we knew.

On September 23, 2001, the second Sunday after the attacks, I watched as the NFL resumed its schedule. The Jets and Patriots—could their names have been any more appropriate?—were playing in Foxboro, Massachusetts. Before the game, three New York City firemen named Andruzzi joined a fourth Andruzzi brother, a Patriots offensive lineman, at midfield for the coin toss. I, along with everyone, wept. Someone in the stands had hung a banner: FOOTBALL HAS PLAYERS. AMERICA HAS HEROES.

It made me think of something Franco said long ago, about football players and plumbers—that the former were treated like heroes only because network television hadn't yet started keeping stats on the latter.

That first Sunday back, I watched the players run and tackle and throw, and for a while at least everything was different. Humility had worked its way inside their limbs. They did their jobs, helped other guys off the turf, trotted back to the sidelines. They didn't bellow like bulls every time they made a play. Linebackers didn't stomp around the head of the man they just tackled. Quarterbacks didn't glare at their receivers when they dropped a ball. I knew they'd get back to that, just like New Yorkers would get back to stealing cabs from one another. But on that day at least, and for a few Sundays afterward, I really enjoyed watching them play football. I liked how they carried themselves. To my eye, they all looked a little bit like Franco Harris.

I almost called him but didn't. A few months later he left a message on my voice mail, wishing happy holidays. I tried him back but he wasn't in. We haven't spoken since.

That was a dark season in New York. It was particularly hard to set aside the fact that, on the other side of the world, it was the 19 hijackers and not the 343 firemen who were the heroes. Our little family, however, found a piece of bright news: Solomon would be gaining a sister. She arrived in February, and we named her Anya Bess. She brought another round of cheer from Gina Harris, another $100 U.S. savings bond, and, best of all, an actual visit.

Without fail, Anya Bess and her brother would lift our thoughts from the darkness of the present. How can you fail to summon hope when you look into a child's eyes? Hope is all you see there.

And I have hopes for them.

May they find people to love, admire, perhaps even emulate. May they discover ideas that are worth living for. May they do well unto others. And this I hope above all: may they be their own heroes.

ACKNOWLEDGMENTS

IN THE END, it is you in a room, alone, for a couple of years. But no writer gets to that room without plenty of help, and I had my share.

Because this book tells the story of my complicated duet with Franco Harris, I won't ramble on about him. But I do thank him for being—long ago and still—himself, which is an awfully hard thing to be. I also thank his mother, and mine, for teaching me that nothing is nobler (or more heart-wracking) than the raising of children.

Other strong women have shored me up. Claire Wachtel at William Morrow is a true editor and true friend. Suzanne Gluck at the William Morris Agency (no relation) is, I believe, without equal. Suzanne and Claire are a pair of firestarters who, miraculously, manage to throw a spark exactly where it's needed but never let the fire get out of control.

My experience with William Morrow/HarperCollins only gets better. Michael Morrison somehow combines unflappability with enthusiasm, and his door is always open. I am thrilled daily to work with him. Cathy Hemming is wisdom incarnate. Then there's the irrepressible Sharyn Rosenblum and the indispensable Jen Pooley. And Lisa Gallagher, Kim Lewis, and Debbie Stier, who are all so good at what they do. At William Morris, I am also lucky to work with Emily Nurkin, Karen Gerwin, Tracy Fisher, Betsy Berg, and Alan Kannof, keeper of the Zelman Moses flame.

To Lisa Chase, Morris Dickstein, Peter Dubner, Adam Moss, Ellen Pall, and Jonathan Rosen: thank you for the best peer review a writer could hope for. I owe you more than these few measly words.

In Pittsburgh, Joe Gordon opened every door and Mike McGough answered every question. They are both fine gentlemen, and it would have been worth writing this book if only to have met them. A few hundred other people came to my aid, telling tales and fielding queries about sports, religion, psychology, hero worship, and so on. I am particularly grateful to: Ernie Accorsi, Bruce Americus, Art and Cynthia Baldwin, Eric Bass, Robin Bernstein, Rocky Bleier, Roy Blount Jr., Ed Bouchette, Enrico Bruschini, Tim Carey, Robert Cialdini, Michiko and Vance Clayton, Josh Cohen, Walter Conti, Myron Cope, James Dabbs, Jerry DiPaola, Pat Doyle, Helen Fisher, Marinella Garbati, Barbara Gilliam and the late Joe Gilliam, Jeffrey Goldberg, Lee Goldberg, Max Gomberg, Stephen Hall, Arthur Hertzberg, Bee Huss, Tunch Ilkin, Julie Irwin, Susie and Chris Kellen, Scott Kerschbaumer, Ed Kiely, Simon Jacobson, Jon Kolb, Richard LaPoint, Chaz Letzkus, Patricia Lowry, Arthur Lubetz, Rev. John Marcucci, Jim Marooney, Gerry Marzorati, Roy McHugh, Lydell Mitchell, Dee and Tom Murrin, Erin Patrice O'Brien, Alan Oirich, Ken Osman, Sandy Padwe, David Potter, Andrew Quinn, Dan Radakovich, Adam Reingold, Art Rooney Jr., Art Rooney II, Dan Rooney, Kathy Rooney, Tim Rooney, Ron Rossi, Gordon Russell, Barry Singer, Fritz Sippel, Eileen and Bill Stewart, Lynn Swann, Ann Terrell, Clarke Thomas, Pat Thomassey, Patrick Tierney, Jason Tyrer, Gene Upshaw, Ron Wahl, Daniel Wann, Shirley Watkins, Daniel Weigand, Dwight White, August Wilson, and Arthur Ziegler. Thanks also to those who, for various reasons, prefer to not be acknowledged in print.

Ruth Wheat of the B'nai B'rith Lecture Bureau has kept me on the road and out of trouble. Carl Koerner gave me a room of my own when I needed one; he and Ivan Kronenfeld provide counsel, much of it sage, and tell great stories. Thanks also to Jordana Levine and Joelle Levine. David Hajdu is a pal; he introduced me to Elba Flanbury, the sort of godmother I wish upon every writer. Thanks to Hugo Lindgren and (again) Adam Moss for helping me tell slivers of this story in the *New York Times Magazine*. And to Michael Murphy, who knew all about Franco but couldn't quite relate, him being a Browns fan.

Katie Brentzel and Benjamin Manges made my time at the Steelers offices worthwhile. Nick Smyth haunted the morgues and libraries of Pittsburgh. And thanks to the following research assistants, who made this book as sharp and true as it could be: Anya Kamenetz, Sarah Richards, Brian Seibert, Rebecca Traister, Brad Tuttle.

Muriel and David Binder are my children's grandparents, and they actually don't seem distressed to have a writer as a son-in-law. David was also my wife's first hero; she chose well. To Solomon and Anya: doo-dah! And to Ellen, the strongest woman of all, I say thank you—and *Sheremetyevo*.

SELECTED BIBLIOGRAPHY

Many of the following works provided specific background material; others offered more impressionistic lessons. And a few, to which I am most indebted, delivered pure inspiration.

BOOKS

Allen, Frederick Lewis. *Only Yesterday: An Informal History of the 1920s.* New York: Harper & Bros., 1931.

Amsel, Nachum. *The Jewish Encyclopedia of Moral and Ethical Issues.* Northvale, N.J.: Jason Aronson Inc., 1996.

Baker, Nicholson. *U and I: A True Story.* New York: Random House, 1991.

Bentley, Eric. *A Century of Hero-Worship: A Study of the Idea of Heroism in Carlyle and Nietzsche, with Notes on Wagner, Spengler, Stefan George, and D. H. Lawrence.* Philadelphia: J. B. Lippincott, 1944.

Benton, Mike. *Superhero Comics of the Golden Age: The Illustrated History.* Dallas: Taylor Publishing, 1992.

Berg, A. Scott. *Lindbergh.* New York: G. P. Putnam's Sons, 1998.

Berger, David. *The Rebbe, the Messiah, and the Scandal of Orthodox Indifference.* Portland, Or.: Littman Library of Jewish Civilization, 2001.

Bierce, Ambrose. *The Devil's Dictionary.* New York: A. and C. Boni, 1925.

Bleier, Rocky, with Terry O'Neil. *Fighting Back.* Briarcliff Manor, N.Y.: Stein and Day, 1975.

Blount, Mel, with Cynthia Sterling. *The Cross Burns Brightly: How a Hall-of-Famer Tackled Racism and Adversity to Help Troubled Boys.* Grand Rapids, Mich.: Zondervan Publishing, 1993.

Blount, Roy, Jr. *About Three Bricks Shy of a Load: A Highly Irregular Lowdown on the*

Year the Pittsburgh Steelers Were Super but Missed the Bowl. Boston: Little Brown & Co., 1974.

Bradley, James, with Ron Powers. *Flags of Our Fathers.* New York: Bantam Books, 2000.

Bradshaw, Terry, with David Diles. *Terry Bradshaw: Man of Steel.* Grand Rapids, Mich.: Zondervan Publishing, 1979.

Bradshaw, Terry, with Buddy Martin. *Looking Deep.* Chicago: Contemporary Books, 1989.

Braudy, Leo. *The Frenzy of Renown: Fame and Its History.* New York: Oxford Univ. Press, 1986.

Braun, Thomas. *Franco Harris.* Mankato, Minn.: Creative Educational Society, 1975.

Burchard, S. H. *Sports Star: Franco Harris.* New York: Harcourt Brace Jovanovich, 1976.

Carlyle, Thomas. *On Heroes, Hero-Worship, and the Heroic in History.* Lincoln, Neb.: Univ. of Nebraska Press, 1966.

Carroll, Bob; Michael Gershman, David Neft, and John Thorn, eds. *Total Football II: The Official Encyclopedia of the National Football League.* New York: HarperCollins Publishers, 1999.

Chabon, Michael. *The Mysteries of Pittsburgh.* New York: William Morrow & Co., 1988.

———. *The Amazing Adventures of Kavalier and Clay.* New York: Random House, 2000.

Cope, Myron. *Double Yoi! A Revealing Memoir by the Broadcaster/Writer.* Sports Publishing Inc., 2002.

Courson, Steve, and Lee R. Schreiber. *False Glory: Steelers and Steroids, the Steve Courson Story.* Stamford, Ct.: Longmeadow Press, 1991.

Cramer, Richard Ben. *DiMaggio: The Hero's Life.* New York: Simon & Schuster, 2000.

Dabbs, James McBride, with Mary Godwin Dabbs. *Heroes, Rogues, and Lovers: Testosterone and Behavior.* New York: McGraw-Hill, 2000.

Dumas, Alexandre. *My Memoirs.* Translated by A. Craig Bell. Westport, Conn.: Greenwood Press, 1961.

Emerson, Ralph Waldo. *Representative Men.* Boston: Houghton Mifflin, 1930.

Exley, Frederick. *A Fan's Notes.* New York: Random House, 1968.

Feiffer, Jules. *The Great Comic Book Heroes.* New York: The Dial Press, 1965.

Feiler, Bruce. *Walking the Bible: A Journey by Land Through the Five Books of Moses.* New York: William Morrow & Co., 2001.

Forster, E. M. *Two Cheers for Democracy.* New York: Harcourt, Brace & World, 1951.

Fox, Larry. *Mean Joe Greene and the Steelers' Front Four.* New York: Dodd, Mead & Co., 1975.

Garber, Marjorie. *Symptoms of Culture.* New York: Routledge Press, 1998.

Graham, Laurie. *Singing the City: The Bonds of Home in an Industrial Landscape.* Pittsburgh: Univ. of Pittsburgh Press, 1998.

Hadas, Moses, and Morton Smith. *Heroes and Gods: Spiritual Biographies in Antiquity.* New York: Harper & Row, 1965.

Hahn, James, and Lynn Hahn. *Franco Harris: The Quiet Ironman.* St. Paul: EMC Corp., 1979.

Hajdu, David. *Positively 4th Street: The Lives and Times of Joan Baez, Bob Dylan, Mimi Baez Fariña, and Richard Fariña.* New York: Farrar, Straus, and Giroux, 2001.

Hameln, Glückel of. *The Memoirs of Glückel of Hameln.* Translated by Marvin Lowenthal. New York: Schocken Books, 1977.

Harris, Gina. *Autobiography of Gina Parenti Harris.* Unpublished.

Harris, Maxine. *The Loss that Is Forever: The Lifelong Impact of the Early Death of a Mother or Father.* New York: Dutton, 1995.

Hertzberg, Arthur. *A Jew in America: My Life and a People's Struggle for Identity.* San Francisco: HarperSanFrancisco, 2002.

Hoerr, John P. *And the Wolf Finally Came: The Decline of the American Steel Industry.* Pittsburgh: Univ. of Pittsburgh Press, 1988.

Hook, Sidney. *The Hero in History: A Study in Limitation and Possibility.* Atlantic Highlands, N.J.: Humanities Press, 1943.

———. Untitled chapter, *The Courage of Conviction.* Ed. Philip Berman. New York: Ballantine, 1985. 125–136.

Hume, David. *The Natural History of Religion.* London: A. and H. B. Bonner, 1889.

Hyman, Merv, and Gordon White. *Joe Paterno: Football My Way.* New York: The Macmillan Co., 1971.

Johnson, Gerald W. *American Heroes and Hero-Worship.* New York: Harper & Bros., 1941.

Johnson, Robert A., with Jerry M. Ruhl. *Balancing Heaven and Earth: A Memoir.* San Francisco: HarperSanFrancisco, 1998.

Kaplan, Fred. *Thomas Carlyle.* Berkeley, Calif.: Univ. of California Press, 1983.

Klapp, Orrin E. *Heroes, Villains, and Fools: The Changing American Character.* Englewood Cliffs, N.J.: Prentice-Hall, 1962.

———. *Collective Search for Identity.* New York: Holt, Rinehart, and Winston, 1969.

Kowet, Don. *Franco Harris.* New York: Coward, McCann & Geoghegan, 1977.

———. *The Rich Who Own Sports.* New York: Random House, 1977.

Kram, Mark. *Ghosts of Manila: The Fateful Blood Feud Between Muhammad Ali and Joe Frazier.* New York: HarperCollins Publishers, 2001.

Lehmann-Haupt, Christopher. *Me and DiMaggio: A Baseball Fan Goes in Search of His Gods.* New York: Simon & Schuster, 1986.

Lorant, Stefan. *Pittsburgh: The Story of an American City.* Lenox, Mass.: Authors Edition, 1964.

Madden, John, with Dave Anderson. *One Size Doesn't Fit All (and Other Thoughts from the Road).* New York: Villard, 1988.

Maraniss, David. *When Pride Still Mattered: A Life of Vince Lombardi.* New York: Simon & Schuster, 1999.

McGinniss, Joe. *Heroes.* New York: The Viking Press, 1976.

McPhee, John. *A Sense of Where You Are: A Profile of Bill Bradley at Princeton.* New York: Farrar, Straus and Giroux, 1965.

Mendelson, Abby. *The Pittsburgh Steelers: The Official Team History.* Dallas: Taylor Publishing, 1996.

Möring, Marcel. *The Dream Room.* New York: William Morrow & Co., 2002.

O'Brien, Jim. *Doing It Right: The Steelers of Three Rivers and Four Super Bowls Share Their Secrets for Success.* Pittsburgh: James P. O'Brien Publishing, 1991.

———. *Glory Years: A Century of Excellence in Sports.* Pittsburgh: James P. O'Brien Publishing, 2000.

———. *The Chief: Art Rooney and His Pittsburgh Steelers.* Pittsburgh: James P. O'Brien Publishing, 2001.

Osborne, Mary Pope. *American Tall Tales.* New York: Scholastic, Inc., 1991.

Pamplin, Robert G., Jr., and Gary K. Eisler. *American Heroes: Their Lives, Their Values, Their Beliefs.* Mastermedia Publishing, 1995.

Pearson, Preston. *Hearing the Noise: My Life in the N.F.L.* New York: William Morrow & Co., 1985.

Pindar. *Pindar: Olympian Odes, Pythian Odes.* Edited and translated by William H. Race. Cambridge, Mass.: Harvard Univ. Press, 1997.

Plimpton, George. *Paper Lion.* New York: Harper & Row, 1965.

Rank, Otto. *The Myth of the Birth of the Hero.* New York: Alfred A. Knopf, 1959.

Reiss, Bob, and Gary Wohl. *Franco Harris.* New York: Grosset & Dunlap, 1977.

Russell, Andy. *A Steeler Odyssey.* Champaign, Ill.: Sports Publishing Inc., 1998.

Sahadi, Lou. *The Steeler Gang: Bradshaw, Harris, and Their Super Teammates.* New York: Scholastic Book Services, 1976.

Sartre, Jean-Paul. *The Words.* Translated by Bernard Frechtman. New York: G. Braziller, 1964.

St. Anthony's Chapel: In Most Holy Name of Jesus Parish. Pittsburgh: J. Pohl Assoc., 1997.

Schochet, Eliyahu. *The Hasidic Movement and the Gaon of Vilna.* Northvale, N.J.: Jason Aronson Inc., 1994.

Shapiro, Irwin. *Joe Magarac and His U.S.A. Citizen Papers.* New York: Julian Messner Inc., 1948.

Simon, Scott. *Home and Away: Memoir of a Fan.* New York: Hyperion, 2000.

Smith, Betty. *A Tree Grows in Brooklyn.* New York: Harper & Bros., 1943.

Smith, Rick. *Ten Super Sundays: The Thrilling Story of the Super Bowl.* New York: Scholastic Book Services, 1976.

Storr, Anthony. *C. G. Jung.* New York: Viking Press, 1973.

Tatum, Jack, with Bill Kushner. *They Call Me Assassin.* New York: Everest House, 1979.

Telushkin, Joseph. *The Book of Jewish Values: A Day-by-Day Guide to Ethical Living.* New York: Bell Tower, 2000.

Tittle de Laet, Dianne. *Giants and Heroes: A Daughter's Memoir of Y. A. Tittle.* South Royalton, Vt.: Steerforth Press, 1995.

Toker, Franklin. *Pittsburgh: An Urban Portrait.* University Park, Pa.: Penn State Univ. Press, 1986.

Tolan, Sandy. *Me and Hank: A Boy and His Hero, Twenty-Five Years Later.* New York: The Free Press, 2000.

Toperoff, Sam. *Lost Sundays: A Season in the Life of Pittsburgh and the Steelers.* New York: Random House, 1989.

Wann, Daniel L., Merrill J. Melnick, Gordon W. Russell, and Dale G. Pease. *Sport Fans: The Psychology and Social Impact of Spectators.* New York: Routledge Press, 2000.

Wecter, Dixon, introduction by Robert Penn Warren. *The Hero in America: A Chronicle of Hero-Worship.* New York: Charles Scribner's Sons, 1972.

Williams, Peter. *The Sports Immortals: Deifying the American Athlete.* Bowling Green, Ohio: Bowling Green State Univ. Popular Press, 1994.

Writers' Program of the Works Projects Administration in the Commonwealth of Pennsylvania. *Story of Old Allegheny City.* Pittsburgh: Allegheny Centennial Committee, 1941.

PERIODICALS

Baker, Stephen, and Roy Furchgott. "A Pigskin Star Runs with Pork." *Business Week,* 16 Sept. 1996.

Benestad, J. Brian. "Paterno on Vergil: Educating for Service." *America,* 2 April 1994.

Billiard, Jules B. "Ever Hear of Joe Magarac?" *Saturday Evening Post,* 22 Feb. 1947.

Blount, Roy, Jr. "The Ascent of an Enigma." *Sports Illustrated,* 23 Aug. 1982.

Callahan, Tom. "Excellence by the Yard." *Time,* 1 Oct. 1984.

Carr, Sam, and Daniel Weigand, and Jason Jones. "The Relative Influence of Parents, Peers, and Sporting Heroes on Goal Orientations of Children and Adolescents in Sport." *Journal of Sport Pedagogy* Vol. 6, No. 2, 2000.

Collier, Gene. "The Ex-Sportswriter: 'I Was Looking for Heroes in All the Wrong Places.'" *Columbia Journalism Review,* Jan.–Feb. 2000.

Davis, Tim R. V., and Bruce L. Darling. "ABC in a Virtual Corporation." *Management Accounting,* Oct. 1996.

DeMarco, Donna. "Assessing Parks' Woes." *Baltimore Business Journal,* 14 Dec. 1998.

Erikson Bloland, Sue. "Fame: The Power and Cost of a Fantasy." *Atlantic Monthly,* Nov. 1999.

Fisher, Helen. "Lust, Attraction, and Attachment in Mammalian Reproduction." *Human Nature,* Vol. 9, No. 1, 1998.

"Football Star Franco Harris." *Kick,* June 1981.

Fraker, Susan, with Stephan Lesher. "Offside in Pittsburgh?" *Newsweek,* 9 May 1977.

"Franco Harris: 'I've Been Lucky—But Only When I've Worked Hard!'" *Ebony,* Oct. 1976.

Hall, Stephen. "The Reluctant Superstar." *Attenzione,* Nov. 1980.

Heinz, W. C. "Brownsville Bum." *True,* 1951.

Higgins, James M. "Innovate or Evaporate: Seven Secrets of Innovative Corporations." *The Futurist,* 1 Sept. 1995.

Irwin, Julie. "Notes on a Fallen Hero." *Minneapolis Review of Baseball,* 1990.

Jenkins, Dan. "The Idea Is to Have Some Fun—And Who Needs to Be No. 1?" *Sports Illustrated,* 11 Nov. 1968.

Jet, various articles.

Livingston, Pat. "Ferocious Franco Sweeps to Rookie Honors in AFC." *Sporting News,* 13 Jan. 1973.

Looney, Douglas S. "'There Are a Lot of People Who Think I'm a Phony and Now They Think They Have the Proof.'" *Sports Illustrated,* 17 March 1980.

Mano, D. Keith. "Say 'Cheese,' Mom and Pop." *Sports Illustrated,* 15 March 1976.

McGregor, Jeff. "Heavyweight Champion of the Word." *Sports Illustrated,* 25 Sept. 2000.

Nack, William. "Bang for the Bucs." *Sports Illustrated,* 23 Oct. 2000.

Oirich, Alan. "Not by Might Alone." *Amit,* Winter 1998.

———. "Move Over X-Men, Here Come the Jewish Super Heroes." *Jewish World Review,* 14 Aug. 2000.

Penn State Outreach, various articles.

Pro Football Weekly, various articles.

Red, White & Green Sports, various articles.

Reid, Ron. "Black and Gold Soul with Italian Legs." *Sports Illustrated,* 11 Dec. 1972.

Shapiro, Michael. "The Fan: 'Sports Journalism Is About Myths and Transcendent Moments.'" *Columbia Journalism Review,* Jan.–Feb. 2000.

Smith, Eric L. "The Immaculate Reception of Parks Sausage." *Black Enterprise,* Sept. 1996.

The Sporting News, various articles.

Sports Illustrated, various articles.

Steigerwald, Bill. "Death by Wrecking Ball: Pittsburgh and the Politics of Eminent Domain." *Reason,* June 2000.

Steinweis, Alan. "Hitler and Carlyle's 'Historical Greatness.'" *History Today,* June 1995.

Wiley, Ralph. "A New Start for an Old Steeler." *Sports Illustrated,* 17 Sept. 1984.

NEWSPAPERS

Associated Press, *Atlantic City Press, Baltimore Sun, Beaver County Times, Burlington County Times, Centre Daily Times* (State College, Pa.), *Chicago Tribune, Cleveland Press, Collegian* (Penn State Univ.), *Courier-Post* (Cherry Hill, N.J.), *Daily News* (Mc-Keesport, Pa.), *Daily News* (New York), *Daily News* (Philadelphia), *Daily Princetonian, Denver Rocky Mountain News, Detroit Free Press, Evening Journal* (Wilmingon, Del.), *Evening Times* (Trenton), *Herald-Dispatch* (Huntington, W. Va.), *Standard-Observer* (Irwin, Pa.), *Jewish Week* (New York), *Kansas City Star, Kansas City Times, Los Angeles Times, Minneapolis Star Tribune, News-Herald* (Uniontown, Pa.), *Newspaper Enterprise Association, New York Newsday, New York Times, Oakland Tribune, Observer-Reporter* (Washington, Pa.), *Patriot-News* (Harrisburg, Pa.), *Philadelphia Inquirer, Pittsburgh Courier, Pittsburgh Post-Gazette, Pittsburgh Press, Pittsburgh Tribune-Review, Schenectady Gazette, St. Louis Post-Dispatch, Tri-State Food News, United Press International, USA Today, Wall Street Journal, Washington Post, Washington Times.*

ABOUT THE AUTHOR

Stephen J. Dubner, the author of *Turbulent Souls: A Catholic Son's Return to His Jewish Family,* is a former writer and editor at the *New York Times Magazine.* He lives in New York City with his family. For more information, visit www.stephenjdubner.com.